23.00

D1262017

"Scott Henderson's *Death and Donation* is the most thorough treatment I know of on the ethical issues surrounding the definition of death and organ donation. Henderson treats with equanimity, patience, and discernment the basic positions on the main ethical questions concerning these issues, and he informs the reader not only of the basic philosophical alternatives but also of the facts needed to evaluate practical alternatives. In my judgment this book will be must reading for anyone interested in these subjects."

—**Patrick Lee**
John N. and Jamie D. McAleer Professor of Bioethics
Franciscan University of Steubenville

"There are few books of which I would say, 'I wish I had written that book myself,' but Scott Henderson's book is one I wish I could have written. It is a well researched, thoroughly philosophical, and scientific critique of brain-death criteria. Henderson's writing is clear and interesting, and the book should be understandable to an educated layperson. Although the book will appeal to a large audience—including physicians and other health care professionals, philosophers, theologians, medical sociologists, and social workers—its chief merit is in its challenge to current standards of the diagnosis of death and to the current practice of organ transplantation."

—**Michael Potts**
Professor of Philosophy
Methodist University

"While Scott Henderson criticizes unambiguously the various definitions of brain death and their use for organ explantation, showing their non-viability from an anthropological, ethical, and scientific-medical point of view, he offers in his conclusions, in an extraordinarily succinct yet complete and well referenced way, a large variety of alternative solutions for organ donation that remain possible after rejecting brain death criteria for organ donation. Death and Donation might just inspire a medical revolution and rethinking of organ donation, holding out many possible ways of furthering patients' health, prolonging their lives, and procuring organs. Some readers might wish a stronger ethical and philosophical judgment on some issues, but the moderate, non-dogmatic, non-fanatical, and elegantly refined way of expressing his clear assessments and replies to the questions posed will secure Henderson even wider respect and acceptance among readers. In a word, a close reading of the text convinced me that the book may be regarded as the single best book-length study on the issues it treats."

—Josef Seifert
Full Professor of Philosophy
Rector of the International Academy of Philosophy

"I was impressed from an early stage by Scott Henderson's grasp of the ethical problems involved in organ transplantation and much admired the tenacity with which he pursued his researches—particularly in what must have been areas unfamiliar to him. He proved most patient and receptive when coming to an understanding of matters clinical and technical, having clearly sought expert advice from the various disciplines concerned where necessary for the accuracy and fairness of his account. In short, I cannot speak too highly of his application and industry in compiling his deeply thoughtful critique of this truly fundamental change in society's attitude to its most defenseless members. As one forced to take an active and continuing interest in this area of medical misadventure, I venture to offer my strongest commendation of his work in the hope that it will be widely read very soon."

—David W. Evans
Fellow Commoner
Queens' College, Cambridge

"Scott Henderson takes us behind the curtain of organ donation and illuminates the life-and-death issues that heretofore were understood only by trained medical personnel. Most donors have not been properly informed about the means and procedures that are often used in securing organs. What Henderson unveils is both fascinating and disturbing."

—Rick Walston
President
Columbia Evangelical Seminary

Death and Donation

Death and Donation

*Rethinking Brain Death as a Means for
Procuring Transplantable Organs*

By D. Scott Henderson

Middlesex County College
Library
Edison, NJ 08818

PICKWICK *Publications* · Eugene, Oregon

DEATH AND DONATION
Rethinking Brain Death as a Means for Procuring Transplantable Organs

Copyright © 2011 D. Scott Henderson. All rights reserved. Except for brief quotations in critical publications or reviews, no part of this book may be reproduced in any manner without prior written permission from the publisher. Write: Permissions, Wipf and Stock Publishers, 199 W. 8th Ave., Suite 3, Eugene, OR 97401.

Pickwick Publications
An Imprint of Wipf and Stock Publishers
199 W. 8th Ave., Suite 3
Eugene, OR 97401

www.wipfandstock.com

isbn 13: 978-1-60899-622-3

Cataloging-in-Publication data:

Henderson, D. Scott.

    Death and donation : rethinking brain death as a means for procuring transplantable organs / D. Scott Henderson.

    p. ; 23cm. — Includes bibliographical references and index.

    isbn 13: 978-1-60899-622-3

    1. Transplantation of organs, tissues, etc. 2. Death—Moral and ethical aspects I. Title.

R725.56 D36 2011

Manufactured in the U.S.A.

To the memory of Andrew Ranger, whose personal encouragement and commitment to truth telling in medical practice inspired me in this endeavor.

Contents

Preface

The boundaries which divide Life from Death are at best shadowy
and vague. Who shall say when the one ends, and the other begins?

~ Edgar Allan Poe

IN EDGAR ALLAN POE's short story, *The Premature Burial*, the un-
named narrator describes in lurid detail his struggle with taphephobia, the fear of being buried alive. His inebriating fear is provoked by
the increasing frequency of attacks of catalepsy, a condition in which he
randomly slips into a death-like trance. Drawing upon the public's fas-
cination with stories of people found to have been buried alive, in some
cases years after their crypts were reopened, the narrator describes how
this crippling phobia worsens his condition making him more prone to
slip into a death-like trance. Obsessed with the possibility of falling into
such a trance while away from home, he takes measures to ensure that
he will not be buried prematurely by eliciting promises from friends,
not venturing away from home, and constructing an elaborate tomb
with devices to signal for help should he awaken after burial. The horror
story ends with the narrator finding himself confined in a small space
in pitch darkness, believing that all his fears have been realized despite
his precautions. As he cries out in utter terror, he is directly restored to
his memory that he has simply fallen asleep in the small berth of a boat.
This shocking incident serves to relieve the narrator's taphephobia thus
restoring him to a life of normalcy.

Poe's story is a reminder of the persistent human fear of being
thought dead while still alive. While modern technologies (the invention

of the stethoscope, for instance) and embalming practices have virtually eliminated the possibility of being buried alive, the fear of a premature declaration of death exists in other modalities. Ironically, modern technologies that brought a sense of relief with respect to the fear of being buried alive have also created new medical situations that perpetuate the question, what is death. Most notably are the perplexing neurological conditions that directly result from the use of life-sustaining technologies. Of particular interest in this work, is the condition known as *brain death*. In this investigation, much attention is devoted to brain death and its concomitant relation to organ donation. This relation raises several questions pursuant to this investigation: Does the permanent loss of all brain function (i.e., brain death) correspond to human death? How did brain death gain acceptance in medical practice and social policy? What is the relationship between brain death and how it is understood and used as the basis for organ donation? What are the implications in other areas including research ethics and experimentation? If brain death were abandoned, how might it affect organ donation? May an exception to the dead donor rule be granted under certain conditions? Such are by no means purely academic questions. The answers to these questions touch upon everyone.

The aim of this investigation is to examine and evaluate the social, legal, medical, and philosophical problems inherent in the current social policy allowing for organ donation under the brain death criterion of human death. The position advanced herein is that brain death is fraught with numerous difficulties that render it ethically untenable in current practice and should be abandoned as a criterion for determining death.

The first chapter chronicles the emergence of brain death and its adoption as a standard of death in both medical practice and legal jurisprudence. The connections with organ procurement, developing new technologies, and the Harvard Committee's recommendation for the adoption of brain death are explored in detail. In addition, this chapter highlights the various discussions following the Harvard Committee's recommendation of brain death, including the search for a coherent conception in support of it culminating in the rationale of the President's Commission Report, and the UDDA (Uniform Determination of Death Act).

The second chapter focuses on the medical problems associated with brain death and organ donation. Areas of exploration include the difficulties of establishing somatic neural dependency with regard to brain-death testing criteria, the questions raised by common clinical anomalies and physical phenomena in brain-dead patients, and the difficulties of maintaining brain death's consistency with traditional cardiopulmonary death. To further the inquiry into conceptual coherency, this chapter examines the clinical tests for brain death and the problems of arbitrariness of application and misdiagnosis of the condition.

The third chapter examines the ongoing problems of brain death's conceptual basis, particularly since its inception with the President's Commission Report and the introduction of the UDDA as the suggested framework for determining death. Accordingly, this chapter highlights various social attitudes and the overall general public confusion surrounding the meaning and application of brain death. To illustrate the extent of this confusion, this chapter underscores the struggles of lawmakers to satisfy the demands of the brain-death standard resulting in statutory irregularities both here and abroad. This chapter also includes the provision of a catalog of statutes representative of how states inconsistently allow death to be defined. The chapter then shifts to a discussion of how brain death is used in other areas, such as medical research and experimentation on the newly declared dead.

The fourth and fifth chapters focus on concerns brain death raises with respect to the philosophical challenges of its relation to defining death. Chapter Four challenges brain death's veracity with respect to its definitional and metaphysical foundation. Accordingly, the chapter discusses the philosophical groundwork and assumptions of the underlying metaphysics for the definition of death under the current paradigm, the theoretical inconsistencies between the organism/substance view and brain death based on the empirical evidence, and particular instances of inconsistencies among advocates of the substantial view. Chapter Five continues along these lines by assessing the various alternatives and modifications to death criteria put forward for the purpose of expanding the pool of potential organ donors. Particular attention is given to higher-brain models of death. These models are evaluated for their philosophical coherence and with current neurological evidence. Moreover, this chapter explores suggestions regarding donation apart from the dead donor rule, particularly with respect to their potential effects on the medical community and society in general. Finally, this chapter considers proposals involving the adoption of conscience clauses for those who oppose the legal standard of death.

In many ways, the sixth chapter is the most important, in that it brings all the relevant data from the previous chapters together in order to assess the ethical viability of brain death as it relates to organ donation. This analysis includes the application of traditional medical ethics to the problems disclosed throughout concerning brain death. Furthering the evaluative purpose of this chapter entails the application of the principles of biomedical ethics and relevant case law to the issue of informed consent for organ donors under the brain-death standard. This chapter concludes by considering the ethical feasibility of grounding brain death on pragmatism as a sufficient reason for its continued use.

The final chapter provides a summary of the major problems with brain death as a means for organ procurement and, in support of the thesis of this work, calls into question the ethical sustainability of current practice. In order to sustain the life-saving practice of organ transplantation, this chapter notes several emerging technologies that may eventually lessen the need for cadaveric organ and tissue donors. The investigation concludes by laying the groundwork for a new policy of death in an effort to further the good of organ donation and transplantation.

Acknowledgments

THIS MONOGRAPH ORIGINATED IN a Ph.D. dissertation submitted to Duquesne University in 2009. There is no shortage of gratitude I have for those who have aided me in this endeavor. First and foremost, I want to thank my wife, Kathryn Reneé, for her encouragement, support, love, and prayers during this long journey. A warm thank you to my children, David Alexander, Ian Eleazar, Ariana Reneé, and Kavan Scott, who patiently endured and supported their father's preoccupation with this project. I am grateful to my parents, David and Elizabeth Henderson, whose unstinting care over the years is beyond measure. I would like to thank my dissertation committee members, Aaron L. Mackler, Rhonda G. Hartman, and William P. Cheshire for their valuable, detailed comments and direction in bringing this work to completion.

Many thanks to Pickwick Publications for their willingness to publish this work. Most especially I am grateful to Charlie Collier and the editorial staff for their hard work in preparing this monograph for publication.

Finally, I want to thank some contemporary scholars who have influenced and encouraged me in the writing of this book: D. Alan Shewmon, whose presentation on brain death over a decade ago inspired me to pursue a Ph.D. in health care ethics and write a dissertation on this topic; Patrick Lee, Michael Potts, and David W. Evans, for their personal words of encouragement and counsel.

1

The Origin of the
Brain Death Standard

DETERMINING THE MOMENT OF human death has always been challenging. In the past, physicians and lay people alike relied upon
the absence of breathing and pulse as indicators of the occurrence of
death. However, in the eighteenth century, accounts of corpses reviving
during funerals and the discovery of exhumed skeletons having clawed
at coffin lids created widespread fear of premature burial. In response, a
number of creative measures were developed, including the sale of coffin lids equipped with speaking tubes or strings linked to bells above
ground and the employment of guards by mortuaries to monitor the
newly dead for life signs.[1] In the years that followed, the medical press
addressed these concerns by proposing various methods for confirming
death.[2] Whether life ceases upon putrefaction of the body, or the point
at which a feather held to the nose ceases to flutter, humans have always
exhibited a keen interest in ensuring the occurrence of death.[3]

Progress in medical technology, developed in the 1950s, brought
with it a new medical phenomenon, which presented new challenges in
the determination of death. Some patients who suffered head trauma or
spontaneous intracranial haemorrhage, would slip into a condition in

1. Alexander, "Rigid Embrace," 25–31.

2. Elliot, "Brain Death," 23. Elliot further notes, "These included observation for the
gradual rusting of a needle inserted into the biceps, the movement of needles with flags
attached inserted transcutaneously into the heart, and absence of organ movement on
X-ray fluoroscopy."

3. Lock, "Inventing a New Death," 97–115.

1

which the brainstem would undergo herniation due to severely elevated intracranial pressure.[4] Indicative of the severest cases is "permanent loss of consciousness, absence of brainstem reflexes, and complete loss of respiratory drive."[5] However, respiratory failure that had previously resulted in the death of these patients could now be delayed through mechanical ventilation. Although the patients would expire within a few hours, or in some cases a few days, their clinical condition would become known as "brain death."[6]

The emergence of brain death stems from two seminal events—one occurring in late 1967 and the other early in 1968. In December 1967, Christiaan Barnard successfully transplanted the first human heart into a patient dying from heart failure in South Africa. Although the recipient died eighteen days later, the well-publicized event led to the advent of heart transplantation, with over one hundred attempted the following year.[7] Early failures were attributed to the problems of organ rejection by recipients' immune systems and organ deterioration due to the need to wait for sufficient time after cardiac arrest to ensure that the donor would not spontaneously resuscitate.[8] Although transplant researchers debated the neurological criteria for determining death, the Harvard report of 1968 marked the first recognized diagnostic criteria for determining brain death. The advantage this offered for transplantation technology was obvious—no longer would transplant surgeons have to wait several minutes after cardiac arrest to retrieve organs for transplantation, thereby risking organ degeneration. It also increased the viability of transplantable organs because, through mechanical ventilation, donors' hearts would continue to beat. Thus, despite the absence of brain

4. Elliot, "Brain Death," 23. Elliot writes: "Most cases of brain death are due to head trauma or spontaneous intracranial haemorrhage. These conditions may lead to herniation of the brainstem through the formamen magnum ('coning'), due to severely raised intracranial pressure. Less often, brain death is caused by severe cerebral hypoxic-ischaemic events, such as after prolonged and/or inadequate cardiopulmonary resuscitation. Brainstem vascular events (infarction or haemorrhage) may lead to primary death of the brainstem, with identical clinical features."

5. Ibid.

6. Today, brain death declarations account for about 1 percent of all deaths.

7. Smith, "Clinical Freedom," 1583. Also see chapter 1 of Singer, *Rethinking Life and Death*.

8. Some reports suggest that the clinical use of heart-beating cadavers as organ sources was taking place years before by some transplant surgeons. See Giacomini, "Change of Heart," 1466.

activity, vital organs were infused with oxygenated blood until the time that the organs were removed.

Despite sporadic objections from physicians and philosophers on both biological and moral grounds, public policy embraced the brain death criterion that was reflected in American law. During the 1970s, the ethical controversy regarding brain death, as well as inconsistencies in legislative initiatives during the 1970s, contributed to the creation of the President's Commission for the Study of Ethical Problems in Medicine and Biomedical and Behavioral Research. The Commission was charged, among other things, with the task to study "the ethical and legal implications of the matter of defining death, including the advisability of developing a uniform definition of death."[9] In 1981, the Commission issued its report, entitled, *Defining Death,* which proposed a "Uniform Determination of Death Act" as a model for legislation. Over the next twenty years, all states adopted, through either legislation or common law, the brain death standard.[10]

Despite its prevalence, brain death continues to generate both controversy and criticism. This chapter will discuss the criticism, particularly with respect to the claim that brain death does not have valid justification other than advancing transplantation research.[11] This chapter, therefore, will investigate the historical development of brain death and critically assess the justifications proffered by various commissions in order to promote its use in medical practice. Specifically, the chapter will provide a brief history of emerging new medical technologies and their effect on medical research and practice. The chapter will then examine the Harvard Ad Hoc Committee's recommendation of the brain death criterion and explore the motivations behind the recommendation. Finally, the chapter will address and evaluate the report of the President's Commission.

THE EMERGENCE OF NEW MEDICAL TECHNOLOGIES

Historically, brain death emerged at the crossroads of two intersecting technological advances in medicine, i.e., artificial life-support

9. President's Commission, *Defining Death,* 1.

10. Menikoff, *Law and Bioethics,* 450.

11. Seifert, "Is 'Brain Death' Actually Death?" 175–203.

mechanisms and organ transplantation.[12] With the advent of flexible plastic tubing and mechanical ventilation,[13] the beating hearts of patients could be sustained through respiratory support when the capacity for breathing was inhibited or lost due to severe or irreversible brain damage. In 1959, P. Mollaret and M. Goulon, two French physicians, published an article describing certain mechanically ventilated patients in a condition they termed *coma dépassé*, or "beyond coma."[14] These patients not only exhibited loss of consciousness, but also "showed apnoea, loss of brainstem reflexes, and other abnormalities (such as hypotension, presumed diabetes insipidus and disturbances of temperature regulation) consistent with the modern concept of brain death."[15] Patients in this condition nevertheless retain hypothalamic-pituitary axis, temperature regulation, and spinal activity for several hours, though no documented case of recovery exists.[16] Earlier that same year, an article was published by M. Jouvet who suggested the use of the electroencephalogram (EEG) for diagnosing the death of the central nervous system.[17] This set the stage for discussions in the decade that followed regarding the ethical and legal aspects of *coma dépassé*.

Although the first successful transplant of a human organ occurred in 1954,[18] organ and tissue transplantation would not thrive until advances in surgical techniques and immunosuppression drugs were developed in the 1960s. Due to these advancements, a growing need for cadaveric organs (particularly kidneys), which living, related donors could not meet demands, prompted discussion concerning the potential source of *coma dépassé* patients.[19] These discussions preceded

12. Pernick, "Brain Death in Cultural Context," 3–33.

13. Mitchell, "Church and the Cultural Imperative," 211. Mitchell writes, "Were it not for flexible plastic tubing, we could not keep patients alive on ventilators and IVs. Without flexible plastic tubing, there would be very few end-of-life decisions to make."

14. Mollaret and Goulon, "State Beyond Coma," 3–15.

15. Elliot, "Brain Death," 24.

16. Saposnik et al., "Movements in Brain Death," 209.

17. Jouvet, "Diagnostic Electrosouscorticographique."

18. The first successful kidney transplant was performed by Dr. Joseph Murray of the Harvard Medical School on December 23, 1954. Dr. Murray transplanted a kidney from one identical twin brother to another, thereby avoiding immuno-system rejection, a practical impossibility at that time.

19. Zamperetti et al., "Irreversible Apnoeic Coma 35 Years Later," 1715–22. Giacomini, "Change of Heart," 1467.

1968, the year in which diagnostic criteria for brain death were formally proposed.[20]

Perhaps the most significant discussions preceding 1968 occurred at the 1966 Ciba Foundation symposium entitled, *Ethics in Medical Progress: With Special Reference to Transplantation.*[21] Included in the discussions were physicians (two-thirds of whom were transplant researchers), legal scholars, journalists, and theologians from the United States and Europe. Their discussions centered on deterioration of organs (kidneys) obtained from cadavers and the possibility of procuring more viable organs from brain-injured patients. With developing diagnostic technology such as the EEG, the use of brain-based criteria for diagnosing death promised to relieve concerns for donor mutilation from live kidney donors, which seemed for some a violation of the ethical imperative to "first do no harm."[22] Nevertheless, some physicians at Ciba were not as optimistic about the prospects of what they considered "redefining death" in order to advance transplant research. These critics charged that proponents of a brain-based criterion were interested only in its use on potential organ donors and showed resistance to its use on themselves or their loved ones should they go on life support.[23] Moreover, there was some question regarding the physiologic meaning of EEG indications in some comatose patients. Particularly, its sporadic use in the study of coma and death raised questions as to its reliability in depicting death. As the conference concluded, more questions were raised than were answered. The apparent unease of many of its participants to propose a new criterion for death reflected an overall concern to safeguard respect for the medical profession.[24] At that time, doctors seemed reluctant to advance a new criterion for determining death due to uncertainties in diagnostics and an awareness that such a venture might have serious ramifications on the reputation of the medical profession. To be sure, beginning in the

20. Giacomini, "Change of Heart," 1467. Although Giacomini employs language indicating the issue to be one of redefining death, it is more accurate to say the issue was one of proposing a new criterion for determining death.

21. Wolstenholme and O'Connor, *Ethics in Medical Progress*. Cited in Giacomini, "Change of Heart."

22. Hippocrates, *Hippocrates, Vol. I.*

23. Giacomini, "Change of Heart," 1467.

24. Ibid.

1960s, medical practitioners began to face challenges from competing claimants of authority with regard to medical treatment decisions.[25] Whatever reluctance existed in 1966, Christiaan Barnard's successful heart transplant in December 1967 seemed to embolden some in the medical community and assuage previous concerns. Indeed an *Ad Hoc Committee to Study the Problems of the Hopelessly Unconscious Patient* convened at the Harvard Medical School in early 1968 to propose new diagnostic criteria for determining death.

THE HARVARD AD HOC COMMITTEE'S RECOMMENDATION

Henry K. Beecher, who was an anesthesiologist and well-known critic of unethical research practices, appealed to Robert Ebert, then Dean of the Harvard Medical School suggesting that a committee be established to consider some new questions.[26] In consultation with Dr. Joseph Murray, a kidney transplant pioneer at Massachusetts General Hospital, Beecher wrote in a letter to Dean Ebert, "Both Dr. Murray and I think the time has come for a further consideration of the definition of death. Every major hospital has patients stacked up waiting for suitable donors."[27] This was not the first time Beecher expressed interest in furthering transplantation efforts. In a seminal article published a year earlier, Beecher wrote a scathing exposé of the exploitation of patients in clinical research. While the article focused on problems of patient consent and protection, Beecher expressed a concern for "the recently added problems arising in the transplantation of organs."[28] In the coming months, news of a modestly successful heart transplant in South Africa would attest to Beecher's expectation of impending advances in transplantation as well as the necessity of preparing the way for its acceptance into medical practice.

---

25. Pernick writes, "decisions previously left to the discretion of individual practitioners began to be contested by other claimants to authority." (4) In this important and influential article, Veatch set forth a challenge to end paternalistic medicine." See Veatch, "Generalization of Expertise."

26. The letter is dated 30 October 1967. Cited in Giacomini, "Change of Heart" and Singer, *Rethinking Life and Death.*

27. Beecher Letter, cited in Singer, *Rethinking Life and Death*, 24.

28. Beecher, "Ethics and Clinical Research," 1354.

Christiaan Barnard, a young heart surgeon who had conducted heart transplant experiments on canines, decided to attempt the new procedure on a human subject.[29] Barnard recounts in his autobiography how Louis Washkansky was initially presented to him as a candidate for open-heart surgery. Despite the experimental nature of the surgery, Washkansky readily accepted the eighty percent chance he was given for the procedure. Although Washkansky's condition deteriorated during the waiting period for a donor heart, finally one was secured when Denise Darvall, a young girl suffering severe brain damage from a pedestrian traffic accident, was brought to the hospital where Washkansky was waiting. As her condition deteriorated, her father consented to the harvest of her kidneys and heart for donation. After a touch-and-go double surgery, surgeons successfully transplanted her heart into Louis Washkansky. Washkansky's death eighteen days later did not diminish media celebration of the world's first heart transplant. To be sure, the considerable publicity after the event focused intently on problems surrounding vital organ donation.[30] Questions regarding the practice of heart transplantation and the conflicting accounts of Darvall's death raised numerous ethical and conceptual concerns. A *Time* editorial illustrated the nature of these concerns: "The real moral and ethical difficulty in heart transplants arises from medical uncertainty. . . . The surgeon wants the donor's heart as fresh as possible . . . that is, within minutes of death. This has raised the specter of surgeons becoming not only corpse snatchers but, even worse, of encouraging people to become corpses. . . ."[31]

Barnard's own account reveals a wait of about three minutes after Darvall's heart stopped before proceeding with its removal.[32] In an interview with *Time* magazine, Marius Barnard, Christiaan Barnard's brother and member of his surgical team insisted that they did not determine death based on a flat EEG as is done in some places. Rather, they followed a more conservative approach in which patient death occurs when heart and lungs cease functioning and no further complexes are indicated

---

29. Barnard and Pepper, *One Life.*
30. Giacomini, "Change of Heart," 473.
31. "Surgery," 64–72
32. Barnard and Pepper, *One Life,* 360.

on the ECG.[33] Indeed, the procedure followed by Barnard is practically identical to what is currently called, *non-beating heart donation.*[34]

Autopsy results revealed that Washkansky's death was caused by lobar pneumonia.[35] During the eighteen days following the transplant, the medical team struggled to control infection, but with aggressive immunosuppression drugs, infection eventually overcame Washkanky's weakened and defenseless body. Nevertheless, the transplant surgery was considered a success. This surgical milestone became the impetus not only for further attempts at heart transplantation, but it also may have provided the incentive for a committee to examine a new criterion of death.

Within a month of the well-publicized transplant in South Africa, Harvard's Dean Ebert approved Beecher's request for convening a committee and appointed him to chair it. Ebert believed Harvard was in the best position to undertake the project, owing to its achievements in transplant technology. In a letter of invitation to committee members, Ebert re-emphasized Beecher's request that further consideration be given to brain death, especially with regard to Harvard Medical School's pioneering interest in organ transplantation.[36]

Ebert appointed a thirteen-member committee, most of whom were physicians and well-acquainted colleagues.[37] The committee finished its work six months later and published its report in the *Journal of the American Medical Association* under the title: "A Definition of Irreversible Coma."[38] The report addressed several items, including the clinical description of irreversible coma, recommended procedures for its diagnosis, and justifications for this new criterion for diagnosing death. Chiefly, the committee established four requirements for a determination of death: 1) lack of reception or response to external stimuli; 2) no spontaneous respiration for three minutes off of a respirator; 3) no reflexes; 4) a flat electroencephalogram for at least ten minutes, repeated after twenty four hours.[39] The most publicized aspect of the report is

33. "Surgery."

34. Shewmon, "'Brainstem Death,'" 125–46.

35. Barnard and Pepper, *One Life*, 463–65.

36. Beecher, "Definition of Irreversible Coma." Cited in Giacomini, "Change of Heart," 1474.

37. Ibid. The committee also included a lawyer, theologian, and historian.

38. "Definition of Irreversible Coma," 337–40.

39. Ibid.

the Committee's rationale behind their recommendation of irreversible coma as a new criterion for determining death. First, they reasoned that due to advancements in resuscitation and critical care measures, some patients survive only partially with irreversible brain damage though still beating hearts. They further reasoned that "The burden is great on patients who suffer permanent loss of intellect, on their families, on hospitals, and on those in need of hospital beds already occupied by these comatose patients."[40] Implicit is the need to remove these patients off of life support without fear of legal reprisals. Second, the new definition was offered as a means for relieving controversy in the retrieval of transplantable organs.

The public's initial impression of these remarks was that the Committee began investigating the features of irreversible coma as a criterion for death and discovered fortuitously the benefits it also would have in obtaining transplantable organs. Scant references to transplantation in the report suggest that the issue was peripheral to the Committee. Gary Belkin, responding to critics of the report, argues that, "A more careful history of the report pushes interest in transplantation to the side," and instead highlights ". . . the combination of ethical concerns and clinical efforts to consider limits on the use of intrusive technologies, framed within emerging paradigms of the neurology of consciousness."[41] While these efforts and concerns contributed to the content of the report's rationale, transplantation interests were far from marginal, as Belkin suggests. Earlier manuscript drafts and memos reveal that the Committee's mission was to advance the cause of organ transplantation.[42] In fact, one early draft concludes with words explicitly demonstrating the centrality of organ transplantation: "The question before this committee cannot be simply to define brain death. This would not advance the cause of organ transplantation since it would not cope with the essential issue of when the surgical team is authorized—legally, morally, and medically—in removing a vital organ. . . ."[43] However, Dean Ebert requested the committee to "tone down" the references pertaining

40. Ibid., 85.

41. Belkin, "Brain Death and the Historical Understanding of Bioethics," 327.

42. Beecher, "Definition of Irreversible Coma." Cited in Giacomini, "Change of Heart."

43. Ibid., 1474.

to the need of transplantable organs to better ensure public acceptance of the report.[44]

Additional evidence of the need to accommodate transplantation surfaces in earlier drafts of the report in which protocols for speeding up the diagnosis of death (to ensure fresher organs) were advanced. For example, originally the report recommended protocols for signs of death at twenty-four-hour intervals over a period of three days before terminating life support.[45] Transplant surgeons, however, objected to this long interval and the committee acquiesced to a twenty-four-hour period. In a later address published in the *International Journal of Clinical Pharmacology*, Beecher remarked that the new definition of death carried with it life-saving potential, "for, when accepted, it will lead to greater availability than formerly of essential organs in viable condition, for transplantation, and thus countless lives now inevitably lost will be saved." He further noted the arbitrariness of defining death and the need to choose a level in which although the brain ceases to function, "usefulness of other organs is still present."[46]

With the rise of advanced transplantation technology in the 1960s, a new form of scarce medical resource was created, viz., transplantable organs. The need for life-saving organ transplants increased exponentially as more patients were added to waiting lists for suitable donors. The new brain death criterion, it was hoped, would facilitate transplantation efforts by increasing the pool of organ donors, thus providing a practical solution to organ shortages. Although the Committee attempted to cast transplantation interests as a secondary concern, the second of the two justifications in the report was heralded (more accurately, perhaps) as the primary justification for brain death by major news reporting

---

44. An earlier draft stated: "With increased experience and knowledge and development in the field of transplantation, there is great need for the tissues and organs of the hopelessly comatose in order to restore to health those who are still salvageable." Ebert responded, "The connotation of this statement is unfortunate, for it suggests that you wish to redefine death in order to make organs readily available to persons requiring transplants. Immediately the reader thinks how this principle might be abused . . . . Would it not be better to state the problem, and indicate that obsolete criteria for the definition of death can lead to controversy in obtaining organs for transplantation?" Cited in Giacomini, "Change of Heart," 1475.

45. Ibid.

46. Beecher and Dorr, "New Definition of Death," 120–21.

agencies from the *New York Times* to the *Chicago Tribune*.[47] From the outset there was public suspicion about the Committee's criterion due in part to both the way in which it was reported and the increasing unease of public sentiment toward the medical profession as a whole. Reports of secret government-sponsored medical experimentation on unknowing human subjects no doubt had affected the public's perception of experimental medicine. Transplantation technology was still considered as experimental in the late 1960s, and thus for many people it represented an uncertain practice. An impression that medical professionals introduced brain death as a way to further organ transplantation likely contributed to public distrust.

The Harvard Committee was less concerned with conceptual abstractions such as personal and organism identity, and more concerned with solving practical problems.[48] In conjunction with the promotion of organ donation, the Committee also wanted to protect the medical profession against critics of transplantation. As Pernick observes, "[Beecher] hoped the Harvard criteria would not only increase the supply of organs but, more broadly, defend the entire medical profession against the public perception that transplant surgeons were organ-stealing killers."[49] In addition, Pernick notes "Beecher's repugnance at what he considered the futile waste of vital resources linked his concerns about transplantation and mechanical ventilation."[50] For Beecher, the use of mechanical ventilation on those who had no use of their organs was a futile endeavor and constituted a waste of transplantable organs. As Beecher himself asks, "Can society afford to discard the tissues and organs of the hopelessly unconscious patient when he could be used to restore the otherwise hopelessly ill, but still salvageable individual?"[51] Moreover, having a keen interest in human experimentation, Beecher recognized the permanently comatose as a potential source of various sorts of medical experimentation. Relying on Beecher's personal correspondences, Pernick

47. Pernick, "Brain Death in Cultural Context." Pernick reports, "Although the Harvard report mentioned both respirators and transplants as reasons for redefining death, all 17 *New York Times* articles on the issue from 1967 to 1970 and 9 of 14 such articles from 1971 to 1974 attributed the need to redefine death primarily to transplantation. The *Washington Post, Chicago Tribune,* and Associated Press followed suit."

48. Ibid. Also see: Giacomini, "Change of Heart."

49. Pernick, "Brain Death in Cultural Context."

50. Ibid.

51. Beecher, "Ethical Problems," 1427.

suggests, "Beecher apparently hoped that experimenting on brain-dead bodies could reduce the need for live human guinea pigs and thereby avoid the ethical complications caused by using live human subjects."[52]

Giacomini offers an expansive contextual analysis concluding that brain death was a social and medical construct.[53] She notes how various competing and cooperating interests negotiated their claims over the new territory represented by the irreversibly comatose body. Giacomini characterizes these discussions as, "A veritable zoo of 1960s-era technologies meandered through early brain death debates." Included among them were successes such as heart transplantation and renal dialysis, and failures (at the time) such as the artificial heart and lung transplantation. One such evolving technology was the EEG, as mentioned earlier. But in 1968 no medical authoritative group considered the EEG as presenting satisfactory diagnostic evidence for determining death.[54] Clearly, transplantation influenced the Committee's deliberations as they hastily deliberated on the heels of the widely publicized first heart transplant.[55]

The Harvard Committee's concerns over solving important practical problems made it vulnerable to criticisms. Central to the criticisms is the lack of supporting evidence substantiating the burden posed by *coma dépassé* patients.[56] The report indicates that these patients pose great burdens on themselves, their families, hospitals, and those who need beds otherwise occupied by comatose patients. While it is difficult to know how patients in this state are a burden to themselves, the notion that care of these patients is a burden on hospital resources seems incredible for two reasons. First, as the Committee noted, most *coma dépassé* patients undergo conventional death within a few hours to a few days. It is unlikely that, in 1968, care for these patients had created a crisis. Second, the burden of transplantation research and its demands on scarce resources far surpassed the burden of care for permanently

---

52. Pernick, "Brain Death in Cultural Context," 10.

53. Giacomini, "Change of Heart," 1478.

54. Ibid.

55. Ibid., 1479.

56. Another similar criticism concerns the lack of scientific evidence provided in the Report to justify its diagnostic criteria. There was no reference to 1959 French report on *coma dépassé* nor to the Ciba symposium. The latter contained discussions on defining death.

comatose patients.[57] Indeed, the survival rate of heart-transplant recipients in the year following Barnard's success was no greater than eleven months. Resources consumed for the first heart transplant in the United States included $30,000 for the transplant surgery and 304 pints of blood that eclipse any other consumption of resources.[58]

Describing the burden posed to families of the permanently comatose, Josef Seifert notes, "The discontinuation of extraordinary means of life-support (artificial respirators, etc.) could be justified without maintaining that irreversible breakdown of brain function is identical with death."[59] Since 1957,[60] Catholic theologians and ethicists have recognized that there is no moral obligation to extend the lives of the gravely suffering or permanently unconscious through extraordinary means. Hence, the first justification of the report that "the burden is great on patients who suffer permanent loss of intellect, on their families, on hospitals, and on those in need of hospital beds already occupied by these comatose patients" is unnecessary. Indeed, some commentators note that physicians, prior to 1968, had long been making decisions regarding foregoing treatment for patients whose conditions they judged as irreversible. Margaret Lock writes:

> Prior to 1968 physicians in North America and Europe had, as a matter of course, quietly turned off the ventilators of patients whose condition they firmly believed was irreversible and would soon result in conventional death. . . . In performing such acts, physicians were participating in a long-standing but discreet medical tradition. As the number of artificial ventilators accumulated in ICUs, intensivists had to deal increasingly with unconscious patients with severe head trauma whose condition was, in their estimation, irreversible. Although many died precipitously, others lingered on for days, and doctors had to decide whether to remove such individuals from life support. Nevertheless, the practice of unplugging the ventilator remained informal, and more or less concealed, in large part because neither the media nor the public evinced much interest in the practice.[61]

57. Giacomini, "Change of Heart," 1471.

58. Titmuss, *Gift of Relationship.* Cited in Giacomini, "Change of Heart." See also Lock, *Twice Dead.*

59. Seifert, "Brain Death and Euthanasia," 206.

60. Pope Pius XII, "Prolongation of Life."

61. Lock, *Twice Dead,* 103. In addition, Giacomini claims that the use of heart-beating

In addition, in public forums during the 1950s and 1960s when criticism of life support appeared, it usually focused more on the extent to which a physician was obligated to postpone the dying process rather than on the criterion of death.[62] Family members often lamented over the indignity imposed on their loved ones due to medicine's ability to prolong the dying process unnecessarily. Hence, the crisis at the time seemed less focused on the uncertainty of a patient's alive-vs-dead status and more on the dreadful prospects of a doctor's ability to prolong death in the hospital.[63] Physicians seemed to find little moral impediment to withdrawing life-support from patients when they deemed that continuation was futile. According to critics, this seriously undermined the legitimacy of the Harvard report's first justification. Its second justification, (Obsolete criteria for the definition of death can lead to controversy in obtaining organs for transplantation), is equally questionable.

In bioethics literature, critics of brain death continue to characterize it as "legal fiction" whose only purpose is to facilitate organ donation.[64] From this perspective, the endorsement of brain death seems to have been a utilitarian move lacking an adequate justification. One writer, for example, characterizes the second justification of the Harvard report as both unnecessary and counterproductive.[65] He notes that the first successful heart and liver transplants in the 1960s were carried out without the need for a brain death declaration. A careful analysis of the harvesting procedure employed in early transplantations suggests that declaring brain dead patients as "dead" may have been unnecessary for the retrieval of their organs. Indeed, Barnard's first heart transplant involved removing the heart and kidneys of a donor post circulatory standstill following the discontinuation of ventilator support. Shewmon presents the procedure as an alternative to brain death for procuring vital organs for transplantation. He writes, "The procedure would not begin until after final (though not yet irreversible) circulatory standstill following discontinuation of the ventilator and after a latency sufficient

---

cadavers as organ sources preceded the deliberations of the Harvard Committee in 1968, noting, "They [heart-beating cadavers] had been used for years prior in kidney transplant experiments." See: Giacomini, "Change of Heart," 1466.

62. Ibid., 1471.

63. Ibid., 1472.

64. Evans and Lum, "Brain Death."

65. Shewmon, "Brainstem Death."

for moral certainty that the heart will not spontaneously start beating again if the body is left undisturbed (probably a couple of minutes would suffice)."[66] Prior placement of arterial catheters in order to perfuse select organs with preserving medications would ensure minimal deterioration upon cardiac arrest. Despite that the heart may still be resuscitatable, Shewmon suggests that if the decision to forego ventilator support is ethical, so would the decision to forego resuscitation of the heart. Hence, the excision of the heart at this point would not alter in any way the physiology of the circulation-less body in the remaining few minutes of the dying process. Understood this way, transplantation techniques could be tailored to accommodate what Shewmon calls the "moral rubic of donation inter vivos" rather than the dead-donor-rule. To be sure, the entire procedure would require prior informed consent.

What Shewmon is describing is a form of NHBD (non-heart-beating organ donation). Although NHBD is currently controversial, it nevertheless represents an alternative to the use of brain death, especially in light of the fact that it was the procedure employed by Christiaan Barnard in the first human heart transplant. However, prior to the use of brain death, this method of procurement ran the risk of producing damaged, unusable organs due to the lack of blood flow during procurement. Today medical advances lessen the problems faced by transplant teams in the 1960s and 1970s and the premature deaths of many organ recipients.[67]

The preceding discussion thus far indicates several important implications. First, initial discussions concerning the permanently comatose patient took place in the context of advancing transplantation interests in the early to mid 1960s. However, due to uncertainties in diagnostics, as well as concern for the reputation of the medical community, it seemed that many physicians were reluctant to advance a new criterion of death at that time. Second, despite these reservations, with the highly publicized success of heart transplantation, this reluctance was overcome when the Harvard Ad Hoc Committee proposed neurological criteria for determining brain death. Though effort was made by the Committee to cast transplantation as a secondary benefit of the new criterion, there is strong evidence that the motivations of the Committee were centered on the advancement of organ transplantation. Third, as

66. Ibid.

67. An ethical assessment of NHBD will be included in chapter 7.

critics note, the Harvard report's dual rationale failed to accord with the concern of the times and rather may have inadvertently caused more confusion and harm to the advancement of transplantation than good. Regardless of these problems, in the decade that followed the new criterion of death found its way into medical practice and law, stimulating further debate and refinements.

THE NEED FOR FURTHER REFINEMENT

In the decade that followed the Committee's recommendation, several crucial activities suggested the need for further refinement. First, "judicial decisions and state legislation created a patchwork pattern of conflicting new and old methods for establishing that a person had died."[68] As early as 1970, "the Kansas legislature took the first legal action in an American jurisdiction recognizing brain-based criteria for the determination of death."[69] The Kansas Legislature drafted a statute employing brain death in response to the developments in organ transplantation as well as medical support of dying patients. The Kansas statute included the traditional heart-lung criterion and the Committee's criteria for determining brain death.[70] Critics of the Kansas statute complained that the language appeared to suggest two separate, conflicting definitions of

---

68. Pernick, "Brain Death in Cultural Context," 8.

69. President's Commission, *Defining Death*, 62.

70. "A person will be considered medically and legally dead if, in the opinion of a physician, based on ordinary standards of medical practice, there is the absence of spontaneous respiratory and cardiac function and, because of the disease or condition which caused, directly or indirectly, these functions to cease, or because of the passage of time since these functions ceased, attempts at resuscitation are considered hopeless; and, in this event, death will have occurred at the time these functions ceased; or a person will be considered medically and legally dead if, in the opinion of a physician, based on ordinary standards of medical practice, there is the absence of spontaneous brain functions; and if based on ordinary standards of medical practice, during reasonable attempts to either maintain or restore spontaneous circulatory or respiratory function in the absence of aforesaid brain function, it appears that further attempts at resuscitation or supportive maintenance will not succeed, death will have occurred at the time when these conditions first coincide. Death is to be pronounced before artificial means of supporting respiratory and circulatory function are terminated and before any vital organ is removed for purposes of transplantation. These alternative definitions of death are to be utilized for all purposes in this state, including the trials of civil and criminal cases, any laws to the contrary notwithstanding." Ibid.

death.[71] Depending on which paragraph is used, a person can be dead or alive.[72] Attempting to correct the problems of the Kansas statute, Professor Alexander Morgan Capron and Dr. Leon R. Kass proposed a model statute in a law article published in 1972. The Capron-Kass proposal more clearly spelled out the synchrony between the two standards of death and avoided language that implied terminating treatment for the dying. This model statute was adopted in some form by seven states.[73]

Between 1970 and 1978, nineteen states adopted legislation recognizing the brain death criterion.[74] In 1975, the American Bar Association House of Delegates formulated a legal definition of brain death. The ABA defined brain death as an "irreversible cessation of total brain function, according to usual and customary standards of medical practice."[75] In 1979, the National Conference of Commissioners of Uniform State Laws approved the Uniform Brain Death Act, which incorporated the ABA's recommended definition.[76]

Despite the approval of legal scholars and practitioners, the act fell short in two important respects: 1) it addressed the concept of brain death only, but not the criteria used to conclude that death had occurred,[77] and 2) it omitted the traditional cardiopulmonary criterion.[78]

To further illustrate these shortcomings, an article published in 1979 by the *New England Journal of Medicine* claimed that, unlike many other countries, no American consensus existed as to which criteria

71. Glaves-Innis, "Organ Donation and Incompetents," 155–63.

72. Ibid., 163.

73. Capron and Kass, "Statutory Definition of the Standards for Determining Human Death," 87–118. A revised version appeared later in 1978 and is as follows: "A person will be considered dead if in the announced opinion of a physician, based on ordinary standards of medical practice, he has experienced an irreversible cessation of respiratory and circulatory functions, or in the event that artificial means of support preclude a determination that these functions have ceased, he has experienced an irreversible cessation of total brain functions. Death will have occurred at the time when the relevant functions ceased." Capron, "Legal Definition of Death," 349–56

74. Glaves-Innis, "Organ Donation and Incompetents," 163.

75. American Bar Association, *American Bar Association Annual Report*, 100.

76. President's Commission, 66: "For legal and medical purposes, an individual who has sustained irreversible cessation of all functioning of the brain, including brain stem, is dead. A determination under this section must be made in accordance with reasonable medical standards."

77. Glaves-Innis, "Organ Donation and Incompetents," 163.

78. Rado, "Cultural Elites," 42–66.

should be used in determining a brain death diagnosis.[79] Moreover, the article pointed out that despite the fact that many articles had been written claiming that brain death criteria were "dependable and duplicable," various advisory groups had recommended over thirty different sets of criteria. Later, the President's Commission would acknowledge the problem of statutory inconsistencies and the need for a uniform standard.[80]

Another major activity in the same decade was the emergence of the bioethics community. Foremost among the issues discussed by members of that community were those related to death. Those issues included whether death was an event or a process, whether whole brain or "higher" brain functional loss was adequate to determine death, and whether certain brain functions could be ignored in declaring patients brain dead.[81] Although these questions were not new, they emphasized the need to conceptualize brain death for both medical practice and legal policy.

In summary, two important factors emerge from the debates over the Harvard criteria in the 1970s. First, the struggle of the medical community to retain its professional power in the face of increasing distrust by the press and public led to the intervention of law in standardizing death. Second, a growing recognition "that the development of criteria for determining death is at once a medical and a philosophical-theological task,"[82] led to the influence of a larger and varied group of cultural elites.[83] This set the stage for the President's Commission whose mandated study included refinement of the definition and criterion of death.

THE PRESIDENT'S COMMISSION REPORT AND THE UDDA

Following developments in transplantation and the Harvard Ad Hoc Committee's report, President Jimmy Carter appointed a Commission for the Study of Ethical Problems in Medicine and Biomedical and Behavioral Research in 1978. Specifically, the President charged the Commission with the responsibility to "study and recommend ways in

79. Black, "Brain Death," 338–34.
80. President's Commission, *Defining Death*, 155–57.
81. Youngner and Arnold, "Philosophical Debates," 527–37.
82. DuBois, "Organ Transplantation," 413–53.
83. See Rado, "Cultural Elites and the Institutionalization of Ideas."

which the traditional legal standards can be updated in order to provide clear and principled guidance for determining whether such [artificially maintained] bodies are alive or dead."[84] Assuming that traditional standards of death were outdated and incapable of accounting for artificially maintained bodies, the Commission sought to discover "whether the law ought to recognize new means for establishing that the death of a human being has occurred."[85] In addition, the Commission endeavored to improve upon the inadequacies of the diagnostic criteria of the Harvard Committee's recommendation. The Commission's report was published in July 1981 under the title, *Defining Death,* in which the Commission defended the concept of "whole brain death." The Commission, working in conjunction with the American Bar Association, the American Medical Association, and the National Conference of Commissioners on Uniform State Laws, recommended in its report a Uniform Determination of Death Act (UDDA). The Act essentially bifurcated the standard of death in the following way:

> An individual who has sustained either (1) irreversible cessation of circulatory and respiratory functions, or (2) irreversible cessation of all functions of the entire brain, including the brain stem, is dead. A determination of death must be made in accordance with accepted medical standards.[86]

Owing to the influence of the President's Commission report, the UDDA's inclusion of brain death into its bifurcated standard has since been adopted in some way by every state.[87]

The reports issued by the President's Commission and the Harvard Committee differed in several important respects. First, unlike the Harvard Committee, which was composed mostly of physicians, less than half of the Commission's members were physicians. This was to ensure that the discussions included the interests and concerns of those outside the medical field. Second, a related but distinct concern was to ensure that there were no conflicts of interest by excluding transplant surgeons from the Commission's make-up. Third, the Commission heard testimony on a range of issues related to a standard for determining death from

84. President's Commission, *Defining Death*, 3.
85. Ibid.
86. Ibid., 4.
87. Menikoff, *Law and Bioethics*, 450.

experts in fields ranging from neurology to philosophy. And finally, a careful review was conducted of the views of prominent members of the right to life movement, to ensure support of the idea of whole-brain death.[88] These measures exemplified the Commission's attempts to propose policy recommendations that would "accurately reflect the social meaning of death and not constitute a mere legal fiction."[89]

Central to the Commission's report is its conceptual foundation for whole-brain death (or simply, brain death), which is attributed to the influence of a group of physicians from Dartmouth. Led by James L Bernat,[90] they argued that the conception behind brain death rested on the notion that the brain was the source of integration for the organism as a whole. As such, when the brain suffers irreversible loss of its integrative functions, then the capacity for organizational function for the organism as a whole is also lost and, hence, the organism is essentially dead. Although artificial support for respiration and heart rate may give the appearance of some organizational unity, the capacity for spontaneous function is, in reality, non-existent. According to the Dartmouth group, this lies in the fact that the human body is an integrated organism of interrelated systems and organs.[91] No single part of the integrated organism constitutes life itself, but rather it is the unitary functioning of the organism as a whole that constitutes a living body. The fact that a

---

88. Lock, *Twice Dead,* 111–12.

89. President's Commission, *Defining Death,* 33. Moreover, the Commission overwhelmingly agreed upon a statutory recommendation of brain death for the following reasons:

    (1) Such a law would establish the legality of pronouncing death based on brain criteria.

    (2) The use of the brain-based standard when the heart-lung standard is not applicable would protect patients against ill-advised, idiosyncratic pronouncements of death.

    (3) Legal recognition of the brain-based standard would remove the doubt that exists in some states over the use of patients without brain functions as organ donors.

    (4) A single set of standards for death pronouncements is appropriate for all legal purposes (encompassing inheritance, taxes and criminal trials, as well as medical treatment).

    (5) Maintaining a dead body on artificial support systems consumes scarce medical resources and may unnecessarily deplete the family's emotional and financial resources. See page 10 of the Commission report.

90. Bernat et al., "On the Definition and Criteria of Death," 389–91.

91. Ibid.

heart can be taken from one body and placed into another indicates that the organizational unity of the body does not necessarily reside in the heart. While the heart is a vital organ, it can be replaced. Not so, however, with the brain. Since the brain is responsible for integrating bodily life, when the whole brain permanently loses it functional capacities, the body is, for all practical purposes, dead. The application of artificial life support, however, maintains a collection of interrelated organs and systems, thereby giving the false impression of a living body.

Following investigation of and debate about the issues, the Commission's report maintained that the whole-brain definition of death is best suited to provide the means for accurately diagnosing the death of the person.[92] Additionally, the report asserted that brain death was a universally accepted concept, although there was no evidence to substantiate that assertion.[93] The Commission seemed inclined to ensure that the new brain death conception appeared consistent with the traditional cardio-pulmonary understanding of death. Some members of the Commission feared that the appearance of a radical "paradigm shift" from conventional death may prevent public cooperation with donation due to the perception that the definition of death was being manipulated.[94] In response to this concern, the report "made clear [that] the traditional means of diagnosing death actually detected an irreversible cessation of integrated functioning among the interdependent bodily systems."[95] Traditionally, heart and respiration were the basic vital signs whose absence denoted the cessation of organic unity. Accordingly, the President's report explains, "Breathing and heartbeat are not life itself. They are simply used as signs—as one window for viewing a deeper and more complex reality: a triangle of interrelated systems with the brain at its apex."[96] Thus, the traditional heart and respiratory means of detecting death are, in fact, detecting the permanent cessation of the integrated functioning of the organism as a whole. In contrast, the brain death criterion allows doctors to see through the mask of artificial life support in order to ascertain whether the integrated functioning of the organism

92 President's Commission, *Defining Death*, 35.

93. Lock, *Twice Dead*. Lock notes that this claim was anecdotal at best.

94. Lamb, *Death, Brain Death, and Ethics*.

95. President's Commission, *Defining Death*, 34.

96. Ibid., 33.

as a whole has irreversibly ceased. In short, this means that the criterion has changed but the conception remains the same.

More to the point, when the use of artificial life support mechanisms obscures the means for viewing the traditional signs of heart and respiration, these vitals are reduced to artifacts of the mechanical life support itself. One approach, which seeks to explain the conception behind the whole brain definition, views "the traditional 'vital signs' of heartbeat and respiration [as] merely surrogate signs with no significance in them."[97] The importance of these vital signs is that when they irreversibly cease, the brain ceases to function.[98] Under this conception, a functioning brain is necessary for regaining consciousness and regulating the vital functions of the body.

Furthermore, the Commission recognized that its work would have ramifications on organ transplantation. While the Commission acknowledged that "advances in organ transplantation were a major impetus in the early development of brain-based criteria for death," it reasoned that current practice indicates, "that the criteria are being applied primarily outside the context of organ donation."[99] For example, a study was conducted in which prolonged ventilator support became the primary qualification for a determination of brain death. Like the Harvard Committee's report, the Commission's report lacked a cohesive legal framework with respect to foregoing life-support and hence saw brain death as a means to relieve the burden of ventilator-supported patients who had no hope of recovery. Even so, transplantation interests influenced the framing and direction of many of the arguments contributing to the uniform standards the Commission recommended. The Commission noted that the internal organs of ventilator-supported patients undergo substantial changes making them less fit for transplantation. Hence, the earlier a brain-death declaration, the sooner transplantable organs can be perfused with organ preserving medications. Moreover, given that these discussions were taking place as new immunosupression drugs

97. Ibid., 34.

98. Ibid. Other signs accompanying these are simply "indicative of loss of the functions of the whole brain." The report also notes: "On this view, death is that moment at which the body's physiological system ceases to constitute an integrated whole. Even if life continues in individual cells or organs, life of the organism as a whole requires complex integration, and without the latter, a person cannot properly be regarded as alive." See page 33 of the Commission report.

99. Ibid., 112.

were becoming available and organ transplants were increasing,[100] it is evident that, as with the Harvard Committee's report, transplantation interests played an important role in the formation of recommendations in the Commission's report.

The Commission, like the Harvard Committee, adopted a neuro-logical conception of death consistent with "irreversible loss of all brain function." This conception distinguishes patients in a persistent vegeta-tive state, whose brain stems continue to function, from those patients who fail to exhibit brain function in either the upper or lower portions of the brain. Patients in a persistent vegetative state (PVS), such as Karen Quinlan[101] and Nancy Cruzan,[102] whose brain stems continue to func-

100. Ibid.

101. In 1975 in New Jersey, twenty-one-year-old Karen Ann Quinlan slipped into a coma and was later diagnosed as PVS. Karen was admitted to an ICU and placed on a vent because of her inability to breathe properly. Her parents were of the Catholic faith and remained hopeful until a meeting in which Karen's physicians informed them Karen would not recover. They understood the Catholic teaching as not requiring ex-traordinary means to prolong life and felt they knew their daughter's wishes. With this in mind Karen's parents asked the physicians to remove the vent and after signing a release form the physicians and hospital agreed. However, the next day the physician informed the Quinlans he could not remove the vent unless they obtained a court order allowing the action. Mr. Quinlan then launched the battle for guardianship of Karen and the right to remove his daughter from the vent. The Quinlan's lost their first round in the NJ Superior Court but they prevailed in the NJ Supreme Court and Mr. Quinlan was granted guardianship. The Quinlan's attorney filed for removal of the vent under: 1) the first amendment: Freedom of Religious Beliefs; 2) the eighth amendment: Cruel and Unusual Punishment; 3) the thirteenth amendment: Liberty. The courts agreed with Liberty, i.e., intimate personal decision-making, and the vent was removed. Karen died nine years later. In this case the courts talked of the need for Ethics Committees.

102. In 1983 a motor vehicle crash left twenty-five-year-old Nancy Cruzan in a per-sistent vegetative state, permanently unconscious and without any higher brain func-tioning. She was kept alive with a feeding tube. After seven years in this state Nancy's parents went to the circuit court on her behalf to ask that the feeding tube be removed. Nancy's parents argued if it was not for the feeding tube she would die of her head injury and the circuit court judge agreed with her parents. However, the Missouri at-torney general appealed to the MO Supreme Court and the decision was reversed. The court ruled that "the state's" interest in life is "unqualified" and that clear and convinc-ing evidence was needed when a life was hanging in the balance. The Cruzans appealed to the US Supreme Court and with a five to four vote the Court ruled the Cruzans needed clear and convincing evidence and there was none that proved Nancy would not want the tube feedings despite what her parents had reported. The family then went back to the MO courts and the courts ruled to remove the feeding tube based on "clear and convincing evidence" after new evidence was presented. Nancy died within a few days of having the tube removed. The case established: 1) state courts can require clear

tion, would not fall under the Commission's criteria for brain death. The significance of this is that such patients, under the Commission's conception, constitute persons, while brain dead patients merely constitute a collection of interrelated organs and systems. Some critics of the Harvard Committee note the lack of clarity of the report and the potential confusion between patients who suffer permanent loss of consciousness and patients who suffer loss of all brain function. In response to this, the Commission sharpened the distinction, thereby rejecting appeals to incorporate neo-cortical death into the standard.

The influence of the Commission's report with respect to social policy is evident in several important cases. Following the UDDA, several courts established legal precedent that recognized the new standard. In 1980, the Supreme Court of Washington took up several questions relating to brain death *In re Bowman*.[103] Five-year-old William Matthew Bowman (Matthew), suffered massive physical injuries which resulted in the irreversible loss of brain activity. The question presented to the court was to whether Matthew had in fact died upon suffering irreversible loss of brain activity, and as a result, medical practitioners were legally protected when removing life support systems from patients suffering from brain death. The trial court employed the UDDA standard, under which the court ruled that Matthew was dead. The State Supreme Court, on appeal, recognized that *Bowman* raised a number of issues involving the cooperation of law and medicine concerning the determination of death. The court ruled that it is for the law to define the standard of death, that brain death should be the standard in Washington, and that it is for the medical profession to apply acceptable medical standards in determining brain death.[104]

Courts have applied the UDDA standard even in the most difficult of cases. *In re T.A.C.P* is instructive in this regard.[105] There, the Florida Supreme Court ruled that the parents of an anencephalic infant could not donate her organs, despite the fact that the child possessed only a brain stem. (In this condition, children lack the ability to develop cogni-

---

and convincing evidence when life is hanging in the balance; 2) there is no "right to die" but instead a right to liberty, which recognizes the right to refuse treatment; 3) the case was instrumental in Congress passing the "Patient Self-Determination Act."

103. *In re Bowman*, cited in Menikoff, *Law and Bioethics*, 444–50.

104. Ibid., 445.

105. *In re T.A.C.P.*, cited in ibid., 455–61.

tion, a sense of pain or sensation, and usually die shortly after birth.)[106] The court reasoned that an anencephalic child does not satisfy Florida's statutory definition of death, and declined to carve out an exception in this case.[107] The court recognized that, according to the UDDA, brain death is defined as the permanent cessation of all functions of the entire brain, including the brain stem. The court reasoned that anencephalic children, though lacking significant parts of their brains (cerebrum and cerebral cortex), nonetheless possess active brain stems. As such, they do not satisfy the brain death criterion.[108] Based upon common law and the UDDA, the Florida court recognized that *T.A.C.P.* was a "live" birth and not a "fetal" death. Although the courts in both *Bowman* and *T.A.C.P.* ruled that brain death was the legal standard, the Washington court held that it was for the law to determine the standard of death, and the Florida court refused to grant an exception to brain death, thus upholding it as the legal standard.

In both of these cases, the courts reached uniform legal conclusions recognizing the legal standard and conception of death as exemplified in the President's Commission report and the UDDA. In short, death is best defined as the death of the organism as a whole, satisfied by either the cardiopulmonary or brain death criterion.

Despite the fact that some state courts and legislatures have struggled to consistently apply the new standard, today all U. S. jurisdictions have accepted brain death as the legal standard underscoring the Commission's success in standardizing death in the United States. Further confirmation of this success is supported by the fact that later commissions have neither sought to revise nor revisit the earlier commission's findings or recommendations. To characterize the two seminal events which brought about the establishment of brain death in the United States, it would be fair to say that while the Harvard Committee

106. See Shewmon's interesting discussion on this issue in Shewmon, "Recovery from 'Brain Death,'" 30–95.

107. As a case of first impression, this court avoided the temptation to craft new law concerning anencephalic infants and organ donation, but rather rendered its ruling in accordance with common law and Florida statutes regarding death.

108. In fact, if the court had granted an exception for anencephaly, it would have implicitly recognized new-cortical death as a viable option, since neo-cortical death focuses on permanent loss of higher brain functions associated with the parts of the brain missing in anencephalic children.

endeavored to frame death as a purely medical matter, the President's Commission transformed it into a matter of law.[109]

CONCLUSION

This chapter explored the historical development of brain death in the context of emerging technologies. In particular, the chapter investigated the criticism that brain death has never been legitimately justified as a valid criterion of death, but instead was advanced by committee in order to promote organ transplantation. This chapter represents one part of a larger analysis in support of the thesis that brain death is fraught with numerous difficulties that render it unethical as a means for determining death.

The boundary between life and death has always been a subject of discussion and controversy. The emergence of new biomedical technologies brought new challenges and controversies concerning the proper diagnostic methods for determining death. The concept of brain death was created in the midst of a complex of 1960s-era technological innovations and interests which involved, in some cases, competing claims over a curious product of medicine's ability to exponentially suspend the dying process, viz., the irreversibly comatose patient.

Historical analysis reveals that the earliest discussions concerning the irreversibly comatose patient took place in the context of developing kidney transplant technology in the 1960s. Due to improvements in immunosuppression, cadaver kidney transplants became realizable as a new source to supplement the scarcity of living kin donors. Recognizing the superiority of heart-beating cadaver kidneys, as well as emerging EEG technology as a potential diagnostic tool, transplant researchers began discussing the possibility of facilitating the brain dead as organ sources. However, most physicians who participated in these early discussions were reluctant to advance a new criterion for death owing to disagreements regarding the signs of death and concern for how respect for the medical community might be affected.

---

109. It is important to note that acceptance of the U.S. brain-death concept has been practically universal. Most other countries have employed it in some way with the exception of the UK and India. In the UK, *brainstem* death is the preference.

Perhaps the most significant influence was the first heart transplant in 1967, which inspired a surge in heart transplants around the world. This was followed almost immediately with the formation of an Ad Hoc Committee from the Harvard Medical School, known for its interest in transplantation, whose purpose was to discuss how best to diagnose neurological death. Though the published report made scant reference to transplantation interests, other documents from committee members reveal transplantation interests to be the primary motivation for advancing a new criterion for death. The memos of Beecher and Ebert document their concerns and interests in advancing transplantation while at the same time attempting to downplay its prevalence in the published report. Additionally, rather than offering support through scientific literature, the report offered two pragmatic justifications: 1) to relieve the burdens posed by permanently comatose patients; and 2) to relieve the controversies surrounding obtaining transplantable organs. Analyses provided by Seifert, Lock, and Giacomini indicate that the degree to which these patients posed burdens upon themselves, their families, and medical resources was little noticed in the late 1960s. Indeed, given that the practice of withdrawing life-support from ventilator dependent patients at that time was morally justifiable and commonplace, it is doubtful that the concerns expressed by the Harvard Committee, at least in this respect, reflected the concerns of the public or medical community in general.

The necessity of advancing a new criterion of death to advance transplantation also was challenged by Shewmon. He noted that early heart transplant surgeries were performed without the need for a neurological criterion, rendering such a move as unnecessary and perhaps counter-productive as an effort to secure more transplantable organs. Pernick suggested that other interests contributed to the motives of the committee headed up by Beecher, including the use of permanently comatose patients for medical experimentation purposes.

Despite general acceptance by the medical and legal press in the decade that followed, some ambiguities remained with respect to the meaning and application of brain death in medial praxis and social policy. In light of varied sets of diagnostic criteria and model statutes, the President's Commission in 1981 published its report, *Defining Death*, in which it proposed a conceptual basis for brain death and a model statute in an attempt to make death uniform. What was lacking in the

Harvard Committee's report, the President's report attempted to clarify and amend, viz., a biological, philosophical, and legal basis for standardizing death.

This chapter has demonstrated that, historically, brain death emerged at the crossroads of intersecting technological developments and interests. In an effort to advance experimental medicine, particularly organ transplantation, some researchers looked to the permanently comatose patient as a means of resolving some practical obstacles in research medicine. In failing to provide an adequate justification for why permanently comatose patients should be considered dead, the Harvard Committee opted to a problems-oriented approach thus disclosing the seemingly dubious priority of advancing research interests over precision regarding the definition and criterion of human death.

Although the President's Commission report enjoyed success in standardizing death in the 1980s and 1990s, further analysis regarding the controversies of the President's Commission's adopted conceptual framework reveal that controversy regarding brain death continues to linger on, and in some cases, has grown in intensity.[110] The aim of chapter 2 is to investigate the conceptual challenges raised by numerous thinkers in regard to the consistency of brain death with the death of the organism as a whole, calling into question its legitimacy in the face of emerging science. Included in the discussion will be an examination into the scientific validity of the criteria and clinical tests for brain death, as well as the doubts and unease exhibited by many clinicians regarding the use of brain death for transplantation. While some have described the issue of brain death as "well settled yet still unresolved,"[111] a closer examination discloses reasons for re-thinking previous conclusions concerning the conceptual basis for brain death as a valid standard of death.

110. Shewmon, "Brain and Somatic Integration," 459.
111. Capron, "Brain-Death."

2

Medical Misgivings with Brain Death

B RAIN DEATH WAS FIRST introduced as a pragmatic solution to the problem surrounding the treatment of *coma dépassé* patients and the removal of donative organs. Although the Harvard Committee recommended tests for determining brain death in patients, the report failed to say why a diagnosis of brain death should be equated with human death. Over a decade later, the President's Commission articulated a conceptual basis for brain death in an attempt to validate its use as a criterion for human death. Additionally, the Commission provided a model statute in an attempt to standardize brain death in the United States. Since that time, there has been global acceptance of brain death. This has led many to conclude that, despite questions that still persist, the issue of brain death is "well settled yet still unresolved."[1]

Specifically, medical experts question the scientific basis for brain death, often pointing to arbitrariness in testing and clinical evidence of long-term survival of some brain dead patients.[2] In 2002, a survey conducted in eighty countries revealed major differences in the procedures for diagnosing brain death in adults.[3] Chief among those differences is the apnea test, which in some cases may lead to a misdiagnosis, or even

---

1. Capron, "Brain-Death," 16.

2. Byrne and Weaver, "'Brain Death.' Is Not Death." Wijdicks, "Diagnosis of Brain Death." Shewmon, "Brainstem Death."

3. Wijdicks, "Brain Death Worldwide."

premature death.[4] Researchers from the Harvard Medical School also have reported that brain death "fails to correspond to any coherent biological or philosophical understanding of death."[5] A growing number of experts in neuroscience, philosophy, and religion claim that a prognosis of brain death, which will inevitably lead to somatic death, is not identical to a diagnosis that somatic death has actually occurred.[6]

The purpose of this chapter is to explore the challenges surrounding brain death and its clinical and scientific basis in particular. This will involve an assessment of its biological conceptual basis, giving particular attention to the difficulties of establishing somatic neural dependency respecting brain death's clinical criteria. Additionally, the chapter will discuss the various clinical anomalies and physical phenomena that occur in brain-dead patients and determine whether they are consistent with the "standard paradigm" as set forth in the brain-death standard. Related to this discussion are the difficulties of using the brain-death criterion along with the cardiopulmonary-death criterion as required by the President's Report.

This chapter deals with the problems of conceptual consistency. Specifically, it explores the evolution of brain death's clinical criteria and tests. This chapter also discloses and assesses data from various surveys of clinicians (doctors and nurses) who deal with brain death and its use in organ procurement.

PROBLEMS OF CONCEPTUAL CONTINUITY

Despite more than thirty years as the standard for determining death,[7] brain death continues to generate confusion and controversy.[8] Beginning in the 1970s, a number of experts challenged the idea that brain death could be conceptually sustained and clinically diagnosed.[9] Bioethics literature reflects criticisms and calls for the abandonment of brain death

---

4. Coimbra, "Implications of Ischemic Penumbra."

5. Truog and Robinson, "Role of Brain Death."

6. Potts et al., "Introduction."

7. Bernat, "Refinements," 83.

8. Shewmon, "Brain and Somatic Integration," 458.

9. Ibid. Shewmon cites the following: Beecher and Dorr, "New Definition of Death." Bryne et al., "Brain Death, the Patient, the Physician, and Society." Evans and Lum, "Brain Death." Youngner and Bartlett, "Human Death and High Technology."

altogether, which medical practitioners and policy makers have tended to ignore. When one considers the implications of the collapse of brain death for solid organ donation, it is not difficult to understand why such calls have been ignored. As several writers note, "The issues of brain death and organ transplantation go hand in hand, for when unpaired vital organs are taken from heart-beating brain dead patients, it causes their somatic death, as in the case of heart transplantation."[10]

Inconsistencies in determining brain death give rise to a three-tiered problem: 1) the tests for diagnosing brain death; 2) the clinical criterion for brain death; and 3) the definition or conception of death.[11] All three must be fulfilled in order to demonstrate cohesion in the paradigm.[12] The definition of death is: "the permanent cessation of functioning of the organism as a whole."[13] The criterion is: "The permanent cessation of functioning of the entire brain."[14] The clinical testing includes: ". . . A battery of tests and procedures, including establishment of an etiology sufficient to account for the loss of all brain functions, diagnosing the presence of coma, documenting apnea and the absence of brain-stem reflexes, excluding reversible conditions, and showing the persistence of these findings over a sufficient period of time."[15]

This interrelationship satisfies each of the three levels; otherwise, serious doubt is cast on the legitimacy of brain death as criterion of death. Brain-death supporters are at great pains to maintain this consistency in the face of growing challenges. Indeed, some researchers maintain that brain death cannot sustain such challenges any longer and therefore should be discarded entirely.[16]

The concept of brain death, originally articulated by Bernat, Culver, and Gert, which had been adopted by the President's Report, rests on two related, though distinct, claims. First, the brain is the source of integration for the organism as a whole, and as such, is consistent with the traditional cardiopulmonary criterion. Consistency is maintained given the fact that after an accurate brain-death diagnosis, cardiopulmonary

---

10. Potts, Bryne, and Nilges, 2.

11. Truog, "Is It Time to Abandon Brain Death?"

12. Ibid., 30.

13. Bernat et al., "On the Definition and Criteria of Death."

14. Ibid.

15. Truog, "Is It Time to Abandon Brain Death?" 30.

16. Ibid.

death quickly follows despite continued intensive care. This is known as the *somatic disintegration hypothesis*.[17] Under this hypothesis, the brain (whole brain) is the critical organ that controls or integrates other bodily systems, and when it ceases to function, the remaining bodily systems are unable to survive.

Early in the debate over the Harvard Report's recommended new criterion of human death, Hans Jonas raised questions regarding the accuracy and sustainability of a brain-oriented definition of death. Parsing out the distinction between "organism as a whole" and "whole organism", Jonas saw the latter as constituting local subsystems (e.g., the continued functioning of cells and tissues) and hence, not "affecting the definition of death by the larger criteria of the whole."[18] He argued that respiration and circulation do not fall into this category because their effect is realized throughout the organism as a whole and "ensures the functional preservation of its other parts."[19] Additionally, introducing the idea of "irreversible cessation" provides no further clarity since it may refer to the function itself or to the spontaneity of the function. Jonas reasoned that a cessation could be either irreversible or reversible depending on which is emphasized. For example, if physicians could do for the disabled brain what they can do for the heart and lungs, i.e., provide an external agency for its continued functioning, such functioning would not matter more so than the lack of spontaneity at its cerebral source.[20] In other words, the location of the agency of functioning, whether interior or exterior, has no bearing on the integration itself. Thus, maintaining cardiorespiratory functions artificially simply does not affect the status of the life of the organism as a whole.

17. Elliot, "Brain Death," 32.

18. Jonas, *Philosophical Essays*, 134–35.

19. Ibid. He further writes: "Why else prolong them artificially in prospective 'cadaveric' organ donors (e.g., 'maintain renal circulation of cadaver kidneys in situ') except to keep those other parts 'in good shape'—viz., alive—for eventual transplantation? The comprehensive system thus sustained is even capable of continued overall metabolism when intravenously fed, and then, presumably, of pretty much everything not involving neural control."

20. At the time of writing, Jonas' hypothetical speculation may have seemed much less convincing than it does today. Today such possibilities are being discussed with all seriousness. See Graham-Rowe, "World's First Brain Prosthesis Revealed." Ivanhoe Newswire, "Artificial Brain Parts on the Horizon."

Another early critic of the whole-brain conception of death is Robert Veatch. For more than thirty years Veatch has challenged brain death on the basis that it cannot be sustained.[21] Focusing on the notion that the entire brain must be dead for the individual as a whole to be dead, Veatch has raised—and continues to raise—doubts about whether a whole-brain conception can be consistently maintained. His main argument is that remaining cellular, electrical, and supercellular functions are ignored as insignificant by brain-death defenders.[22] To be sure, today it is universally recognized that many brain-dead patients who satisfy all the standard clinical tests continue to exhibit integrative functions of the brain.[23] Some of these functions include: 1) continued functioning of the auditory pathways as evidenced by brainstem evoked potentials; 2) continued cortical functioning as evidenced by EEG readings;[24] and 3) continued retention of free-water homeostasis through the neurologically mediated secretion of arginine vasopressin, as evidenced by serum hormonal levels and the absence of diabetes insipidus.[25] The arbitrary way in which these qualifications occur hardly represents the idea that the whole-brain must be dead in order to declare an individual dead. If one accepts that all functions of the entire brain must permanently cease for an individual to be dead, then it is difficult to justify why certain functions can be ignored in clinical testing.[26]

These concerns have not gone unanswered. While recognizing that all functions of the brain must cease irreversibly before declaring that an

21. Veatch, "Whole-Brain Oriented Concept of Death."

22. Veatch, *Transplantation Ethics,* 104–5. Veatch cites Bernat who justifies ignoring supercellular functions when he writes: "the bedside clinical examination is not sufficiently sensitive to exclude the possibility that small nests of brain cells may have survived . . . and that their continued functioning, although not contributing significantly to the functioning of the organism as a whole, can be measured by laboratory techniques. Because these isolated nests of neurons no longer contribute to the functioning of the organism as a whole, their continued functioning is now irrelevant to the dead organism." Bernat, "How Much of the Brain Must Die on Brain Death?" 25.

23. Ibid., 73.

24. Ibid. The first two are observations provided by Brody.

25. Truog, "Is It Time to Abandon Brain Death?" 30. That is to say, brain mediated hormonal releases continue to be exhibited in patients who meet the clinical criteria for brain death.

26. In light of the evidence, it should be obvious that the attempt by some to analogize the brain death patient with a decapitated corpse proves to be a false analogy. See Lizza, "Conceptual Basis for Brain Death Revisited."

individual is dead, Bernat suggests that not every function of the organism as a whole must permanently cease in order to satisfy brain death.[27] In an effort to refine his earlier account of brain death, Bernat suggests that the term *critical* be used to qualify the functions to which one must appeal in determining the death of the organism as a whole. He defines the critical functions as those necessary for the continued health and life of the organism as a whole.

While many functions are attributable to the organism as a whole, only the critical functions such as breathing, circulation, and awareness matter in assessing whether the critical system of the organism as a whole has been destroyed. Bernat makes clear that it is these critical functions that he and President's Commission had in mind when they used the term *functions*.[28]

Bernat further suggests that when the critical system of the organism is destroyed, entropy and deterioration increases until the systems of organism lose their capacity to operate.[29] His suggestion is based on a thermodynamics theory in which the brain governs entropy production. "When the brain is destroyed," he explains, "the critical system is destroyed and the organism can no longer survive in a state of minimal entropy production."[30] The loss of all critical systems of the brain entails the beginning of this process, in which case, the death of the organism as a whole has occurred.

Such refinements like that offered by Bernat have not satisfied critics of brain death who argue that Bernat's criteria seem arbitrary[31] and *ad hoc*.[32] In particular, they complain that Bernat dismisses any evidence or anomaly contrary to the standard paradigm simply because it does not comport with the notion that the brain is the primary integrator of the organism's critical functions. It is unclear as to whether narrowing the sense of integrated functioning to include only those functions that are consistent with maintaining the current standard is justifiable. Indeed, due to the more dynamical-systems-enlightened biology of the 1990s a broader reading of integrated functioning suggests that integra-

27. Bernat, "Refinements in the Definition and Criterion of Death," 86.

28. Ibid., 87.

29. Ibid.

30. Ibid.

31. Youngner and Arnold, "Philosophical Debates."

32. Potts, "Requiem for Whole Brain Death."

tion is not localized in any one part of the body, including the brain.[33] This broader reading poses a direct challenge to the claim that the brain is the primary source of integration. This challenge, among others, will be considered in the next section.

ARBITRARINESS OF THE CRITERION

According to the current standard that comprises brain death, death occurs when the whole brain irreversibly ceases to function. As Bernat explains:

> [I]t is primarily the *brain* that is responsible for the functioning of the organism as a whole: the integration of organ and tissue subsystems by neural and neuroendocrine control of tempera-ture, fluids and electrolytes, nutrition, breathing, circulation, appropriate responses to danger, among others. The cardiac ar-rest patient with whole *brain* destruction is simply a preparation of unintegrated individual subsystems, since the organism as a whole has ceased functioning.[34]

Alan Shewmon, a pediatric neurologist, has scrutinized Bernat's ratio-nale in light of the empirical evidence opposing the idea of the brain as the organ of somatic integration. The criterion rests on the idea that the brain serves as the integrator of the organism as a whole. That is, the integrated unity of the organism as a whole is sustained and directed primarily by a functioning brain. If this claim is mistaken, the concep-tual basis for brain death is untenable. Shewmon, whose multiple con-versions, from neo-cortical death to whole-brain death, and finally to a holistic, systems oriented criterion of death, offers criticisms that are instructive on this point.[35] Many physicians cite Shewmon's work and that the role of the brain, with regard to its contribution to the organism as a whole, is best described as a modulator and enhancer of integration rather than the integrator itself.[36] Viewed this way, integration may not be reducible to a single part or organ of the body. Rather, as Shewmon explains, "Each part of the body, especially the brain, contributes to the

---

33. Shewmon, "Brain and Somatic Integration," 473.
34. Bernat, "Refinements in the Definition and Criterion of Death," 36.
35. Shewmon, "Recovery from 'Brain Death.'"
36. Shewmon, "Brain and Somatic Integration," 471.

stability, robustness, and richness of the body's vitality and unity, but no one part or even combination of parts constitutes that vitality or unity."[37] Thus, the essence of integration is neither localizable nor reducible but rather enhanced throughout the interaction of all the parts, cells, and tissues of the body and "mediated in mammals by circulating oxygenated blood."[38] This suggests that the traditional cardiopulmonary criterion (or some modified form of it) is best suited for determining the death of the organism as a whole.

In support of his claims, Shewmon documents 175 brain-dead patients whose survival rates varied from one week, to several months, and, in one case, to fourteen years.[39] The greatest survival rates were among children who had exhibited a remarkable capacity for prolonged survival. Other cases include brain-dead pregnant women and other adult patients whose survival rates were significantly less. Shewmon concludes that the data discloses: 1) cardiac arrest is not necessarily imminent in brain dead patients; 2) survival rates are better explained by non-brain factors; and 3) stabilization is possible for some patients to the point of being discharged at home on a ventilator.[40]

Some brain-death defenders have challenged the diagnoses in Shewmon's cases. Wijdicks and Bernat,[41] for example, raised doubts given the incomplete information provided by the cases. Particularly, they cite to the lack of a 'denominator' and the exclusion of information regarding drug effects as well as the details of apnea testing as shortcomings. Yet, as Elliot notes, "It seems unlikely that all of these cases could have been misdiagnoses," otherwise, "the implication must be that many other misdiagnosed patients have had support discontinued, or have been subjected to organ harvesting."[42]

To further support his claim that brain-death criteria are arbitrary, Shewmon refers to sixteen non-brain integrative 'holistic' functions

---

37. Ibid., 472.

38. Ibid., 473.

39. Shewmon, "'Brainstem Death.'" Regarding the case of fourteen years, Shewmon details this interesting case in the above article. I should note that in a personal conversation (November, 2006) with Dr. Paul Byrne, a neonatologist who treated TK, he disclosed that TK lived five more years before passing away at age 23.

40. Ibid. Emphases in original.

41. Wijdicks and Bernat, "Chronic 'Brain Death.'"

42. Elliot, "Brain Death," 32.

of patients who had been declared to be brain dead.[43] These functions varied in patients and include fighting infections, sexual maturation, improvement in general health, and the ability to survive outside a hospital with little medical intervention.[44]

Furthermore, Shewmon claims that most brain-mediated integrative functions are not somatically integrating. While many of these integrative functions are endogenous within the brain, very few have to do with the integration of the body. As such, they do not confer unity upon the body; rather they enhance or preserve the somatic unity that is already present. Consider breathing and nutrition, for example. If breathing is understood as a brain-mediated function, then it constitutes only the moving of air in and out of the lungs (in the bellows sense) involving the "the phrenic nerves, diaphragm and intercostals muscles."[45] However, as Shewmon notes, given that "fetuses in utero and patients on cardiopulmonary bypass or extracorporeal membrane oxygenation are quite alive without movement of air driven by either brain or ventilator," breathing in the bellows sense is best understood as "merely a *condition* for somatic integration to take place under ordinary circumstances, not an essential aspect of somatic integration itself."[46] If breathing is understood as respiration (the exchange of oxygen and carbon dioxide), then breathing is not mediated by the brain. Similarly, if nutrition is understood as eating and drinking or merely swallowing, it is a brain-mediated function. But if it is understood as the break down of food into smaller elements for absorption into the body's structure, it is not.

The somatic disintegration hypothesis is further weakened when the integrative capacities of certain brain-dead patients are considered.[47]

43. Shewmon, "The brain and somatic integration," 460–62. Further documented cases of maintained survival of brain dead patients include: Bernstein et al., "Maternal Brain Death." Field et al., "Maternal Brain Death During Pregnancy." Iwai et al., "Effects of Vasopressin."

44. See the complete list: Shewmon, "Brain and Somatic Integration," 467–68.

45. Ibid., 464.

46. Ibid.

47. Other researchers report interesting anomalies as suggestive of continued signs of integrative functioning. Common physical phenomena include: unusual spontaneous movements, such as the "Lazarus" sign, unusual extension and rotation of limbs, referred to as "decerebrate posture," spinal reflexes, enteric nervous system reflexes, local cardiac reflexes, renal function, and the continuation of heart rates for brain dead patients for months, and sometimes years. All of these phenomena are indicative of some remaining integrative function in the so-called "dead brains" of patients who

Perhaps the greatest difficulty for advocates of the brain-death standard, and the one that some have suggested is "the straw that breaks
the conceptual camel's back,"[48] is found in brain-dead pregnant women
who are sustained on life support and continue to carry developing children in their wombs to near full term delivery (in one case 107 days).[49]
Commenting on the implications of this phenomenon, a Japanese cardiologist, Dr. Yoshio Watanabe, explains:

> if the entire brain including the brain stem has indeed sustained
> irreversible damage, cardiorespiratory arrest would inevitably
> ensue, bringing about the person's death. However, the duration
> of this stage may well last for several days to several weeks when
> a respirator is used and hence, this stage at best only predicts
> that death of the individual is imminent, not that it is confirmed.
> The fact that some brain dead pregnant women have given birth
> to babies can be taken as strong evidence that the person is still
> alive, and the use of terms such as biomort or heart-beating ca-
> daver is nothing but a sophism to conceal the contradiction in
> transplant protagonists' logic.[50]

It seems difficult for those who advocate the brain-death standard to
account for this phenomenon if the brain provides the integrative functioning of the organism as a whole. As Karen Granstrand Gervais observes, "The organism as a whole must be functioning for the uterus to
remain a hospitable environment for the developing fetus."[51]

The preceding discussion suggests several implications. First,
the rationale for the brain-death criterion, as developed and articulated by Bernat, et al, continues to be challenged in spite of refinements.
Specifically, recent findings by Shewmon disclose that brain-dead patients exhibit a litany of biologically integrative activity indicative of
somatic life, not death. As a result, many thinkers no longer consider
the somatic disintegration hypothesis a legitimate conceptual basis for
brain death. The influence of Shewmon's work is particularly trouble-
some for brain-death advocates. In a recent exchange between James

---

satisfy the tests. See: Roper, "Unusual Spontaneous Movements." Marti-Fabregas et
al., "Decerebrate-Like Posturing." Shewmon, "Chronic Brain Death." Döşemeci et al.,
"Frequency of spinal reflex movements in brain-dead patients."

48. Siegler and Wikler, "Brain Death and Live Birth," 1101.

49. Bernstein et al., "Maternal Brain Death and Prolonged Fetal Survival."

50. Watanabe, "Brain Death and Cardiac Transplantation," 192.

51. Gervais, *Redefining Death,* 146.

Bernat and another researcher, he candidly admits, "Alan Shewmon has written convincingly that the integration argument alone is inadequate. After numerous conversations with him over the years I have come to conclude that he is probably correct. I have struggled to discern what else is important in addition to the integrator theory."[52] Nevertheless, the problems surrounding the brain-death standard do not end here. They include the difficulty of maintaining consistency in clinical testing. This difficulty is central to the standard as a whole, which will be critiqued in the next section.

INCOHERENCIES OF THE CLINICAL TESTS

Maintaining conceptual clarity requires consistency with regard to the clinical tests-criterion relation for determining brain death. Since its inception, brain-death testing guidelines have undergone numerous revisions. The Harvard Committee recommended testing to determine the following: 1) lack of reception or response to external stimuli; 2) no spontaneous respiration for three minutes off of a respirator; 3) no reflexes; and 4) a flat electroencephalogram for at least ten minutes, repeated after twenty four hours.[53] Missing from the Committee's report was data from studies that qualified uses of these tests. In 1971, two Minneapolis neurosurgeons published their study of twenty-five brain-dead patients.[54] Of the twenty-five, only nine had EEG testing and of those, two had biologic activity after having been declared brain dead. The Minnesota Criteria, as it became known, not only removed the necessity of EEG testing, but also reduced the twenty-four hour period for neurologic confirmation of no spontaneous movement to twelve hours. The most significant study to date was conducted by the National Institute of Health.[55] This Collaborative Study was conducted on 804 patients, with data provided for only 503 of them. The limits of the study resulted in a recommendation for a larger clinical trial, which has not occurred as of the writing of this project. In contrast to the thirty sets

---

52. Personal correspondence cited in: Whetstine, "Examination of the Bio-Philosophical Literature," 122.

53. See "A Definition of Irreversible Coma."

54. Mohandas and Chou, "Brain Death: A Clinical and Pathological Study.

55. National Institute of Health, "Appraisal of the Criteria of Cerebral Death."

of criteria that were used as the basis for brain death during the 1970s, today there are over forty.

While brain death has gained global acceptance, the criteria for determining brain death varies considerably from country to country, and in different areas of the same country. In 2002, neurologist Eelco Widjicks published a study on brain death, which consisted of a survey of eighty countries regarding diagnostic testing procedures.[56] Of the eighty countries, Widjicks found that seventy had adopted guidelines permitting a brain-death diagnosis. Although relative uniformity exists with respect to the definition of brain death, the requirements for diagnosing the condition can differ. In some countries, several specialists must confirm the clinical diagnosis, while in others a single physician can make the diagnosis.

Of specific concern to Widjicks are the differences between countries regarding confirmatory testing, such as the apnea test. Variations in guidelines for apnea testing indicate these tests are not conducted uniformly. In fact, some countries do not accept apnea testing as confirmatory, while others vary in the timing of its application.[57] A study conducted by Coimbra suggests that apnea testing may result in a misdiagnosis of respiratory center failure if inadequately stimulating, and if stringently applied may induce brain death.[58] Apnea testing is carried out by disconnecting the patient from the ventilator over a period of

---

56. Wijdicks, "Brain Death Worldwide."

57. Randell, "Medical and Legal Considerations," 140–41.

58. See Coimbra, "Implications of Ischemic Penumbra for the Diagnosis of Brain Death." The conclusion of this study is: "Patients declared brain-dead may actually sustain global or regional (brain-stem) ischemic penumbra and respond to moderate hypothermia and/or thrombolysis. Time-consuming procedures currently in use may induce rather than diagnose irreversible brain damage. The thirty-year-old guidelines for diagnosis of brain death are to be urgently reconsidered." Norm Barber explains:

> Coimbra shows there are two ways of treating severe brain injury that may produce recovery even in apparently hopeless situations. One is hypothermia that reduces the brain's use of oxygen and gives doctors more time to treat the patient before further damage occurs due to lack of oxygen.
>
> Another is the controversial, and some say unproven, hyperventilation that is intended to increase the amount of oxygen reaching the brain. Both treatments are intended to minimize oxygen deprivation in the brain, hyperventilation by maximizing oxygen reaching the brain and hypothermia by minimizing the brain's oxygen requirements by slowing the metabolism.

Barber, *Nasty Side of Organ Transplantation*, 13.

time (up to ten minutes) allowing for a specified build-up of carbon dioxide in the blood sufficient to exceed the threshold level for stimulation of the respiratory center. Simultaneously, oxygen is delivered at a high flow rate directly through the trachea throughout the period of disconnection to protect transplantable organs from hypoxic damage. The problem is that the addition of oxygen to protect wanted organs removes the stimulus for spontaneous breathing in patients who may have lost their hypercapneic respiratory drive. In addition, when CO_2 levels rise in the brain, additional swelling occurs which may further compromise an already damaged brain.[59] If the apnea test is stringently applied prior to other bedside reflex testing (as is often the case), it practically ensures patient failure of the other tests. Coimbra suggests that some patients could have survived if organ removal had not been rushed.

> [A] review of the literature shows that some of even the most severely head-injured patients (GCS of 3 or 4, with pupils fixed to light) who are not subjected to apnoea may recover to normal life. Early labeling of these patients as dead (for transplant purposes) during the past 3 decades has diverted medical researchers away from developing novel therapeutic resources that could already have saved many thousands of human lives throughout the world.[60]

Surely a test that predisposes a patient to be declared brain dead is unacceptable.

Doctors in the United States also are inconsistent when determining brain death in patients. For example, in diagnosing brain death in children, special (and in some cases exclusionary) criteria must be considered.[61] This is due to "many factors including difficulties of clinical assessment, determination of proximate cause of coma, and certainty of the validity of laboratory tests" unique to infants and children.[62] In addition, variations exist from state to state. For example, while most states require one physician to make the determination, others require a

59. Evans, "Demise of 'Brain Death' in Britain," 147–48.

60. Coimbra, "Implications of Ischemic Penumbra for the Diagnosis of Brain Death."

61. Currently, the U.S. criteria for adults are described in terms of practice parameters by the American Academy of Neurology. See American Academy of Neurology, "Practice Parameters for Determining Brain Death in Adults."

62. Wijdicks, "Brain Death Worldwide."

second independent physician to confirm the diagnosis.[63] In two states, a nurse can determine that a patient is brain dead, provided that a physician confirms that determination within twenty-four hours. The New Jersey State Board of Medical Examiners has recently considered easing brain-death testing criteria in an effort to procure more transplantable organs.[64] If approved, the new criteria would require only one physician to make the diagnosis instead of two, and furthermore, eliminate the need for a neurologist or neurosurgeon to confirm the condition. As previously discussed in relation to the problem of clinical confusion, these changes also may increase the potential for misdiagnoses.

Of particular concern is the exclusion of EEG testing.[65] In the United Kingdom, EEG tests are not required because the death of the brainstem is sufficient to produce the irreversible loss of consciousness and the capacity to breathe.[66] If EEG testing is eliminated from the testing protocol, it is possible that some patients who satisfy the other tests may nonetheless retain some neocortical activity which suggests the possibility of minimal consciousness in some of these patients. More troubling is the fact that even if EEG testing is applied, it only is capable of evaluating the outer part of the cortex. Most investigators conclude that brain-dead patients lack consciousness when the anatomic seat of consciousness is destroyed. However, some investigators suggest that it is not possible to exclude the possibility that some deeply comatose patients who satisfy standard clinical testing may retain preserved cerebral hemispheres, and hence might be capable of thinking, feeling, etc.[67] Given the subjective nature of consciousness, "...even though wakefulness may be permanently lost, the preformed content of consciousness may still reside intact in the cerebral hemispheres—at least in the cases of 'BD' [brain death] where there is real electrical cerebral activity—but it is impossible to be inspected directly."[68]

The preceding discussion discloses several implications. First, although the Harvard Committee recommended tests for determining

63. The Iowa statute 702.8 entitled *Death* required two physicians for a determination. See "Death," in *Iowa Code.*

64. White, *New Jersey Looking to Harvest More Organs.*

65. Karakatsanis and Tsanakas, "Critique of the Concept of 'Brain Death.'"

66. Elliot, "Brain Death," 26.

67. Karakatsanis and Tsanakas, "Critique of the Concept of 'Brain Death,'" 138.

68. Ibid.

brain death, a substantial clinical trial confirming diagnostic tests has never occurred. As a result, over forty different sets of criteria are presently in use worldwide. For many, this generates further confusion and controversy with respect to the meaning of a brain-death diagnosis. More troubling is the questionable nature of some confirmatory tests for brain death, such as the apnea test, which may induce brain death in patients, when stringently applied. In addition, the use of the EEG, as a confirmatory measure, lacks universal application. This is due in part to the ongoing complexities surrounding the nature of consciousness. To be sure, variations in diagnostic criteria for brain death signify the difficulties of satisfying a perpetually qualified criterion, calling into question the clinical tests-criterion relation. Indeed, some proponents of brain death admit that the criterion and related testing seem arbitrary.[69] Robert Truog, a critic of brain death, calls into question whether brain death can be accurately diagnosed prior to cardiopulmonary death. He writes:

> Unfortunately, a study of over 500 patients with both coma and apnea (including 146 autopsies for neuropathologic correlation) showed that "it was not possible to verify that a diagnosis made prior to cardiac arrest by any set or subset of criteria would invariably correlate with a diffusely destroyed brain." On the basis of these data, a definition that required total brain destruction could only be confirmed at autopsy. Clearly, a condition that could only be determined after death could never be a requirement for declaring death.[70]

Physicians and nurses acutely experience these uncertainties, particularly those who are involved in organ procurement and transplantation procedures. While many clinicians "feel comfortable" with brain death as the standard by which to declare human death, others are uneasy with it in practice. The nature of their uneasiness will be the focus of the next section.

---

69. Wijdicks, "Diagnosis of Brain Death," 1216.

70. Truog, "Is it Time to Abandon Brain Death?" 32. Truog cites Molinari, *Nincds Collaborative Study*.

DOUBTS AMONG CLINICIANS

Chief among clinicians' doubts is the way in which the brain-dead display behavior indicative of life, not death. Many patients who satisfy the standard tests for brain death often exhibit unusual physical movements. These include, unusual spontaneous movements, such as the "Lazarus" sign[71], unusual extension and rotation of limbs, referred to as "decerebrate posture,"[72] and the continuation of heart rates for brain-dead patients for months, and sometimes years.[73] For some clinical investigators, this indicates that continued brain function remains. As David Hill, an anaesthetist, expressed: "A measure of life is the continuing hypothalamic function which controls body temperature. If the patient is warm then that part of the brain is functioning."[74] All of these phenomena, it is argued, are indicative of some remaining integrative function in the so-called "dead brains" of patients who satisfy the tests.

Those who are most closely associated with the removal of donor organs express unease and doubts that brain death is not actually death. When considering the experiences of surgical organ transplant team members involved in organ retrieval, it is easy to understand why. Brain-dead "corpses" rarely act like other corpses. When surgeons insert scalpels to surgically remove the organs from the brain-dead corpses, the heart rates and pulses increase and bodily movements suggest "fear and panic."[75] In some cases, the reactions suggest "coordinated attempts to 'grab the knife.'"[76] The solution to this reaction is to immobilize the patient by administering paralyzing drugs. An anaesthetist in the United Kingdom has expressed the concerns of many surgeons who have participated in the procurement of organs: "Almost everyone will say they have felt uneasy about it. Nurses get really, really upset. You stick the knife in and the pulse and blood pressure shoot up. If you don't give anything at all, the patient will start moving and wriggling around and it's

71. Roper, "Unusual Spontaneous Movements in Brain-Dead Patients."

72. Marti-Fabregas et al., "Decerebrate-Like Posturing with Mechanical Ventilation in Brain Death."

73. Shewmon, "Chronic Brain Death."

74. Hill, "Brain Stem Death," 144.

75. Barber, *Nasty Side of Organ Transplantation*, 10.

76. Ibid.

impossible to do the operation. The surgeon always asked us to paralyze the patient."[77]

These concerns have prompted one physician to quip, "I don't carry a donor card at the moment because I know what happens."[78] Indicative of this uncertainty is the reluctance of many intensivists to become organ donors. One survey discloses that among intensivists, only about nineteen percent are card-carrying organ donors.[79] Lock reports that none of the reasons given for failing to sign organ donor cards is convincing.

Reports of uneasiness from nursing staff and physicians of transplant teams are not uncommon. Such uneasiness stems from the belief that they actually killed the organ donors.[80] Nurses, too, believe this and have recorded the time of death of donors *after* the retrieval surgery.[81] Perhaps the most difficult task for nurses in the management of patients who have been diagnosed as brain dead is to suppress their own intuitive sense that the patient is not yet dead.[82] This counter-intuitive notion is further confounded when the brain-dead are seen to yawn, cough, or cry.[83] While most accept the rationale for brain death, it is nonetheless taxing on one's acuity to consider a patient who remains warm, pink, with an independently beating heart as dead. Moreover, transplant surgeons convey continued uneasiness with the difficult job of organ procurement even after multiple surgeries. Dr. David Evans, for example, states that surgeons do not seem to get over the uneasiness of organ procurement, despite doing it many times.[84]

In the study of organ procurement, Margaret Lock reports that, although all of the physicians she interviewed agree that accurate brain-death diagnoses are robust, simple, and infallible, they do not believe that patients are biologically dead when taken to the operating room for organ retrieval. She reports that none of the physicians interviewed thinks brain death is the end of biological life, though they believe that

77. Ibid.
78. Ibid.
79. Lock, "Inventing a New Death."
80. Shewmon, "Recovery from 'Brain Death,'" 81.
81. Ibid.
82. Edwards and Forbes, "Nursing Practice and the Definition of Death."
83. Lock, *Twice Dead.*
84. Ibid.

brain death is an irreversible diagnosis.[85] Despite uniformity among clinicians regarding the irreversibility of brain death, doubts and uncertainty still remain as to its accuracy in depicting human death.

Given the prevalence of doubts and uncertainties among health care professionals who diagnose and declare brain death, it seems sensible to think that similar doubts and uncertainties about brain death exist in the community at large, including a deep-seated fear of being declared dead while still alive. As Michael Potts points out, "A deep seated fear may yet be rational."[86] Further investigation regarding public sentiment on brain death will be the subject of chapter 3.

CONCLUSION

In the previous chapter a historical analysis was conducted in an effort to chronicle the development of brain death as well as the rationale for its incorporation into medical praxis and social policy. It was argued that the proposed justifications for advancing a brain-based criterion for death were based not on conceptual or biological grounds, but rather on desires to advance experimental medicine—most directly transplantation efforts. In support of the central thesis of this work, this argument demonstrates that the way in which the brain-death standard arose has contributed greatly to ongoing controversy and confusion regarding its meaning and application in law and medicine.

The focus of this chapter was to explore the clinical and scientific challenges to brain death. Specifically, several important implications emerged. First, this chapter began by exploring the conceptual foundation for brain death as advanced by Bernat and colleagues in conjunction with the President's Commission report. From its inception, brain death, understood as the permanent cessation of all functions of the entire brain, has been criticized at its conceptual basis. Critics, such as Jonas and Veatch, who pointed out that despite satisfying all the standard clinical tests, many brain-dead patients continue to exhibit neurological activity in some form. Additionally, clinical anomalies and physical phenomena in brain-dead patients suggest that not all neurological functions have ceased. In full recognition of these problems, brain-death

85. Ibid.
86. Potts, "Letters," 598.

supporters have attempted to qualify which functions (deemed "critical") should count in constituting the conceptual foundation that the brain is the primary integrator of the organism as a whole.

Their attempts notwithstanding, it is increasingly apparent that the conceptual foundation for brain death is crumbling. There is substantial evidence for continued somatic integrative life in brain-dead patients. The evidence included a litany of non-brain integrative functions that continue in patients, despite satisfying the clinical tests for brain death. Perhaps the greatest challenge to the somatic disintegration hypothesis, is brain-dead pregnant women who continue to provide a hospitable environment for fetal development. Yet some still seem to ignore the mounting evidence against neurologic somatic dependence in these patients. This seems arbitrary, at best. Given Bernat's admission that somatic integration is insufficient to ground brain death, the first claim upon which the conception is based collapses. Simply put, most integrative functions are not brain mediated. As such, the primacy of the brain with respect to somatic integration is seriously challenged.[87] It would seem that brain-dead individuals are alive as long as at least one integrative bodily system remains in tact (the circulatory system being the key).[88]

Moreover, the second claim regarding consistency within the bifurcated standard cannot be sustained. When the brain dies, bodily functions may continue for some time when life-support measures are provided. Jonas has pointed out that maintaining cardiorespiratory functions "artificially" does not affect the life of the organism as a whole. Given that certain capacities can be supplemented, as is the case with brain-dead patients, such capacities cannot be said to constitute life, or with their permanent loss, death. Rather, it is what these capacities do that constitute life, i.e., sustaining bodily functioning. Since these capacities can be supplemented, then life can continue despite the loss of certain capacities. Advanced technologies will no doubt continue to supplement the loss of particular brain functions.[89] Should they become

---

87. As Shewmon writes: "Under ordinary circumstances the brain participates intimately and importantly in this mutual interaction, but it is not a *sine qua non;* the body without brain function is surely very sick and disabled, but not dead." Shewmon, "Brain and Somatic Integration," 473.

88. Potts, "Requiem for Whole Brain Death."

89. Graham-Rowe. "World's First Brain Prosthesis Revealed."

readily available, then it appears Jonas' inquiry concerning what matters most (i.e., the functioning itself or the lack of spontaneity at its cerebral source) becomes all the more relevant. Understood in this way, brain death may be a form of reductionism, particularly when viewed as a lack of capacity for consciousness, respiration, and heart rate, even when these capacities are supplemented.

While brain death has been accepted worldwide as the standard for determining death, clinicians' inability to uniformly apply the testing criteria suggests that the concept of brain death is flawed as well. In particular, section 2.4 revealed the lack of coherence with respect to the criterion-tests relation. While brain death has been accepted by most modern countries, clinical testing varies greatly from country to country, state to state, and in some cases from hospital to hospital, depending on which of the forty available sets of criteria are utilized. Currently lacking is a thorough clinical trial capable of establishing uniformity with respect to the proper diagnostic tests in confirming the criterion. Recent challenges regarding confirmatory testing, such as the use of the apnea test or the meaning of EEG analysis, demonstrate a lack of understanding with regard to the proper tools for confirming a diffusely destroyed brain. Indeed, data indicates that, at present, brain death cannot be confirmed prior to autopsy following cardiopulmonary death.

Adding to these concerns are the doubts and unease of clinicians who are directly involved in the organ procurement process. Given that brain-dead patients often exhibit behavior indicative of life, not death, some transplant team members struggle in their efforts to suppress their intuitive sense that those who are declared to be brain dead are not really dead. That these uncertainties are influential is evidenced by the fact that few clinicians directly involved in organ procurement carry organ donor cards. But if the analysis to this point is correct, it is not clear why clinicians and patient relatives ought to suppress their intuitions concerning the brain dead. Perhaps, as Potts has suggested, fear has its basis in reason.

At this juncture, it is appropriate to relate how the conclusions of this chapter contribute to the overall purpose of this work. Thus far, it has been noted that the conceptual foundation for brain death is crumbling due to the overwhelming data contradicting both its biological basis as well as its clinical coherency. Contributing to the analysis undertaken in this investigation to examine the social, legal, medical, and philosophical problems of brain death, this chapter contributes to the central thesis that brain death is ethically untenable due to its lack of a biologically coherent foundation.

Further analysis entails an examination of social policy issues related to brain death. Chapter 3 examines the ongoing problems of brain death's conceptual basis, particularly since its inception with the President's Commission Report and the introduction of the UDDA as the suggested framework for determining death. Various social attitudes and overall general public confusion surrounding the meaning and application of brain death are explored. To illustrate the extent of this problem, the struggles of lawmakers to satisfy the demands of the brain-death standard resulting in statutory irregularities both here and abroad are underscored. Chapter 3 catalogs how states define death. Moreover, it is important to discuss how brain death is used in other areas, such as medical research and experimentation on the newly declared dead. These uses generate important moral, ethical, and policy questions regarding the scope and extent of application.

3

Social Policy Problems
with Brain Death

Prior to the advent of advanced medical technologies, the moment of death seemed clearly definable; namely, when all visible life signs have ceased, then the person is dead. For most, the absence of such signs was definitive and final. Public attitudes about death were shaped largely by shared experiences often steeped in religious and family traditions. Common deathbed scenes at home with families gathered around a loved one waiting in vigil for the final draw of breath and exhalation reflect a by-gone era.[1] Today, medical institutions regulate and organize death to such an extent that families often have to be told when their loved ones have died. Life-sustaining technologies not only expand the time to death, but also have altered, in some cases, the way in which death is now conceived. Most important among these advanced medical technologies is the influence of organ transplantation. In previous chapters it was argued that the need for obtaining transplantable life-saving organs from cadaver donors has in large measure shaped and expanded the criteria of death, which ultimately led to the inclusion of brain death. That process, beginning in the late 1960s has been little informed, if any, by public attitudes and opinions. For the most part, the debate about brain death has occupied a relatively small group of professionals. Although a clear consensus of acceptance exists, the public in

---

1. My father relayed to me the scene of his grandmother's death at his Pennsylvania childhood home in the 1950s. Following the death rattle, and when all life signs had ceased, family members placed a rolled-up cloth under her chin and coins on her eyes.

general remains confused and poorly informed about the controversies surrounding brain death and organ donation.

Additional confusion is evident as lawmakers attempt to craft statutes in order to satisfy a standard about which they have little understanding. Though most states follow the Uniform Determination of Death Act as the framework for the determination of death, applying the bifurcated standard does not lead to consistency in how states allow for a determination of death. Statutory irregularities are common, indicating for some that defining death is outside the purview of law.[2] This is significant, given the overall goals of both the President's Commission and the UDDA to facilitate termination of treatment, improve organ supply, and make death uniform. Despite widespread adoption of brain death, problems of "overtreatment—the continuation of life-sustaining treatment on patients who have no reasonable prospects for meaningful survival and often no clear interest in or desire for such treatment"[3]—and a widening gap between organ supply and demand indicate the problems are more widespread today than in 1968.

Although brain death is most often associated with organ donation, many are unaware of its unsettling use in certain areas of medical research and development. Performing medical procedures on the newly dead or dying is a traditional training activity among physicians.[4] Experiments and other procedures vary from endotracheal intubation and central venous catheter insertion to the administration of certain drugs to measure effectiveness. It is argued by some physicians that since corpses no longer have autonomy, and families have limited determination over a decedent's remains, consent is unnecessary for training purposes. Issues of informed consent and the treatment of the dead come into question upon consideration of the methods of experimentation and resuscitation of the newly dead for research purposes. What is more, if the brain dead (sometimes referred to as "biomorts") are not really dead, then further troubling implications arise, deserving careful examination.

This chapter examines the ongoing problems of brain death's conceptual basis, particularly since the President's Commission Report and the introduction of the UDDA as a model framework for standardizing

2. Frost, "Unimportance of Death."
3. Ibid., 175.
4. Berger et al., "Ethics of Practicing Medical Procedures."

death in the US. This will involve an assessment of social attitudes and ongoing public confusion surrounding the meaning and application of brain death. Related to this discussion is the way in which influential pro-life groups have rationalized their acceptance of brain death. Additionally, the chapter will discuss the measure of success purported by supporters of the UDDA, despite ongoing inconsistencies in statutory law. Finally, this chapter considers how brain death is used in other areas, such as medical research, training, and experimentation on the newly declared dead.

This chapter deals with the problems of general societal confusion. This includes an exploration of the rationale of various pro-life groups regarding their acceptance of brain death. Additionally, the chapter assesses the way in which some states have attempted to incorporate the UDDA into statutory from. Finally the chapter discloses the way in which brain death is applied into areas of medical training and experimentation.

SOCIAL ATTITUDES AND PUBLIC CONFUSION

There is little doubt that public attitudes regarding the diagnosis of death were aroused as news coverage of Christaan Barnard's first heart transplant raised ethical concerns about the practice. As early as 1968, a survey of public attitudes toward the determination of death revealed that popular awareness had been influenced by the reports. Of the 112 people surveyed, about sixty percent indicated they had "[given] thought to the issues of how death is determined." Nevertheless, only nine percent "thought of death in terms of irreversible loss of cerebral function."[5] A few years later, another survey indicated that sixty percent of lay people, forty-two percent of medical students, and forty-six percent of physicians did not consider brain death an adequate criterion for death.[6]

In the decade that followed, the popular press and scholarly publications continued to question the theoretical and moral bases of neurological death.[7] Regardless of these challenges, more recent evidence suggests a greater acceptance of brain death, due in great measure to its

5. Arnold et al., "Public Attitudes," 1953–54.

6. Delmonico and Randolph, "Death: A Concept in Transition."

7. Siminoff and Bloch, "American Attitudes," 184.

commonplace use. Yet what is unclear is whether the term brain death is sufficiently understood by both laity and professionals alike.

Youngner, in a 1992 article, notes the problems of linguistic ambiguity regarding the use of the term *brain death* and the ongoing debate concerning the whole-brain and higher-brain definitions of death.[8] Any semblance of consensus, he notes, is both superficial and fragile, given public confusion on the meaning of the term. In a noteworthy study delivered at the 1996 Annual Meeting of the Division of Transplantation, significant gaps were found to exist in families' understanding of brain death despite the fact that 95.7 percent discussed brain death with their relatives' physicians. Indeed, of the 164 donor and non-donor families surveyed in the study, forty-five percent could not differentiate between brain death and coma, and 31.7 percent believed that a brain dead patient could recover.[9]

More recent surveys of public attitudes and beliefs about death and donation reveal similar findings.[10] Of particular note is a recent survey revealing that, "in every country 20 to 40% of the population doubts the idea of brain death."[11] In the United States, Siminoff et al.[12] report that while ninety-eight percent of survey respondents were aware of the term "brain death", only about one third believed that a brain-dead patient is legally dead. While roughly eighty-six percent were able, under a certain scenario, to identify a brain-dead patient as dead, about fifty-seven percent confused patients in a coma as dead and 34.1 percent identified PVS (persistent vegetative state) patients as dead. Regarding the desire to donate organs under different scenarios, most respondents were unwilling to violate the dead donor rule. However, a substantial minority (33.5 percent) was willing to donate the organs of patients under certain scenarios they classified as still alive. This study concluded with a call for further public dialogue and education concerning brain death and donation.

The preceding chapter illustrated substantial variation with regard to the clinical testing methods employed by health-care professionals to

8. Youngner, "Defining Death."

9. Franz, *Study of Donor and Nondonor Families*. Quoted in Siminoff and Bloch, "American Attitudes".

10. Siminoff et al., "Death and Organ Procurement."

11. Morioka, "Reconsidering Brain Death," 41.

12. Siminoff et al., "Death and Organ Procurement."

determine brain death. Among those professionals who should have intimate knowledge of brain-death criteria and its application, further detailed examination of their knowledge reveals that misinformation and confusion still exists. One survey reports that of the 195 physicians and nurses likely to be involved in organ procurement, only thirty-five percent were able to correctly identify both the legal and medical criteria for brain death.[13] Another study reveals that one-half of ICU nurses believe physicians were unsure of the criteria for determining organ donor eligibility, while one-third of nurses also expressed their own uncertainty of the criteria.[14] Moreover, a 2006 article reported a survey that revealed "significant confusion about the concept of brain death among pediatric intensivists."[15] In an effort to determine whether pediatric intensivists are aware of the controversies surrounding the concept of brain death, the authors reported that among those comfortable diagnosing brain death, only twenty-two percent identified brain death with the loss of integration of the organism as a whole. The report concluded with a call to the medical community to reconsider whether brain death is equivalent to death.

Additionally, this author conducted formal and informal surveys among physicians in three community hospitals in West Virginia and Ohio.[16] Physicians who had experience with cadaveric organ procurement registered significant opposition to the use of brain death. Some of these physicians indicated that their experience led them to oppose organ donation and admitted encouraging other health-care providers to do the same because of their first-hand knowledge of the details of the organ procurement process.[17] While most physicians indicated they were organ donors and encouraged their patients to become donors,

13. Youngner et al., "Psychological and Ethical Implications," as quoted in Siminoff and Bloch, "American Attitudes."

14. Daneffel et al., "Knowledge and Attitudes," as quoted in Siminoff and Bloch.

15. Joffe and Anton, "Brain Death."

16. These surveys spanned the years 2004–2007. Formal surveys were in the form of an annotated questionnaire while informal surveys were in the form of personal conversations with physicians. Of the former, I received about a dozen responses from various physicians. Regarding the latter, most were the product of informal conversations with several physicians, some nurses, and one hospital administrator some of whom served on the ethics committee at Trinity Medical Center in Steubenville, OH.

17. One physician, who had witnessed the procurement of tissues and organs from one of his patients in a California hospital, described the procedure as "ghoulish."

many of these same physicians exhibited a lack of awareness with regard to the controversies surrounding brain death. More than two-thirds expressed they were concerned or troubled upon disclosure of the details of these controversies.[18] In the final analysis, most physicians, while able to identify the brain-death criterion as stated in the UDDA, nonetheless exhibited confusion and uncertainty with respect to the legitimacy of its application in the clinical setting.

This confusion and uncertainty extends to the experiences of donor families as well. Commenting on his personal experiences with donor family members, one bioethicist writes,

> When members of the family later investigate and find out, for instance, sometimes for the first time, that organs are taken while the heart still beats, or that the practice is to administer a general anesthetic to donors for the harvesting operation (which the relatives often interpret as implying the need to suppress capacity to feel pain indicating continued brain function), they may be extremely distressed and feel exploited.[19]

He further notes that in many of the accounts given by donor families, "the matter of being confronted by the concept and reality of death by brain death, and being asked for consent to donation, was later seen as part of the original trauma."[20] In other words, the trauma of events which occur for the sake of organ donation, added to the devastating events of the brain injury suffered by the relative, often cause family members to feel assailed or assaulted. Indeed, many times after having agreed to organ donation, family members expressed doubt as to whether their loved one was in fact dead at the time of organ procurement. Often overlooked is the fact that the grieving process experienced by family members can be greatly complicated in such circumstances by the notion that they have betrayed their loved-one.[21]

In the aftermath of the surgical removal of their children's organs, mothers often express a sense of betrayal and guilt for their consent to a procedure and event (brain death) the details of which they were uninformed. As a case in point, one mother describes the pressures and uncertainties of being confronted with the prospects of donating her fifteen

18. The disclosure included information from the first three chapters.

19. Tonti-Filippini, "Revising Brain Death," 51–72.

20. Ibid.

21. Ibid.

year-old son's organs after he suffered a tragic accident and was later diagnosed as brain dead. She laments, "The doctor urged us to consent as there were other parents being as desperate as we sitting at the bedside of their children but we were able to help them! I didn't want anyone to die neither my child nor any other children."[22] Depicting her uncertainties about the meaning of her son's brain-death diagnosis, she expresses how she "had to say goodbye to him forever while he was still treated while he was warm while the monitors were on and while he was given infusions." She continues, "I failed to see that he was 'dead', but believed in what the doctors said and trusted them."[23] However, after looking through the medical report and discovering three different death notices, she asks, "How often can a human being die, how many deaths can he die?" To complicate matters further, the family discovered after the surgery that, unknown to them at the time, their consent included their son's heart, liver, kidneys, eyes, and the removal of his pelvic bones, which were sold. In an expression of guilt and betrayal, the boy's mother writes, "Our consent to the removal of one organ had been changed into a multi-organ removal without asking us. The last sight of my child burnt itself into my soul. When I think of him I have to fight the horrible impression that he was looking so undignified and exploited. This sight of my son still haunts me in my dreams."[24]

This mother is not alone in expressing her doubts and anguish concerning her personal experience in consenting to donation under the brain-death criterion. After exhibiting similar frustrations with the process of consenting to donation of her son's organs, another mother quips, "The lives of a lot of donor families have been shaken, and many of us have lost their [sic] peace of mind."[25] Believing that the process lacks relevant disclosure for informed consent, she offers this eight-fold advice:

- You have the right simply to say NO, especially when they ask you about the presumed will of your brain dead family member.

- If you are willing to donate your organs, insist on your rights!

- Make sure that you get all the relevant information.

---

22. Greinert, "Renate Greinert's Story."
23. Ibid.
24. Ibid.
25. Focke, "Renate Focke's Story."

- Discuss organ donation with your family because it will have an impact on their mourning.

- Decide which organs and tissues you are willing to donate and which not.

- Insist on a general anesthesia during the organ removal.

- Your next of kin has the right to see your dead body right after the organ removal operation.

- Your next of kin has the right to inspect the files.[26]

Although lack of education about brain death and organ donation may account for some of the above data, there remains for many the difficulty of reconciling common-sense notions about death with a corpse that exhibits many characteristics indicative of organizational life. As R. Taylor notes, "Persons who meet whole-brain criteria of death, if mechanically ventilated, typically remain normothermic, continue to grow hair and fingernails, often retain spinal reflexes, maintain cardiac and circulatory function, digest and absorb food, filter blood through both liver and kidneys, urinate and defecate, heal wounds and may even gestate fetuses.[27]" Peter Singer observes that the view of life and death implicated in the concept of brain death is counterintuitive even to those who employ it.[28] In an attempt to ease the counterintuitive reactions of family and medical staff that the brain dead are still alive, these systemic integrative activities are often attributed to remaining insignificant vestiges of non-integrated biological activity.[29] As one commentator remarks, "The antagonism between the perception of a warm and breathing body and the notion of death is rationalized by proponents of 'brain death' as an opposition between sensual perception and intellectual knowledge."[30] In assessing what to do with patients who are diagnosed as brain dead, it is argued that conclusions should not be based on empirical observations but rather on rational grounds.[31] As such, brain death is thus

---

26. Ibid.

27. Taylor, "Reexamining the Definition."

28. Singer, "Is the Sanctity of Life," as quoted in Steineck, "Brain Death."

29. Ibid., 234.

30. Ibid., 237. Brain death, as is clear from the previous chapter, rests more on a rationalistic conception than an empirically based one.

31. Ibid.

depicted primarily as a rationalistic conception, which boasts a superior epistemic foundation for distinguishing between reality and illusion.[32]

However, as previous chapters indicate, there is little by way of scientific reason to substantiate the conceptual coherence of brain death. As a valid rational conception, it must withstand challenges to its internal coherence and remain impervious to empirical challenges. The tendency to dismiss any empirical evidence that challenges the rationalistic framework of brain death reveals the assumptive nature indicative of a purely rationalistic approach. Indeed, the *a priori* dismissal of the intuitive notions of family and medical staff reveals the ongoing lack of import from the public that has characterized the emergence of brain death from its inception.

Regardless of these epistemological gaps, the fact remains that brain death has slowly gained acceptance since its introduction in 1968. Important to this chapter is an examination of several dominant religious groups, particularly those identified as pro-life. Given the sociological impact that these groups continue to have on social policy, it is worth exploring and evaluating the rationale behind their acceptance of brain death.

SOCIAL INFLUENCE OF PRO-LIFE GROUPS

Michael Potts notes, "One of the most remarkable aspects of the introduction of brain-based criteria for human death . . . has been its almost universal acceptance by society, both among the intelligentsia and people in general."[33] Few seem willing to challenge the fundamental change in the way life and death is construed with the acceptance of the brain-death standard. Of particular note is the seeming lack of resistance by traditional pro-life groups. Peter Singer, commenting on this point observes: "But the most extraordinary aspect of the process was the lack of opposition from the groups that could be expected to protest vigorously against any attempt to deny the sanctity of any member of our species, from the point of conception onwards. Where was the pro-life movement? Where was the Roman Catholic Church?"[34]

32. Soccio, *Archetypes of Wisdom*, 550.

33. Potts, "Pro-Life Support," 121.

34. Singer, *Rethinking Life and Death*, 28–29.

Singer suggests that the acceptance of brain death in 1968, and later confirmed in 1981 by the President's Commission Report, served as a turning point away from the traditional Judeo-Christian ethic, which upheld the absolute wrongness of taking innocent human life. He further suggests that society now seemed willing to accept that a certain group of individuals could be "excluded from the community of human persons,"[35] and be killed for the sake of others.

Singer offers two suggestions to explain the lack of substantial pro-life opposition to the proposed brain-death criterion. First, in a 1958 address by Pope Pius XII to an International Congress of Anesthesiologists,[36] the Pope seemed to suggest that defining death belongs to the physician alone, exclusive of theological or philosophical input. Hence, when a group of physicians, such as the Harvard Ad Hoc Committee, recommended a new way for determining death, it was only reasonable for Roman Catholics to embrace it.

Second, Singer says those in the pro-life movement "were worried that the wave of support for turning off the respirators on those whose brains would stop working would sweep over into other areas and, in particular, euthanasia."[37] In an effort to work more effectively to ban euthanasia, pro-life strategists embraced the rationale, beginning with the Harvard Committee and culminating in the President's Report, that the permanent loss of all brain function indicates the loss of organic integrated unity and the death of the organism as a whole.

A third reason is suggested by Potts. He proposes that widespread acceptance of organ transplantation made it difficult to argue against the new criterion of death without appearing to be anti-life.[38] For if the brain dead are not dead, he argues, then removing their vital organs for transplantation would be the direct cause of their deaths. A strict sanctity of life ethic opposes the intentional direct killing of an innocent person. However, people who receive vital organs would die without them.[39]

35. Potts, "Pro-Life Support," 121.

36. Pope Pius XII, "Prolongation of Life." The statement in question is: "It remains for the doctor, and especially the anesthesiologist, to give a clear and precise definition of 'death' and the 'moment of death' of a person who passes away in a state of consciousness."

37. Singer, *Rethinking Life and Death,* 29.

38. Potts, "Pro-Life Support," 122.

39. Pope John Paul II illustrates the dilemma as follows: "How does one reconcile respect or life—which forbids any action likely to cause or hasten death—with the

Given the overwhelming wave of support for organ transplantation, and in an effort to avoid appearing to oppose life-giving organ donation, the pro-life movement accepted brain death. This section will explore the rationale for pro-life acceptance of brain death in light of the above suggestions.

Strong papal support for organ donation comes directly from Pope John Paul II's encyclical letter, *Evangelium Vitae*. In an effort to promote and build up a culture of life, the Pope speaks of the everyday heroism exhibited by various individuals. As an example he promotes organ donation as a heroic measure when he writes, "A particularly praiseworthy example of such gestures is the donation of organs, performed in an ethically acceptable manner, with a view to offering a chance of health and even of life itself to the sick who sometimes have no other hope."[40] Some conservative Catholic groups maintain that the Church's official teaching embraces brain death as a moral means for organ procurement. Supportive of this claim are certain comments in an address given by Pope John Paul II to the XVIII International Congress of the Transplantation Society. In words reminiscent of Pope Pius XII, John Paul II writes:

> With regard to the parameters used today for ascertaining death—whether the "encephalic" signs or the more traditional cardio-respiratory signs—the Church does not make technical decisions. She limits herself to the Gospel duty of comparing the data offered by medical science with the Christian understanding of the unity of the person, bringing out the similarities and the possible conflicts capable of endangering respect for human dignity. Here it can be said that the criterion adopted in more recent times for ascertaining the fact of death, namely the complete and irreversible cessation of all brain activity, if rigorously applied, does not seem to conflict with the essential elements of a sound anthropology.[41]

In these two paragraphs the Pope seems to confirm that defining death primarily resides in the realm of medical science. Since medical science

---

potential good for humanity if the organs of a dead person are removed for transplanting to a sick person who needs them, keeping in mind that the success of such an intervention depends on the speed with which the organs are removed from the donor after his or her death?" Quoted in ibid., 122.

40. Pope John Paul II, *Evangelium Vitae*, 86.

41. Pope John Paul II, *Address of John Paul II*.

has, in recent times, expanded the criteria for determining death to include the irreversible cessation of all brain activity, then there seems to be no conflict with the anthropology taught by the Church.

Further recognition of this is evident in the commentary on brain death offered by the National Catholic Bioethics Center, a group devoted to the teaching Magisterium. They contend that the use of neurological criteria (brain death) is legitimate according to the Catholic Church, noting that, " Pope Pius XII and Pope John Paul II both said the Church has no competency in determining death; this properly belongs to medical science."[42] They further note that those who reject brain death as a viable criterion for determining death "are in tension with sound Catholic teaching." This, of course, presupposes that medical science offers a coherent biological basis that supports brain death as human death. In same address, the Pope writes, "Acknowledgement of the unique dignity of the human person has a further underlying consequence: vital organs which occur singly in the body can be removed only after death—that is, from the body of someone who is certainly dead." However, what is evidently uncertain, as previous chapters indicate, is that the brain dead are in fact certainly dead.

Other Catholic writers reveal the same presumption as they attempt to qualify consistency of brain death with traditional Christian anthropology.[43] Traditional Christian anthropology construes a living human person as an essential unity or composition of body and soul.[44] Following Thomas Aquinas, this view rejects a strict dualism of body and soul, as Plato and Descartes held, while recognizing a duality of body and soul, in which the soul informs or animates the body as the life-giving principle. As long as organizational integrity is intact, then the soul's presence remains.

Jason Eberl argues that a Thomistic understanding of death entails that, "A human being dies when her body ceases to function as an *organism* with integrative unity."[45] Eberl articulates Bernat's conceptual basis of brain death and then applies the single organ hypothesis to the integrative functions of the whole brain. While St. Thomas contended that organizational unity is maintained by the heart, Eberl suggests that were

42. National Catholic Bioethics Center, *FAQ's on Brain Death*.

43. DuBois, "Organ Transplantation."

44. LaRock, "Dualistic Interaction."

45. Eberl, "Thomistic Understanding," 47.

St. Thomas alive today, he would recognize, based on current medical opinion, that the brain is the organ of integration. In concert with this understanding, a Working Group with the Pontifical Academy of Science issued a statement in which they conclude: "It appears evident that the establishment of total and irreversible loss of all brain functions is the true medical criterion of death and that this criterion can be established in two ways. Either by establishing the cessation of circulation and respiration or directly by demonstrating the irreversible loss of all brain function (brain death)."[46]

It is significant to note that Catholic authorities are more careful than some of their interpreters to avoid absolute language with regard to their acceptance of brain death. Notice that "it appears" in the above paragraph and "does not seem to contradict" in Pope John Paul II's statement reflect a cautious embracing of the conclusions of medical science. This is understandable given the tentative nature of general scientific conclusions, which are subject to modification and change. Moreover, these statements reflect that current accepted medical criteria for defining death do not "constitute binding magisterial teaching."[47]

A second large constituancy of the pro-life movement are Evangelical Protestant Christians. Though diverse in many respects, this group maintains a core of five fundamental doctrines of belief. They are: (1) the innerrancy and infallability of the Bible; (2) the deity of Jesus; (3) the substitutionary atonement of Jesus; (4) the literal, physical, bodily resurrection of Jesus; and (5) the literal, bodily return of Jesus from heaven to earth.[48] Additionally, many Evangelical Christians hold to a central conviction regarding the sanctity of life from conception to natural death. Their greatest social concerns include the issues of abortion and euthanasia, both of which are viewed as moral evils plaguing secular society. These Christians, under the dictate to be "salt and light," see themselves as preservers of truth and light in a morally decaying and dark world.

Having a high regard for Scripture, Evangelical scholars generally attempt to ground their thinking on principles and commands derived either explicitly or inferentially from biblical texts. Working from premises built on the conception that humans are created in God's

46. White et al., *Determination of Brain Death*, 82.

47. DuBois, "Organ Transplantation."

48. Torrey, *Fundamentals*.

image, human life is held in high regard as being under the domain of God's sovereignty. Life and death are in the control of God who gives breath (Gen 2:7) and takes it away (Ps 104:29). Humans are therefore accountable for their moral choices, which are expressed in the value of stewardship.[49]

Discussions regarding the definition of death are most likely situated within the context of the social acceptance of euthanasia. Social policy that attempts to revise death in order to facilitate organ procurement is viewed as a means to hasten death for the comatose and other vulnerable patients. The most ardent opposition regarding the debate on how death should be defined concerns the use of the neo-cortical or higher-brain criterion.[50] The fear is that as the line of demarcation between life and death is moved forward, more vulnerable populations are put at risk. As John M. Frame notes: "Without a strict criterion of death, it is difficult to guard against abuses, such as hastening a declaration of death to obtain organs for transplant."[51]

While emphasizing a "rigorous medical definition of death," most evangelical scholars nevertheless embrace brain death. J. Kerby Anderson expresses his acceptance when he writes, "A comatose patient without any brain wave activity (A flat EEG, electroencephalogram) should be removed from life-support systems; he is considered to be already dead."[52] Similarly, Norman L. Geisler expresses a cautious embrace of brain death when he writes: "Death is difficult to define, but in general terms it means vital signs are lacking, such as breathing, pulse, nerve reaction, or brain wave (EEG). This does not mean that after the person dies that the body cannot be kept "alive" by machine to prevent organ decay. It simply means that we should not hasten death in order to get a fresh organ."[53] In sync with Roman Catholic authorities, Evangelicals

---

49. Campbell, "Fundamentals of Life and Death," 197–98.

50. Vautier, "Defining Death."

51. Frame, *Medical Ethics*, 62.

52. Anderson, "Biblical Appraisal of Euthanasia," 198.

53. Geisler, *Christian Ethics*, 185. Under the principle of charity, Geisler strongly advocates organ donation when he opines: "'Greater love has no one than this, that he lay down his life for his friends (John 15:13).' I find it hard to imagine giving an eye, lung, or kidney to someone who has none, yet some human beings have done this. How little sacrifice is required to do so when we are dead and no longer in need of these organs!" See 184–85.

tend to express concern as to how death is defined, while nevertheless generally accepting the medical consensus regarding brain death.[54]

Judaism, "guided by the concept of the supreme sanctity of human life and of the dignity of man created in the image of God,"[55] also has a stake in the debate about death. Although the idea of ethics is not found in Jewish thought, latter-day scholars have attempted "to describe the methods and concepts implicit in the tradition itself."[56] In so doing, certain statements are gleaned from the tradition providing guidelines for adjudication in moral matters. The process by which this is accomplished proceeds out of a deep respect for *halakhah*[57] (Jewish Law). Halakhah encompasses the legal aspect of Judaism and "embraces personal, social, national, and international relationships, and all the other practices and observations of Judaism."[58] It may be said that it provides the basis, or story, for meaning in the ascertainment of duty and obligation in the world. This story contains the narrative of creation and the responsibilities for which beings created in God's image are accountable. It also includes the story of the fall resulting in a broken world and adding to the responsibilities of which human persons are obligated to each other, and ultimately to God to maintain.

The traditional methodology for deliberation concerning current ethical discussions is characterized as a legal process by which individual texts are sought out for application. The process includes examining commentaries and previous legal decisions of these texts in an effort to discover their applicability to current situations. David Novak explains:

> The basic scriptural norm is located, its rabbinical elaborations are traced through the Talmud and related literature, its authoritative structure is determined, relevant precedents (if any) are culled from the vast literature of legal responsa by individual rabbinic authorities, and finally the person accepted by a

54. Two other prominent Evangelical scholars who accept brain death are: Moreland and Rae, *Body & Soul.*

55. Rosner, "Definition of Death in Jewish Law," 211.

56. Dorff and Newman, *Contemporary Jewish Ethics,* 9.

57. Literally, "to go" or "to walk." It includes the written Torah (Five books of Moses), the Mishnah (a list of legal decisions), Talmud (a series of debates on various topics), commentaries on the Talmud, Responsa (case law rulings), and various legal codes.

58. "Halakhah," in *Encyclopedia Judaica.*

community of Jews as their legal authority frequently seeks the council of learned colleagues.[59]

This method is by no means easily achieved. It is a careful process that recognizes human fallibility by including minority opinions and interpretations of biblical texts. The sources from which one must cull are vast containing many legal decisions, propositions, narrative accounts, and debates. As Jewish thinkers grapple with the relation between tradition and modernity, they vary in opinion on the criterion of death, often engaging in intense debate. However, what is rarely at issue among Jewish thinkers is the question of whether Jews should donate organs.[60]

Jewish thinkers, like their Catholic and Evangelical Protestant counterparts, express concern that organ donors may be killed for their transplantable organs. Thus, in matters of organ donation, defining criteria appropriately consistent with traditional modalities is crucial for Jews. In accordance with Jewish methodology, rabbinic opinion is by no means unitary with regard to whether brain death is an acceptable criterion for human death. It is a well-known fact that some Orthodox Jews do not accept brain death, and that significant segments of their population in the state of New Jersey have influenced the passage of a statutory exception regarding the use of brain death for religious reasons.[61] J. David Bleich, an Orthodox Rabbi states: "It is axiomatic, according to Halakhah, that death coincides with cessation of respiration."[62] Owing to the Scriptural references "God breathes life into Adam" (Gen 2:6) and ". . . all in whose nostrils is the breath of the spirit of life" (Gen 7:22), Jewish sources (e.g., *Yoma* 85a) indicate that evidence for life resides at

59. Novak, "Judaism," 1302.

60. While some rabbis limit the scope of organ transplantation, Jewish opinion is, for all practical purposes, uniform with respect to the need for Jews to become organ donors. In fact, it is the official policy of the Conservative movement within Judaism that provision of organ donation upon one's demise is "not simply a voluntary act of beneficence but a commanded obligation." See: Dorff, *Matters of Life and Death*, 228.

61. Signed April 8, 1991, the New Jersey Declaration of Death Act reads in part: "'The death of an individual shall not be declared upon the basis of neurological criteria . . . of this act when the licensed physician authorized to declare death, has reason to believe, on the basis of information in the individual's available medical records, or information provided by a member of the individual's family or any other person knowledgeable about the individual's religious beliefs that such a declaration would violate the personal religious belief of the individual. In these cases death shall be declared, and the time of death fixed, solely upon the basis of cardio-respiratory criteria."

62. Bleich, "Establishing Criteria of Death," 300.

the nose. However, after citing a variety of opinions from Jewish sources, he concludes that death only occurs at the cessation of both cardiac and respiratory functions, due to the fact that the "lack of respiration is also indicative of prior cessation of cardiac activity."[63] According to Bleich, Halakhah does not permit the use of brain death as a criterion of death. In fact, Halakhah obligates medical treatment and resuscitation for all human beings, no matter how debilitating their injury.

Nonetheless, other Orthodox Jews are more willing to accept brain death. They cite sources in the *Talmud* and *Codes of Jewish Law* which indicate that a criterion of irreversible cessation of respiration in an individual who shows no movement and is unresponsive to stimuli is to be considered dead. Fred Rosner notes, "Jewish writings provide considerable evidence for the thesis that the brain and brainstem control all bodily functions, including breathing and heartbeat."[64] Hence, cessation of all brain function, including the brainstem, is an acceptable criterion for determining death. Further qualification of the acceptability of the brain-death criterion is advanced by a figurative analogy with the thesis of physiological decapitation. Based on a talmudic discussion regarding individuals who had sustained broken necks, these persons are considered dead despite retaining for a short period of time spastic, convulsive movements and heartbeats. Since the brain dead exhibit similar phenomena, these thinkers suggest that one may therefore conclude they are the functional equivalent of a decapitated body.

The physiological decapitation thesis receives favorable attention from many commentators and is deserving of evaluation.[65] Though some have found the analogy convincing, questions pertaining to the critical differences between decapitated individuals and the brain dead suggest the thesis involves a faulty analogy. As Paul A. Byrne et al note:

> It may be noted that decapitation is not the cutting off of a brain but of a head, with all its arteries and veins, bony and muscular structure, and upper spinal cord, so that neither literal beheading nor its equivalent through having one's head smashed in an accident is the same as "brain death." In decapitation, the heart quickly stops and the rest of the body begins to disintegrate. By no means is the brain alone affected. Indeed, one could argue that

---

63. Ibid., 301.

64. Rosner, "Definition of Death in Jewish Law," 20.

65. Lizza, *Persons.*

death by decapitation comes primarily from cardio-respiratory failure.[66]

Despite the lack of similarity between a decapitated body and a brain-dead patient, the decapitation thesis continues to be the primary mode of persuasion for many, including those who would not necessarily describe themselves as pro-life. In fact, a participant in a recent discussion on brain death by the President's Bioethics Commission relayed to this writer that the main argument upon which its continued acceptance rests, is the decapitation thesis.[67] This is unfortunate given the fact that the empirical evidence renders the thesis demonstrably false. As one former supporter of this thesis notes:

> Until relatively recently (1992), as an ethicist, I was myself misled in this respect, having had brain death explained to me and seen it explained to donor families many times as the brain event equivalent of having been guillotined. Having now studied the medical literature I know that to be false, and more than that, it was known to be false as early as 1977 following the multi-center study funded by the National Institutes of Neurological Disease and Stroke.[68]

Other Jewish thinkers accept brain death on other grounds. Since 1976, Conservative Jews have embraced, as sufficient for determining death, a flat electroencephalogram (EEG), which indicates "succession of spontaneous brain activity."[69] Their willingness to adopt the new criterion rests on the fact that since "ancestors determined Jewish law in light of medical practice of their time,"[70] it seems reasonable to accept testing that conforms to current medical practice. In 1988, the Chief Rabbinate of Israel demonstrated its approval of a flat EEG when it approved heart transplantation, since the test "guarantees that a patient can no longer

66. Byrne et al., "Brain Death-the Patient," 37.

67. This information was relayed to me by Patrick Lee, a former colleague of mine, and Professor of Bioethics at Franciscan University of Steubenville. In 2007, he was invited by Robert George, a member of the President's Bioethics Commission, to observe and participate in the panel's discussion on brain death. He provided helpful information relevant to the current misunderstandings surrounding the decapitation hypothesis.

68. Tonti-Filippini, "Revising Brain Death: Cultural Imperialism."

69. Dorff, *Matters of Life and Death*, 229.

70. Ibid.

independently breathe or produce a heartbeat."[71] Elliot Dorff, commenting on the use of brain death for the procurement of organs says, "If a flat electroencephalogram is confirmed, the donor is officially dead within the terms of Jewish law as now interpreted, and the transplantation is permissible."[72]

In summary, it may be noted that dominant pro-life religious groups share a number of concerns and agreements regarding brain death and organ donation. All three groups recognize the life-saving potential of donation and, to varying degrees, endorse organ donation as an act of heroism, charity, and in some cases a legal obligation. Also noteworthy is the fact that, despite the claims of Singer that pro-life groups have abandoned their traditional sanctity of life ethic, all groups surveyed share a uniform concern over the criterion of death, founded upon the sanctity of life. What Singer seems to overlook is that pro-life thinkers are dependent upon the medical community for providing a biologically coherent model reflective of their theologically (and to some degree, philosophically) informed anthropology. Now that more investigators are recognizing the faulty foundation upon which brain death rests, it remains to be seen whether pro-life groups will continue to support a criterion that fails to represent the death of the organism as a whole.[73] Legislation is based on public policy, and the next section will consider the UDDA's success in 'standardizing' death.

STATUTORY IRREGULARITIES

Death marks the end of bodily life, a curiosity shrouded in mystery. On an individual level, it represents the end of a person's temporal existence in human society. As such, the moment death occurs is of profound importance to the individual.[74] Moreover, on a social level, "death represents a tearing of a large web of social relationships."[75] In both representations, society has an interest in protecting the rights of individuals to pursue

71. Ibid.

72. Ibid.

73. It should be noted that pro-life thinkers are among the most vigilant in criticizing the brain-death criterion. Indeed, the number of critics among pro-lifers is growing. See: Potts et al., "Introduction."

74. Byrne et al., "Brain Death—the Patient, the Physician, and Society."

75. Ibid.

life as far as possible, and to ensure that the social fabric is protected from great harm when death severs social ties. It is on this point that the law has profound interests in protecting human life and ensuring that the societal web of relationships is safeguarded. Social policy, therefore, must attempt balance between the interests of the individual and society in such a way that ensures the least amount of harm to the security of all citizens.

While the law's role in standardizing death principally involves the task of framing a legal rule, the procedure is dependent upon the nodes of interaction between various disciplines which inform the direction of social policy.[76] Defining death is, by all accounts, multi-disciplinary. Laypersons and experts alike rely on religion, philosophy, medicine, law, and everything in between, to reflect on the meaning of death.[77] The law's interest in framing social policy concerning death utilizes the disciplines of medicine and philosophy to a large degree. If ambiguity exists in medicine and philosophy with regard to the diagnosis and definition of death, legal framers have little hope of capturing the level of coherence necessary for a uniform policy.

The Uniform Determination of Death Act (UDDA) issued by the National Conference of Commissioners on Uniform State Laws states:

> Any individual who has sustained either (1) irreversible cessation of circulatory and respiratory functions, or (2) irreversible cessation of all functions of the entire brain, including the brain stem, is dead. A determination of death must be made in accordance with accepted medical standards.[78]

It is important to note that the uniform act not only codified the common law standard but also extended it to address the problem of brain death. Though some states directly employ the language of the UDDA, others have opted to utilize it as a framework leading to some inconsistencies in how states allow for a determination of death. In states like Nebraska and South Carolina the UDDA standard is specifically applied. In South Carolina, Article 6, section 44-43-460 of the *Uniform Determination of Death Act*, states:

---

76. Capron, "Bifurcated Legal Standard."

77. Menikoff, *Law and Bioethics.*

78. Uniform Determination of Death Act § 1, 12 U.L.A. 340 (Supp. 1991).

An individual who has sustained either (1) irreversible cessation
of circulatory and respiratory functions, or (2) irreversible cessation of all functions of the entire brain, including the brain stem,
is dead. A determination of death must be made in accordance
with accepted medical standards.[79]

From here states deviate from the UDDA in at least four different ways.

First, some states have crafted death statues that fail to address any
situation other than those with patients on artificial life support. For
instance, the Florida statute provides:

For legal and medical purposes, *where respiratory and circulatory
functions are maintained by artificial means of support* so as to
preclude a determination that these functions have ceased, the
occurrence of death *may* be determined where there is the irreversible cessation of the functioning of the entire brain, including
the brain stem, determined in accordance with this section.[80]

As Menikoff observes, "The statute does not purport to codify the common law standard applied to other jurisdictions, as does the uniform
act."[81] Although the statutory framers expressly limit the statute to those
cases in which "respiratory and circulatory functions are maintained by
artificial means of support," Menikoff further notes, that "the use of the
permissive 'may' in the statute" suggests that the legislature envisioned
other ways to diagnose death. This is made evident in a later subsection
which declares:

Except for a diagnosis of brain death, the standard set forth in
this section is not the exclusive standard for determining death
or the withdrawal of life-support.[82]

Thus, the Florida legislature appears to have struck out on its own in its
departure from the bifurcated language of the UDDA.

A second way that states have deviated from the UDDA is by employing language more closely resembling the brain-stem criterion. For
example, the Iowa statute 702.8 titled *Death* includes this provision:

In the event that artificial means of support preclude a determination that these functions have ceased, a person will be

---

79. "Uniform Determination of Death Act," in *South Carolina Code of Laws*.

80. Cited in Menikoff, *Law and Bioethics*, 458.

81. Ibid.

82. Ibid.

considered dead if in the announced opinion of two physicians, based on ordinary standards of medical practice, that person has experienced an irreversible cessation of *spontaneous brain functions*. Death will have occurred at the time when the relevant functions ceased.[83]

Similarly the Texas death statute states:

If artificial means of support preclude a determination that a person's spontaneous respiratory and circulatory functions have ceased, the person is dead when, in the announced opinion of a physician, according to ordinary standards of medical practice, there is irreversible cessation of *all spontaneous brain function.* Death occurs when the relevant functions cease. (c) Death must be pronounced before artificial means supporting a person's respiratory and circulatory functions are terminated.[84]

These provisions suggest that the determination of death rests solely on the irreversible cessation of brain-stem functions. As such, they do not reflect the "whole-brain" criterion of death specified in the UDDA by the phrase, "irreversible cessation of all functions of the entire brain, including the brain stem."

The third way in which states deviate from the UDDA concerns how states incorporate clinical criteria into their statues in place of the UDDA's somewhat ambiguous phrase, "A determination of death must be made in accordance with *accepted medical standards.*" The difficulty posed by the lack of specificity as to what constitutes "accepted medical standards" has caused some legislatures to incorporate their own clinical criteria into their death statutes. Several examples are worth noting. In Delaware, the same bifurcated approach is applied but with some qualification regarding the details of diagnosis. Section 1760, titled *Determination of Death* says:

A determination of death pursuant to the provisions herein may be made, by a physician admitted to practice under this chapter, by either: (1) Personal examination, or (2) By the use of information provided by an EMT-P (paramedic) using telemetric or transtelephonic means in accordance with protocols approved by

---

83. "Death," in *Iowa Code* (1999).
84. "Death and Disposition of the Body," in *Texas Statute.*

the Board of Medical Practice, following recommendations of its
Advanced Life Support Committee.[85]

In Virginia, a registered nurse may pronounce death, if the following
criteria are satisfied:

> (i) the nurse is employed in this Commonwealth by a home
> health organization, by a hospice, or the department of correc-
> tions; (ii) the nurse is directly involved in the care of the patient;
> (iii) the patient's death has occurred; (iv) the patient is under the
> care of a physician when his death occurs; (v) the patient's death
> has been anticipated; (vi) the physician is unable to be present
> within a reasonable period of time to determine the death; and
> (vii) there is a valid Do Not Resuscitate Order.[86]

Moreover, Oregon statute 432.300 titled, *Determination of Death*, carves
out another difference not seen in other states, when it says: "For the
purposes of this section as it relates to fetal death, heartbeats shall be
distinguished from transient cardiac contractions and breathing shall
be distinguished from fleeting respiratory efforts or gasps."[87] Although
these particular differences may seem peripheral to the standard, they
nevertheless reflect the difficulties law makers face when confronted
with standards that "vary both geographically and from hospital to
hospital."[88] Indeed, many physicians readily acknowledge *de facto* violations of the dead donor rule due to the difficulties in attempting to satisfy a conceptually flawed criterion of death.[89] Variations in the criteria
for determining BD, coupled with statutory irregularities, raise doubts
about accuracy of the brain-death standard.

However, the most serious challenge to the goal of the UDDA is
exemplified by the State of New Jersey's legislative initiative which recognizes a personal religious exemption for those objecting to the brain-
death criterion. Signed into law in 1991, the New Jersey Declaration of
Death Act provides a statutory exception to the brain-death criterion,
specifically for those in the Orthodox Jewish, Japanese, and Native
American communities, who adhere to a belief that life is primarily

85. "Determination of Death," in *Delaware Laws*.

86. "Determination of Death," in *Code of Virginia*.

87. "Determination of Death," in *Oregon Statue* (1997).

88. DeMere, "Statement," as quoted in Bryne et al., "Brain Death—the Patient, the
Physician, and Society."

89. Greenberg, "As Good as Dead"; Youngner and Arnold, "Philosophical Debates."

identified by the circulatory and respiratory activities of the body. The
Act provides:

> The death of an individual shall not be declared upon the basis
> of neurological criteria . . . of this act when the licensed physi-
> cian authorized to declare death, has reason to believe, on the
> basis of information in the individual's available medical records,
> or information provided by a member of the individual's family
> or any other person knowledgeable about the individual's reli-
> gious beliefs that such a declaration would violate the personal
> religious belief of the individual. In these cases death shall be
> declared, and the time of death fixed, solely upon the basis of
> cardio-respiratory criteria.[90]

The rationale for the act rests in the recognition that "when death
occurs [it] is not solely a medical judgment about a biological fact, it is
also a value judgment, which for some rests on personal religious beliefs
for moral convictions."[91] New Jersey's legislative body reasoned against
the "state's general interests in uniform legal recognition of neurological
death" as justifying the law to "compel those with contrary personal religious beliefs to accept neurological criteria for declarations of their own
deaths."[92] Instead of embodying the position advanced by the President's
Commission, (that societal interests in a uniform standard of death precludes a statutory recognition of a conscious clause), the State of New
Jersey struck out on its own in order to accommodate the personal interests of a minority group whose religious beliefs and the exercise thereof
were being threatened.[93]

While some commentators have seen the New Jersey legislative initiative as a model for expanding the law to satisfy the demands of greater
pluralism regarding the definition and criterion of death,[94] others see it
as a threat to the judicial stability evinced by a uniform standard. For
example, Capron writes:

90. "New Jersey Declaration of Death Act," in *New Jersey Statutes Annotate* (1991).

91. Olick, "Brain Death, Religious Freedom, and Public Policy," 54.

92. Ibid.

93. Also noteworthy is the similar conclusion reached by the New York Task Force
on Life and The Law. New York consequently has adopted legislative provisions for
"reasonable accommodation" of religious objections to brain death. The New York Task
Force on Life and The Law (1986). See also New York Codes (1987).

94. Engelhardt Jr., "Redefining Death."

> By providing that the neurological standard should not be ap-
> plied when a physician has reason to believe that a brain-based
> declaration of death would "violate the personal religious beliefs"
> of the patient (in which case "death shall be declared, and the
> time of death fixed, solely upon the basis of [the] cardio-pulmo-
> nary criteria" specified elsewhere in the statute), the New Jersey
> law sows confusion and invites litigation.[95]

The concern rests on the prospects of a dispute arising due to the religious beliefs of a patient whose condition satisfies one set of findings
while not another. The situation could produce confusing "oscillat-
ing results (alive, not dead, not alive, and so forth) depending upon
fluctuation in the resolution of the dispute."[96] In other words, a policy
that fails to provide the uniform stability necessary to resolve disputes
concerning the timing of death invites greater confusion to an already
delicate process.

As the preceding discussion of state statutes demonstrates, though
states have the ability to draft statutes to better suit their jurisdictions,
the purpose of the UDDA was to standardize laws. The two primary elements exist in most of the statutes unchanged, but there are clear inconsistencies that challenge the overall success of the brain-death standard.
The fact that policy makers struggle to write laws in accordance with
a poorly conceived medical condition prone to perpetual qualification
further substantiates what may be called "the mirage of consensus."[97]
There should be little expectation that these social policy problems will
be resolved as long as a technically latent, medically confused concept
continues to be embraced by law and medicine.

APPLICATIONS TO MEDICAL RESEARCH

A less publicly known and perhaps portentous application of the brain
death criterion is its unsettling utilization in certain areas of medical
research and development. A little over a decade after the Harvard
Committee recommended tests for determining the condition known
today as brain death, reports of medical experimentation on brain dead

95. Capron, "Bifurcated Legal Standard," 130.
96. Ibid.
97. Engelhardt Jr., "Redefining Death."

patients began to emerge. The first of these reports involved the use of children who satisfied the brain death criterion.[98] Several years later, a report documenting the experimental use of an adult diagnosed as brain dead was published.[99] While some of these experiments involved the administration of certain drugs, other more invasive procedures include: endotracheal intubation, central venous catheterization, peripheral venous and artery catheterization, thoracentesis, pericardiocentesis, and temporary transvenous pacemaker insertion.[100] These reports resulted in a small spate of articles evaluating the ethical issues associated with research on the newly dead.[101] The primary focus centered on the need to secure consent for medical experiments on the newly dead either by the deceased prior to death or from the deceased's family after death. Among these commentators, there was general agreement that such experiments are justified if consent is obtained.

Although a survey of the early literature suggests concord regarding the requirement of consent for medical experimentation on the newly dead, Mark R. Wicclair notes, "That whatever the merits of their arguments, opponents of consent significantly outnumber its proponents among those who practice procedures on the newly dead."[102] More recently, Wicclair reports that discussions have centered on the issue of whether the standard of consent pertaining to research on living patients is applicable to post-mortem research as well. According to some opponents of the consent requirement, the right to make decisions concerning one's bodily integrity is a personal one, which ends with death.[103] A dead body is no longer a person possessing autonomous rights that can be violated.[104] Moreover, given the irrational reactions to death by the next-of-kin, presumed consent is preferable in that it

98. de Frias et al., "Inappropriate Secretion of Antidiuretic Hormone."

99. Coller, "Newly Dead."

100. Berger et al., "Ethics of Practicing Medical Procedures," 775.

101. Robertson, "Research on the Brain-Dead."

102. Wicclair, "Informed Consent and Research," 352. Wicclair cites a report in which only 10 percent of all programs that use the newly dead for teaching purposes require consent from the families of the deceased.

103. Sperling, "Breaking the Silence," 400.

104. As Iserson suggests: "Simple as the concept is, corpses no longer are individuals, and so they cannot be the basis for either autonomy or informed consent. They are merely symbols." Iserson, "Live Versus Death," 262.

eliminates heightened grief or anxiety over family members consenting to such practices.

Recall that one of the advantages of brain death envisioned by Henry Beecher was the use of brain dead bodies for research, which could potentially eliminate many of the ethical problems associated with the difficulty of obtaining informed consent from living patients. In keeping with this vision, many researchers simply do not see how nonautonomous corpses can be abused or harmed by experimentation that promises to benefit society as a whole. Indeed, as some opponents of consent suggest, "Patients who die in emergency departments have implicitly given at least limited consent to practice and teach life-saving techniques by using the services of emergency medical personnel and by merely living in modern society which provides everyone a right to this care."[105] Hence, it is argued, "The absence of harm to patients in conjunction with the benefits from training opportunities support training procedures independent of family consent."[106]

Proponents of informed consent for research on the newly dead generally focus on the nature of the harm that obtains upon failure to respect pre-mortem preferences and values, even in the absence of advance directives indicating personal preferences. Typically, harm refers to the negative effects an action or event may have on the well-being of an individual. Wicclair asks, "Can actions and events that occur after a person has died affect that person's well-being?"[107] Not according to a mental state criterion of well-being. Since the dead are incapable of good and bad experiences, medical experimentation proffers no harm to their well-being. However, according to a desire-based or preference theory,[108] in which well-being is defined exclusively as a function of desire or preference satisfaction, a different answer emerges. Wicclair offers the following illustration:

> Professor Perkins, a Constitutional scholar, is dying of cancer. She has spent the last five years writing a book on the Second Amendment. Since she is too frail to read the publisher's response, her husband opens the letter. It states that reviewers

105. Sperling, "Breaking the Silence."

106. Berger et al., "Ethics of Practicing Medical Procedures," 775.

107. Wicclair, "Informed Consent and Research," 357.

108. Kagan, *Normative Ethics,* as quoted in Wicclair, "Informed Consent and Research."

rejected the manuscript because it was based on claims that have been decisively refuted in a soon-to-be published monograph. Professor Perkins' husband cannot bring himself to tell her the truth. Instead, he tells her that the manuscript was accepted for publication, which causes her to feel very happy. She dies without discovering the truth . . . [A]ccording to a desire-based or preference conception, even though she was unaware of the negative assessment of her work and felt good about what she falsely believed she had accomplished, the fact that she failed to achieve her goal of making a significant scholarly contribution had a negative effect on her well being.[109]

The preference theory of well-being accords with many cultural norms, as well as ethical principles well established in medical practice. Central among these principles is that in the absence of pre-mortem consent, the sensibilities and preferences of the deceased's family members ought to be respected.[110] Highly regarded medical associations, representing the interests of physicians, including the AMA, the AHA, and the *Report of the President's Commission for the Study of Ethical Problems in Medicine and Biomedical and Behavioral Research*, support the position that research on the newly dead should proceed only when consent has been obtained by a substitute decision maker, next-of-kin, or family member.[111] Common among health care providers is the concern that public awareness of practicing procedures on the newly dead, absent consent, may "undermine generally held faith in physician fidelity,"[112] eroding public trust of the medical profession.[113]

Public trust relies on disclosure, truth-telling, and consent. Society expects the medical profession to respect the values and preferences of patients, even after death. Individuals who agree to be organ donors may not be aware of the scope of their "anatomical gifts." In some states,

109. Ibid., 358.

110. Wicclair argues: "Generally, family members are most likely to be familiar with the deceased's premortem preferences and values; they are likely to have the most care and concern for the deceased; and it seems reasonable to assume that most people would want family members to make such decisions. Accordingly, if there are any legitimate protective functions at play in research on the newly dead, it is reasonable to presume that they are primarily the responsibility of family." Wicclair, "Informed Consent and Research," 359.

111. Sperling, "Breaking the Silence."

112. Berger et al., "Ethics of Practicing Medical Procedures," 776.

113. Sperling, "Breaking the Silence."

the "organ donor" designation printed on a driver's license includes authorization for transplantation, therapy, research, and education.[114] Instead of allowing people to restrict the scope of their anatomical gift, they are simply asked, "Do you wish to have the organ donor designation printed on your driver's license?" without any disclosure on all that entails.[115] Meaningful consent about the scope of anatomical gift includes informing organ donors and their families that such gifts cover therapy, research, and education as well. Additionally, opportunity should be given to limit or restrict an individual's gift according to his or her preferences.[116]

However, it remains unclear as to whether this satisfies consent to the degree to which it is informed. As Wicclair notes, "When the scope of post-mortem research includes uncommon and potentially controversial activities, it is not sufficient to refer generically to 'research' in consent instruments."[117] Moreover, as Susan R. Martyn observes, it is doubtful whether individuals would conceive of post-mortem research as including mechanically ventilated, heart-beating corpses.[118] Assuring consent is properly informed requires some detail of the particulars of the research to be conducted.[119]

114. Wicclair, "Informed Consent and Research," 36.

115. 20 Pa. C. S. § 8619.

116. An important legal case evinces this point as well. In *Moore v. Regents of the University of California*, John Moore's physician failed to disclose that his cells were being used for research and profit. The court, while not applying conversion liability, struck a balance between a competent patient's right to make informed autonomous decisions, based on the longstanding principles of fiduciary duty and informed consent, and the need to avoid threatening potentially useful research with civil liability. The court ruled in favor of Moore in regard to his complaint stating a cause of action for breach of fiduciary duty and lack of informed consent. This case is instructive to the issue at hand. Since patients who agree to be organ donors are not informed with regard to the extent of their gift, it could be argued that a legal violation of informed consent occurs practically every time an individual agrees to be an organ donor. See: "John Moore v. Regents of the University of California," in *51 Cal.3d 120* (Supreme Court of California, 1990).

117. Wicclair, "Informed Consent and Research," 365.

118. Martyn, "Using the Brain Dead."

119. More troubling, however, is the relatively unknown details of the extent of use of body parts and tissues in the American body processing industry. Donors and their families are unaware that tissue taken from their bodies may be used for cosmetic surgeries such as "reducing or enlarging breast size and thickening penises." Human tissues and bones from donors are used for a variety of things, including cosmetic

Some researchers may worry that specific disclosure may have serious effects on future research and training efforts deemed invaluable for the progress of life-saving intervention techniques in emergency medical situations. For them, disclosure practically ensures the elimination of these vital training and research efforts, which society cannot afford to lose. It is worth noting, however, that advances in resuscitative training tools, such as mannequins and computer simulators, is increasingly narrowing the advantage of using corpses.[120] Furthermore, as Sperling notes, "It has been indicated that using only mannequins and didactic sessions for teaching these skills is not less successful than using cadavers."[121] Whatever advantages corpses had in the past is increasingly being supplemented by developing technology for research education.

CONCLUSION

There is little doubt that the way in which death is managed today differs greatly from the past. Medical practitioners regulate death to the extent that it is estimated that the timing of eighty percent of deaths in hospitals is chosen.[122] The import of public opinion in the debate about brain death remains scant, at best. Surveys indicate confusion abounds, even when the attempt is made to disclose the meaning of the diagnosis. Given that life support mechanisms sustain life signs in patients who have suffered chronic cognitive and physiological impairment, family members are sometimes reluctant to accept that their loved one has died. At other times, people simply cannot understand the complexity of terms meant to convey various levels of cognitive impairment, the details of which their own physicians may be uncertain. Indeed, most people simply accept their doctors' assurances that their loved one has died, without knowledge of the controversies surrounding brain death and organ donation. Whatever consensus about brain death exists in public opinion rests on an uncertain foundation.

---

products, dental dust, and bone putty. A single cadaver can generate products worth up to two million dollars. For more on this, see Barber, *Nasty Side.*

120. Berger et al., "Ethics of Practicing Medical Procedures."

121. Sperling, "Breaking the Silence," 403.

122. Orr and Meilander, "Ethics and Life's Ending."

Various pro-life groups also have helped shape public opinion through their acceptance of brain death. This is significant, given the fact that ongoing moral controversies in society (e.g., abortion and euthanasia) are supported by these groups' reliance upon a sanctity-of-life ethic that highly values the lives of all human beings, particularly the most vulnerable. It is evident that while some explanation exists in the efforts of these groups' authorities to remain relevant and mainstream, the most influence comes from reliance upon the medical community's acceptance that brain death is the death of the organism as a whole. With this biological basis now in question (see Chapter Two) it remains to be seen whether these groups will continue to support a condition that fails to represent the death of the organism as a whole.

Statutory irregularities are an indication of the struggles of lawmakers to apply a conceptually confused criterion of death. Variation in the clinical tests for determining brain death contributes to the arbitrariness in the way in which states determine how brain death should be applied. Though most states incorporate the two main elements provided in the UDDA, variations in the statutes lead to inconsistencies between jurisdictions. This "trickle-down" effect underscores the need for a more coherent conceptual foundation that better provides for a legal framework that can guarantee the legal protection society depends upon for a web of social relationships.

Finally, the most disconcerting aspect brought out in this chapter is the problem of consent with regard to how the brain dead are exploited for medical training and research purposes. It is highly questionable whether consent is possible, given that the details of extent of one's anatomical gift are rarely disclosed. Researchers who propose that corpses have no autonomy and interests, fail to appreciate that people in general care deeply about their interests, including what happens to their bodies after they die. As acute as this concern seems to be, it is further heightened when consideration is given to the ambiguity regarding the physiological status of the brain dead. If indeed, as previous chapters maintain, the brain dead are not dead, then consent to post-mortem research under the brain-death criterion is not possible. These concerns invite a larger conceptual analysis, which will include a philosophical investigation of brain death in the following two chapters.

4

Philosophical Problems
with Brain Death

THE STANDARD PARADIGM FRAMING current discussions about
death represents a multi-level debate concerning: (1) the concept
or definition of death; (2) the criteria for determining death; and (3)
the diagnostic testing for the clinical signs of death.[1] In previous chapters the medical criteria as well as the clinical tests for brain death were
discussed in detail. Chapter One revealed the historical development of
levels two and three in which a new criterion (brain death), along with
clinical tests, was adopted in what may be described as a conceptual
vacuum.[2] Based on pragmatic concerns, brain death was initially adopted in medical practice and social policy, despite having no theoretical
basis for explaining why it represents human death. But since the use of
particular tests is contingent upon particular criteria, and the use of particular criteria rests on a particular conception of death, it follows that
a constructional definition is central to understanding why a criterion
is valid. Recognition of this is evident in the fact that various theorists,
since the Harvard Committee, have attempted to construct a conceptual
basis consistent with the criteria and tests adopted in practice and law.
Considered this way, it appears that the development of brain death has
occurred exactly backwards than it should have. Normally, one starts
with a particular paradigm and then proceeds to identify corresponding
criteria and the various tests consistent with the paradigm. Instead, the

1. Bernat et al., "On the Definition and Criteria of Death."
2. Gervais, *Redefining Death*, 156.

Harvard Committee simply identified tests for a medical condition and then recommended that condition as a criterion for death. Failure to appreciate the importance of an underlying philosophical conception to ground the criterion may be the primary reason for the controversy and misunderstanding surrounding the use of brain death. David Lamb expresses the importance of philosophical clarity with regard to defining death as follows:

> Clarity concerning the concept of death provides a point of reference when deciding upon criteria, but some definitions of death are philosophically inadequate despite the fact that criteria can be logically derived from them. Consequently an investigation of the philosophical basis of any concept of death is important . . . .[3]

In a previous chapter, it was suggested that the problems evident in the tests-criterion relation would ultimately be found in a faulty relation with the definition. Bernat articulates the definition of death as "the permanent cessation of functioning of the organism as a whole."[4] If this definition is accepted, then the definition ought to be sufficiently consistent with its corresponding criteria (cardiopulmonary death and brain death). It has been demonstrated in the analysis in Chapter Two that there is plausible evidence that the diagnostic tests fail to comport with the brain-death criterion. This chapter aims to carry the analysis further by critiquing the criterion-definition relation in the standard paradigm. The purpose of this chapter is to challenge brain death's veracity with respect to its definitional and metaphysical foundation. Accordingly, this chapter addresses the philosophical groundwork and assumptions of the underlying metaphysics for the definition of death under the current paradigm. Specifically, the chapter discloses the theoretical inconsistencies between the organism/substance view and brain death based on the empirical evidence as well as particular instances of inconsistencies among advocates of the substantial view. Finally, the chapter presents several important objections to the substance view and briefly highlights some responses from substance advocates.

3. Lamb, *Death,* 12.
4. Bernat et al., "On the Definition and Criteria of Death."

PHILOSOPHICAL GROUNDWORK AND ASSUMPTIONS

Philosophical notions of personal identity, though notoriously contro-versial, are essential for laying the groundwork for thinking about many important biomedical issues. Exactly how one thinks about what consti-tutes being human in general and being a person in particular directly translates into how one formulates positions on issues such as abortion, embryonic stem cell research, and defining death. Indeed, many of the issues currently under discussion among bioethicists today hinge on the underlying metaphysical assumptions regarding the constitution of hu-man persons. As J. P. Moreland and Scott B. Rae note: "Philosophical clarity and, especially, careful metaphysical distinctions are crucially relevant to the task of assessing various views of human persons and the ethical positions that follow from those views."[5] Failure to recognize the importance of metaphysical starting points with regard to defining death leaves out the philosophical scaffolding necessary for constructing medical criteria and tests consistent with the death of human persons. In short, failure to adequately address the philosophical underpinnings in the debate about death would amount to, at best, the establishment of criteria and tests on *petitio principii* grounds.

Among many theorists, there tends to be a generally accepted distinction between psychological-based criteria and organism-based criteria for death. If one adopts and defends a higher-brain model, then one has adopted a psychological-oriented conception of human death. If, on the other hand, one adopts and defends something beyond the higher-brain model, (i.e., the whole brain model) then one is usually characterized as having an organism-oriented conception.[6] So, the two models evidently depend on two conceptions of "person." The former asserts that persons come to be when certain properties or functions emerge associated with a human organism, and with the permanent loss of those properties or functions, the person ceases to be. The latter, however, asserts that personal identity is congruent with the life of the organism as a whole, from its coming to be as a human organism to its ceasing to be as such. Hence, the question ultimately is one that con-cerns the ontological status of the brain-dead individual. Put differently, the question concerns whether it is correct to think that human persons

5. Moreland and Rae, *Body & Soul*, 50.
6. Gervais, "Advancing the Definition of Death."

are human organisms who cease to be when the organism ceases to be, or are persons who are something different than the human organisms with which they are associated.

When the President's Commission defined death as "that moment at which the body's physiological system ceases to constitute an integrated whole,"[7] the Commission unambiguously adopted an organism-based conception of human persons. The Commission was deliberately conservative in their deliberations and chose to base them on the idea that humans have been traditionally viewed as organisms belonging to a substantial kind. This is evident in the parts to whole relation in the Commission's rationale for opting to an organism-oriented view of death. The Commission's report states:

> The functioning of many organs—such as the liver, kidneys, and skin—and their integration are "vital" to individual health in the sense that if any one ceases and that function is not restored or artificially re-placed, the organism as a whole cannot long survive. All elements in the system are mutually interdependent, so that the loss of any part leads to the breakdown of the whole and, eventually, to the cessation of functions in every part.[8]

Desiring to maintain constancy with a more traditional view of life and death, and to avoid the perception of a radical shift in the definition of death, the Commission recognized that "the adoption of a higher brain 'definition' would depart radically from the traditional standards" implying "that the existing cardiopulmonary definition had been in error all along."[9] Thus, the President's Commission was deliberate in opting away from a psychological-oriented view and instead chose a definition of death consistent with the idea that humans are organisms of a substantial kind. The question of conceptual continuity between the definition and the proposed criterion depends on whether brain death is consistent with the metaphysical theory that avers human persons to be essentially physical organisms.

An organism-based conception of human persons is indicative of a substance view of human persons, the metaphysics of which requires some explication. As in any philosophical discussion, the level of coherence will depend on the clarity of the terms employed. Imprecision

7. President's Commission, *Defining Death*, 33.
8. Ibid., 32.
9. Ibid., 40–41.

undoubtedly leads to confusion about how data is incorporated into the philosophical framework. While a detailed explication and defense of the metaphysics of substances is beyond the scope and purpose of this investigation, it is nevertheless necessary to carefully define the relevant terms employed by contemporary proponents of the substance view in order to assess the coherence of brain death with the metaphysics implicitly adopted by the President's Commission.[10]

The traditional view of a substance (in accordance with Aristotle and Thomas Aquinas) suggests several features indicative of the core of substantial identity. Norris Clarke sets forth four characteristics of a substance:

> (1)it has the aptitude to exist *in itself* and not as a part of any other being; (2) it is the unifying center of all the various attributes and properties that belong to it at any one moment; (3) if the being persists as the same individual throughout a process of change, it is the substance which is the abiding, unifying center of the being across time; (4) it has an intrinsic dynamic orientation toward self-expressive action, toward self-communication with others, as the crown of its perfection, as its very *raison d'etre*. . . .[11]

Substances, therefore, are basic individual wholes or unities of properties, parts, and capacities and are capable of maintaining absolute identity or sameness through change. The idea of change indicates sameness. If something has undergone a change, then something has to remain the same, otherwise nothing has changed. Human persons, for instance, undergo various changes throughout their existence, such as gaining consciousness and growing in rationality, but nevertheless remain the same thing, the same substance, throughout these changes.

Unlike the weak unity a pile of junk on the curb might have, substances possess a deeper unity of parts. Indeed, the parts of a substance obtain their identity with respect to their connection to the substance as a whole. As Moreland explains:

> The parts of a substance are united in such a way that the whole is ontologically prior to its parts in this sense: the unity of a substance is basic and primitive, it is not derived after its parts come

10. Much of this section is derived from Moreland and Rae, *Body & Soul.*
11. Clarke, *Explorations,* 105.

together, and the parts of a substance are what they are in virtue
of the role they play in the substance as a whole.[12]

To illustrate, the parts of a human heart are what they are by virtue of
the role they play in relation to the heart as a whole; the heart is what it
is by virtue of the role it plays in relation to the circulatory system; and
the circulatory system is what it is by virtue of the role it plays in relation to the organism as a whole. If a part is removed, then the relation
is severed, thus effecting a relational change in the identity of the part.[13]

Important to substantial unity is the way in which capacities
(sometimes called potentialities, tendencies, or predispositions) adhere
in a substance. Among different substances are natural groupings of
capacities, with each natural group containing a hierarchical ordering
of capacities. The human substance has various capacities that other
substances do not possess. For instance, humans have the capacity to
believe and think certain things, as well as to feel and to choose in ways
other beings do not. Humans are of a particular identifiable substance by
virtue of their natural grouping of capacities such as intellectual, emo-
tional, and volitional.

In addition to natural groupings, capacities also come in hierarchies. Hierarchies may be divided into first-order, second-order, and so
on until ultimate capacities are obtained. Moreland explains:

> . . . if Sue can speak English but not Russian, then she has the
> first-order capacity for English as well as the second-order capac-
> ity to have this first-order capacity (which she has already devel-
> oped). Sue also has the second-order capacity to speak Russian,
> but lacks the first-order capacity to do so.[14]

In other words, second-order capacities are realized only when first-order capacities are first developed. A tomato seed has the ultimate capacity to produce tomatoes, but this ultimate capacity cannot be actualized
until lower-order capacities are developed first, such as developing a
root system. The only things preventing the natural development of the
lower-order capacities necessary for the substance to realize its ultimate

---

12. Moreland and Rae, *Body & Soul*, 71.

13. The substance view thereby recognizes that when an organ is removed from one
individual and transplanted into another, a different substantial relation obtains and
hence a new identity.

14. Moreland and Rae, *Body & Soul*, 72.

capacities are a suitable environment and possible defects in lower order capacities. Consequently, when a substance fails to develop its ultimate capacities due to some defect or some other factor that prevents the development of a lower-order capacity, the substance cannot be said to lose its ultimate capacity, but rather "lacks some lower-order capacity it needs for the ultimate capacity to be developed."[15]

Hence, all the capacities of a substance find their culmination in a set of ultimate capacities which are possessed by a particular thing by virtue of its belonging to a natural kind. It is the inner structure or nature of a substance that orders and directs the development of lower-order capacities necessary for the realization of its ultimate capacities. Failure to fully develop ultimate capacities, or lose the capacity to exhibit them once obtained, is not necessarily tantamount to a substantial loss or change in identity. As long as the substance remains a member of its natural kind, at whatever level of development or diminished capacity, it retains its substantial identity.

Important to advocates of the metaphysics of substances is the contrast made with artifacts (sometimes referred to as property-things.) Unlike substances, which are internally structured according to a set of internal relations, artifacts are structured entirely by a set of external relations. While a pile of junk on the curb contains a weak unity of sorts, artifacts represent a deeper unity in that the parts constitute a whole by virtue of their ordered relations. The kind of order or unity obtained by an artifact is imposed on its pre-existing parts. For example several parts, such as four legs and a top, compose a table. The external relation imposed upon the parts makes it a structured thing. But the parts, legs and top, are what they are by virtue of their ordered relations. Metaphysically speaking, unlike substances whose unity is prior to its parts, the parts of artifacts are prior to the whole. Clearly, the unity of parts is not derived and ordered according to an internal nature within the being of the table. Rather, the table is structured completely by a design previously conceived in the mind of a designer. Hence the unity of the table does not "spring from within the parts . . . or within the [table] taken as a whole: it resides merely in the designer's mind."[16]

15. Ibid., 73.
16. Ibid., 81.

Moreover, an artifact has no capacity to realize "new kinds of properties not already resident in [its] parts."[17] For instance, tables cannot actualize new parts latent in their previously existing parts. At best, new spatial relations may be imposed on tables which rearrange their parts in different locations. But this new arrangement is not due to an internal agency directing from within. Rather it is due to an external imposition of spatial relations already existing in the parts prior to its existence as a whole.

Finally, artifacts also are subject to a change of identity in ways that substances are not. Recall that for a substance, events such as losing or gaining a part do not constitute a change in identity. However, when an artifact loses or gains a property (or part) something about its identity changes. As new parts replace the old parts of a table, the table itself would undergo a change in identity and literally become a different table. This is due to the idea that "[artifacts] are mereological compounds, systems constituted by separable parts standing in external relations."[18] In other words, the individual parts are essential to its identity; and thus with respect to an artifact's loss or gain in its network of parts, a new entity emerges.

Another way to understand the nuances of the substantial view is by considering its philosophical roots in the metaphysics of Aristotle and Thomas Aquinas. Through the philosophical literature of Aristotle, Aquinas develops a composite view of living organisms. For Aquinas, "Every natural body which has life in it is a substance in the sense of a composite."[19] That is to say, every living being is composed of two metaphysical components: form and shape. As Ric Machuga explains, "'Form'" is that which makes something *what* it is. 'Shape'. . . refers to the totality of a thing's physically quantifiable properties, i.e., its physical shape, size, height, weight, chemical composition, etc., *in its most complete description.*[20]"

For Aristotle and Aquinas, the study of shape belongs to the physical sciences, such as chemistry, biology, and physics. Form, however, belongs to the category of ontology and hence takes on a more abstract point of view. While chemists, biologists, and physicists concern

---

17. Ibid.
18. Ibid.
19. Aristotle *De anima* II, I, 412a15.
20. Machuga, *In Defense of the Soul.*

themselves with questions of how physical, bodily processes work, the ontologist takes up the question, "What sorts of things exist?" To further elaborate, when one asks a question such as, "What is a table?", for Aquinas, an adequate answer requires delineating between whether the question concerns the physical properties of the particular table in question (its shape), or the nature or essence of a table in general (its form.) The latter is an ontological question concerning "what is" a table. The answer to the question that limits itself to physical descriptions of the table's shape is insufficient to convey fully what is a table. To answer that question fully one needs to address the nature of tableness in general, (i.e., its form or essence).

A living thing is a composite of substantial form (called a thing's soul), and body (the shape or expression of substantial form.) Regarding the former, soul is the metaphysical principle of identification for living organisms belonging to a universal kind (a thing's *whatness*). Concerning the latter, body represents a particular instance of the universal form (a thing's *thisness*). More than that, soul represents the vital activity of body. Since matter *qua* matter is itself lifeless, that is, life is not intrinsic to body as body, Aquinas contends that soul is the animating principle or source of life for the body. He writes:

> For it is clear that to be a source of life, or to be a living thing, does not belong to body as a body, since, if that were the case, every body would be a living thing, or even a source of life, as a certain kind of body . . . . Therefore, the soul, which is the source of life, is not a body, but the actuating form of a body.[21]

For biological organisms, soul is the organizing principle which brings all the parts of an organism into a unitive expression of its substantial form. As such, organizational life is a feature of soul that cannot be reduced to the "stuff" of physics or chemistry. M. Green writes, "Organized systems cannot be understood in terms of their least parts alone, but only in terms of those parts *as organized* in such systems."[22] Rather, soul is that which organizes and directs bodily parts and systems into an organized whole. As such, the soul is the organized organizer of the body.

These distinctions represent a minimal set of characteristics necessary for understanding the metaphysical foundation for human persons

21. Aquinas, *Treatise on Man.*
22. Green, "Aristotle and Modern Biology," 411.

as organisms of a substantial kind. The next section undertakes assessing the substance view of human persons (human persons as organisms of a specific kind) in relation to the current evidence regarding the brain-death criterion. The measure of success for this chapter will be whether the conceptual resources for the substance view, as represented in the current paradigm, are consistent with the brain-death criterion as proposed by its advocates.

BRAIN DEATH AND SUBSTANTIAL IDENTITY

Though the definition of death under the current paradigm is the death of the organism as a whole, brain-death defenders, such as James Bernat, clarify that it is the critical functions necessary for the continued health and life of the organism as a whole that represent the necessary and sufficient conditions for human life. Thus, in the assessment of a human organism's functional capacity, only certain requisite functions count in the determination of whether an organism has sustained irreversible functional loss. These functions fall into three biological categories, all of which must be irretrievably lost in order to constitute the death of the organism as a whole. Bernat cites these as: 1) *vital functions* of spontaneous breathing and autonomic control of circulation; 2) *integrating functions* that assure homeostasis of the organism, and 3) *consciousness*. Bernat further explains, "The presence of any of the three elements constitutes sufficient evidence for life."[23]

Crucial to a proper understanding of what constitutes the necessary and sufficient conditions for life is the underlying distinction between "whole organism" and "organism as a whole." In an attempt to maintain consistency with an organism-based definition, Bernat explains:

> "The organism as a whole" is an old biological concept that refers not to the whole organism (the sum of its parts) but to that set of vital functions of integration, control, and behavior that are greater than the sum of the parts of the organism, and that operate in response to demands from the organism's internal and external milieu to support its life and to maintain its health. Implicit in the concept is the primacy of the functional unity of the organism.[24]

23. Bernat, "Defense of the Whole-Brain Concept of Death."
24. Ibid.

It should be clear that Bernat's rejection of the former category (whole organism) is an implicit rejection of an artifactual (property-thing or functional) view of human persons. Hence, by accepting the latter category, Bernat has, in some sense, embraced a substance view, since substantial identity is rooted in the idea that persons are greater than the sum of their parts. At least this much is consistent with the substance view as delineated earlier in this chapter.

However, the manifest difficulties of reconciling brain death with the death of the organism as a whole (as detailed in chapter 2) suggest that brain death does not mark the end of human integrated functioning. Indeed, many of the functions necessary for maintaining organic integration can be supplemented by medical technology. For instance, with the use of a ventilator the diaphragmic muscles can operate to provide oxygenated air allowing for the respiratory system to maintain its continued functional capacity for O_2 and CO_2 exchange.[25] In this sense, respiratory function has not been destroyed. Moreover, artificial maintenance of other critical functions, such as the regulation of blood pressure through vassopressors, the maintenance of body temperature, and the suspension of rapid asystole through synthetic arginine vasso-pressin (ADH) and epinephrine, suggest that the idea that brain death inevitably leads to bodily disintegration is overstated.

Additional evidence concerns the dozen or more documented brain-dead pregnant women who, with the aid of medical support, retained integrated organic functioning and were able, in many cases, to gestate fetuses to near full term. Mark Siegler and Daniel Wikler note that these sorts of cases contribute to the ambivalence associated with "corpses" that exhibit functions indicative of living patients. They write:

> It has been known for some time that brain-dead patients, suitably maintained, can breathe, circulate blood, digest food, filter wastes, maintain body temperature, generate new functions, and fulfill other functions as well. All of this is remarkable in a "corpse." Granted, these functions could not be maintained without artificial aid and, even so, will cease within a few weeks. However, many living patients depend on machines and will not live long; they are not thereby classified as (already) dead.[26]

25. Potts, "Pro-Life Support," 129.
26. Siegler and Wikler, "Brain Death and Live Birth," 1101.

Perhaps the most devastating critique of brain death, as highlighted in chapter 2, concerns the work of Alan Shewmon. Recall that Shewmon, a pediatric neurologist, has advanced considerable empirical evidence in direct opposition to the idea that the brain is the organ of somatic integration, a necessary condition for the viability of the criterion. If the brain serves as the integrator of the organism as a whole, then the integrated unity of the organism as a whole is sustained and directed primarily by a functioning brain. When the brain loses its functional capacity, cardiac arrest will follow shortly.

However, observations made by Shewmon demonstrate that "if 'brain-dead' patients are supported during the acute phase of their illness, cardiac arrest is now not certain."[27] As the number of counter examples grows (Shewmon alone documents some 175), there no longer remains any reason under the current paradigm to accept the claim that brain death marks the end of bodily integration.[28] As a case in point, Shewmon has carefully documented a noteworthy example of prolonged somatic survival for a patient who survived more than fourteen years after a brain-death diagnosis. Despite claims of misdiagnosis by critics, the autopsy showed a completely destroyed brain.[29] As one neurologist confirms, "Recent evidence shows that survival is possible in the environment of modern Intensive Care Units—and even out of these—despite the fact that the whole brain seems destroyed, as happened with a series of patients reported by Shewmon."[30]

The substance view is capable of accounting for the organizational unity present in medically supported brain-dead patients. The distinction between lower-order and higher-order capacities is crucial on this point. With respect to the loss of lower-order capacities, supplementation through external means makes little difference with respect to the life of the organism as a whole. Many higher-order capacities indicative of organizational life continue despite the fact that some lower-order capacities are derived through means external to the patient. Thus, brain-dead patients may lack some lower-order capacities, but still retain higher-order capacities indicative of living persons. In this sense, the external agencies of lower-order capacities are, as Tom Tomlinson

27. Karakatsanis, "'Brain Death': Should it be Reconsidered?" 398.

28. Shewmon, "Brainstem Death."

29. Repertinger et al., "Long Survival."

30. Karakatsanis, "'Brain Death': Should it be Reconsidered?" 398.

notes, "The functional equivalent of the destroyed brain stem."[31] As far as the substance view is concerned, continued organizational unity is indicative of the continued presence of the inner nature, which is constituent of human persons.

The fundamental inconsistency in the standard paradigm concerns the insistence of internally based functions as necessary conditions for organizational unity.[32] However, if patients who are not brain dead are dependent on external sources for lower-order capacities (or functions), then by that criterion they lack the necessary conditions for organizational unity as well. Two counter examples from Robert Truog and J. T. Fletcher highlight the problem. They are: 1) individuals who, due to spinal cord injuries, rely on mechanical ventilation for support; and 2) patients who rely on pacemakers for effective heart functioning.[33] Withdrawal or removal of these external agencies of support would quickly result in the lack of "integrated organic functioning," and yet no one would consider these patients dead.

Stuart Younger and E. T. Bartlett provide a hypothetical situation that bears further consideration. They ask us to imagine a case in which "someone has suffered neo-cortical ('higher brain') death, and is no longer conscious."[34] If the patient retains the capacity for temperature regulation, then according to the brain-death criterion, he would still be alive. Suppose that this same patient suffers a stroke in the area of the brain stem that controls temperature regulation; nevertheless, temperature is maintained through medical support. They ask, "Is he still functioning as a whole?"[35] Suppose further that the patient suffers another stroke affecting his respiratory and circulatory centers. Added supportive measures are taken, such as placing him on a ventilator and regulating his blood gases. If we continue to imagine further compromises, with each function supplemented by ICU staff, at what point should we conclude that organizational unity has sufficiently ceased? The evidence suggests that integrated organic functioning remains at all stages of lower-order functional loss. According to the substance view, as long as

31. Tomlinson, "Conservative Use of the Brain-Death Criterion."

32. Recall that the bedside testing procedures for brain death focus on automated reflexes, including spontaneous breathing.

33. Truog and Fletcher, "Brain Death and the Anencephalic Newborn."

34. Youngner and Bartlett, "Human Death and High Technology."

35. Ibid.

organizational unity is present, despite the loss of lower-order capacities, the brain-dead patient retains his or her higher-order capacities for bodily integration. Thus, the substance-view advocate, if he or she is to be consistent, must maintain that brain-dead patients do not lose their substantial identity. They neither "become members of another species" by virtue of severe brain damage, nor are they mere aggregates of persons who were once associated with bodies.[36]

Since physical organisms undergo constant change throughout their lives, constancy is explained at the level of substantial form. As an organism gains new parts or loses old ones, it is its substantial form (as the organized organizer) that directs these changes according to its essence, or natural kind. In the case of brain-dead patients, certain physical parts become damaged (constituting a loss of parts) which results in the loss of certain lower-order capacities. However, since these lower-order capacities are supplemented through artificial support mechanisms, the substance retains the capacity for many of its higher-order capacities. The inability of a particular substance/organism to actualize all its capacities at a given time is irrelevant as long as the organism as a whole continues to exhibit organizational capacities. As one substance advocate notes, "A substance has a set of capacities that are true of it even though they are not actualized."[37]

These considerations lead to the conclusion that since brain-dead patients retain integrated organizational unity, these individuals, at least under the substance view, are living human beings. While it is true that such individuals have experienced the loss of certain capacities, because these capacities are supplemented by medical support, what remains under this view is not the mere "residual countenance of a person."[38] Rather, the brain dead, at least from a substantial perspective, remain persons, albeit severely disabled. In the next section, consideration is given to particular instances of inconsistency among proponents of the substance view.

36. Jones, "Metaphysical Misgivings," 108.
37. DeWeese and Moreland, *Philosophy Made Slightly Less Difficult*, 44–45.
38. Jonas, *Philosophical Essays*.

INCONSISTENCIES AMONG SUBSTANCE ADVOCATES

Among substance-view advocates, the majority embraces the reasoning set forth in the President's Commission report as consistent with their view that death should be declared only when organic unity in the body breaks down. They argue, in conjunction with the Commission's report, that without the unique integrated functions of the entire brain, organic functioning of the body is lost. Typically, substance advocates argue that a human person comes to be when the human organism comes to be (at conception) and ceases to be when the organism as a whole dies. The question of whether these advocates can maintain consistency based on their claims about the status of the human organism at the beginning of life with the empirical evidence now uncovered regarding the human organism that has been declared brain dead is worth considering.

The substance view is most often offered as a means to assess the abortion debate.[39] Proponents present the view as an attempt to argue that a "human being is intrinsically valuable because of the sort of thing it is, and the human being remains that sort of thing as long as it exists."[40] According to the substance view, a human being throughout its development and decline does not undergo any substantial changes that alter its identity until the organism as whole dies. Indeed, it remains numerically identical to itself as long as it exists even when it is unable to exhibit those functions normally associated with healthy adult human beings. Hence, mere membership in the species *homo sapiens* is sufficient reason to attribute intrinsic value and rights to any human individual in recognition that it is "one of us."

Patrick Lee, an advocate for the substance view, presents a form of the argument in five steps:

1. You and I are intrinsically valuable (in the sense that makes us subjects of rights).

2. We are intrinsically valuable because of what we are (what we are essentially).

3. What we are, is each a human, physical organism.

4. Human physical organisms come to be at conception (a biological proposition: a new and distinct human organism is gener-

39. Lee, *Abortion and Unborn Human Life.*
40. Beckwith, "Explanatory Power."

ated by the fusion of a spermatozoon and an oocyte).

5. Therefore, what is intrinsically valuable (as a subject of rights) comes to be at conception.[41]

Lee, et al note three important points regarding the substantial identity of the human embryo.[42] First, they note an embryo is from the start *distinct* from any cell of the father and mother. This is due to its internal, directed, and distinct growth toward maturation. Second, the embryo is *human* with a genetic make-up characteristic of humans. Third, the embryo, though immature, is a *complete* or *whole* organism that will, barring disease, violence, or variation in environment, direct itself toward full expression of its essence. All of these features are present in the embryo and none of the changes it undergoes during its development generates a new direction of growth.[43]

Of specific note is the fact that for those thinkers who employ these sorts of arguments, the necessity of a functioning brain to denote the presence of a person is not required. For them, a proper view is one in which personhood is defined in biological but not necessarily strictly neurological terms. As John S. Feinberg and Paul D. Feinberg note, "Whatever is or potentially is genetically a person counts as a person and has a person's rights."[44] Yet the necessity of having a partially functioning brain as a condition for personhood in parallel cases with the life of the fetus is deemed unnecessary by many defenders of the substance view, this despite the fact that many of these same thinkers consider having a (partially) functioning brain necessary at later stages of the human being's life. Consider Lee's comments on the matter:

> The reason why irreparable cessation of brain functions constitutes death is not because having a brain is at all stages of the human being's life a necessary property, but because in the mature human being the brain is the organ which organizes all the systems of the human organism. So when the brain ceases to function (totally and irreparably) in a mature human being, the various tissues and organs cease to form an organism. Now a human being is essentially an organism (a specific type of

---

41. Lee, "Pro-Life Argument," 250.

42. Lee and George, "Wrong of Abortion."

43. Ibid.

44. Feinberg and Feinberg, *Ethics for a Brave New World*, 123.

organism), and so if the tissues and organs cease to constitute an organism, then the human being has ceased to be.[45]

Similarly, in an effort to distance their view from a higher-brain formulation of death, Moreland and Rae state, "Biological functioning is important to a substance view since it holds that the human person is an organic unity grounded in an individual essence."[46] Yet, a few sentences later they state, "The whole brain definition is consistent with a substance view of the person since once the entire brain ceases to function, heartbeat and respiration will cease as well."[47] Consistent (in their view) with their claim that human persons are organisms (or substances) of a specific kind, they write: "Whole brain definitions of death are most consistent with a substance view of a person, in which the person is a unity of biological, mental, and spiritual components, grounded in an individuated essence—one's human nature."[48]

A final example is from Elio Sgreccia, a proponent of the Aristotelian/Thomistic substance view articulated earlier in this chapter. He argues that the mental and spiritual components of persons belong to the substantial character of the human organism. In contrast to the dualism implicit in higher-brain death, he contends, "The body does not have its own private existence aside from the spiritual soul. The unity of the person lies in this fact: there is a single existence for these two components."[49] Attempting to maintain distance from the higher-brain criterion, he further maintains that the brain-death criterion must not be understood "in the sense that one wants to identify the part (the encephalon) with the whole (the body separate from the soul)." Rather, he argues, the brain-death criterion is commensurate with the death of the organism as a whole since "once the functions of the entire encephalon have been irreversibly lost, including those of the encephalic trunk, which governs the cardio-respiratory function, the organism loses the unifying principle of life that defines it as a living organism."[50] He goes on to note that this is true regardless of the use of mechanical ventilation,

45. Lee, *Abortion and Unborn Human Life,* 76.
46. Moreland and Rae, *Body & Soul,* 336.
47. Ibid., 337.
48. Ibid.
49. Sgreccia, "Vegetative State and Brain Death," 362.
50. Ibid., 364–65.

serving merely as a substitute for spontaneous breathing, which permits the heart to continue to beat for the maintenance of organs to be retrieved for transplantation.

What all these substance advocates have in common is their acceptance of organizational unity as the defining feature of the presence of the human person from conception to the death of the organism as a whole. Though at earlier stages of development the human organism does not require a functioning brain, at later stages the unifying principle of life is present only in those organisms with lower-brain function intact. As noted in the last section, the discrepancy lies on the insistence that internally based integrated functions are a necessary condition for the life of the organism as a whole. Patients who rely on artificial or external means for these same lower-brain functions maintain unified organic function, as exemplified in cases of brain-dead pregnant women. Given the empirical evidence to the contrary, substance advocates like those highlighted above can no longer maintain that their acceptance of brain death is consistence with the death of the organism as a whole.

Though these problems are indicative of the substance view as articulated by those holding to an organism view of human persons, other thinkers have criticized the metaphysical foundation upon which the organism view is grounded. These critics, most of whom embrace a dualism of one kind or another, generally approach the issue from a psychological-oriented view of personhood. They maintain that the problem with the current paradigm lies not in the brain-death criterion, but rather in the definition of the death of the organism as a whole. In the following section, several objections to the substance/organism view are presented.

SOME OBJECTIONS TO THE ORGANISM/SUBSTANCE VIEW

As previously noted, psychological-oriented conceptions of human persons tend to be dualistic—often distinguishing between the psychological self which comes to be and may cease to be at times other than the organism with which it is associated. Advocates of the psychological ilk often criticize the organism view on the basis of its inability to satisfy contemporary emphases and advances in metaphysics and biology. While variations at the theoretical level are wide, a few instances should suffice to illustrate the challenges leveled against the substance/organism view.

The question raised by some current thinkers regarding the traditional substance view pertains to its inadequacy in accounting for both biological and mental structures. William Hasker, a prominent emergentist proposes a dualism based on the idea that the conscious mind, which constitutes psychological identity, emerges at a time different than that of the organism itself. Representing a growing trend among some philosophers of mind, his dualism rests on the recognition that the unity of conscious experience cannot be accounted for by virtue of its relation to physical properties and parts. He argues that if it is taken seriously the vast amount of data coming out of neuroscience, as well as that of the phenomena of the mind itself, it is clear that a mechanistic/reductionistic view is unable to supply an adequate accounting of both fields of data. On the mechanistic view, mental properties are properties of brain. Although the brain is an extremely complex organ consisting of identifiable sub-organs, which in turn consist of billions of neurons, the brain nonetheless consists of these parts. So whatever is done by the brain must also consist of "the properties of, and relations between the parts of the brain."[51] However, when the application of this is made to conscious experience, a certain incongruity results. When one views a complex scene, such as a landscape interplayed with multiple objects, colors, and depths, the image is experienced by the person as a unity, not a cacophony of fragmented parts. As Hasker notes, "It is simply unintelligible how this experience can consist of activities of and relations between parts of the brain each of which does not have the experience in question."[52] Something over and above the parts must be posited in order to account for the unity in question.[53] This is best explained by a substantial form that organizes the complexity of the parts and their operations into a unified conscious experience. This view is dualistic in that it distinguishes between the bodily substance and the mental substance, the latter of which has some reliance for its emergence and operation on the brain and is indicative of the conscious self.

51. Hasker, "Persons as Emergent Substances," 111.

52. Ibid.

53. Some functionalist materialist philosophers have attempted to account for unity by referring to a set of functional states defined in terms of causal relations. For a rebuttal of these contentions, see LaRock, "Dualistic Interaction."

Hasker objects to the Aristotelian/Thomistic substance view by noting that current biology has done away with the need for postulating *form* as the organizing and life-giving principle of body. Reflecting on what he considers an untenable metaphysics, he notes: "Aristotelian souls are responsible for energizing bodily functions such as digestion, growth, and reproduction as well as for consciousness, sensation, and reasoning: this runs head-on into the commitment of contemporary biology to mechanistic explanations of such biological processes."[54] Hasker is suggesting that current biological explanations are capable of adequately accounting for the biological processes formerly attributed to form by Aristotle and Aquinas. Implicitly, he suggests that notions of an immaterial form responsible for bodily integrity are outmoded in light of contemporary biology.

Advocates of the substance view may respond in two ways to this sort of objection. First, they might respond by claiming that it is a mistake to assume that scientific descriptions of biological processes constitute a complete explanatory account of life. While the sciences can describe to us which arrangements are associated with certain functions, they are nonetheless inept to explain why the mere arrangement of material parts generates the kinds of effects observed in various organisms (much more why these parts should arrange in the way they do in the first place.) Rich Machuga explains:

> There is absolutely no good reason why nerve cells attached to a central nervous system should be able to feel, whereas cambium layers attached to roots and leaves should not be able to feel. It is no use saying that nerve cells are necessary conditions for the ability to feel and since trees lack nerve cells they can't feel. The problem is that "nervous system" *means* a system which is able to feel. Or as a mocking Moliere might say, the reason animals are able to feel is because of their sentient powers![55]

Applied to other bodily functions, including digestion and growth, organization and causation are irreducible to physics and chemistry. Indeed, these functions are only properly understood with respect to their functional roles in the organism as a whole. Meaning, therefore, resides in the parts only in terms of their relation to the whole.

54. Hasker, *Emergent Self.*
55. Machuga, *In Defense of the Soul*, 39.

A second, though related point, concerns the need for a unifying principle to account for holistic integration. One view, called the *genocentric view*, attempts to explain organizational unity and causation through the encoded DNA, which serves as the ordering principle of aggregated parts into a whole. This view depicts a mechanistic and hence, a property-thing view of human organisms in which a single aggregate part orders and directs other aggregate parts to form a living whole. Problematic to this view is that it assumes DNA molecules are self-actualizing. That is, it assumes that since DNA contains the fundamental building blocks of life, which constitute the core elements of human persons, then DNA must also possess the capacity "to initiate the complex set of chemical reactions necessary for cellular growth and development."[56] However, current genetic science reveals that this form of genetic reductionism lacks explanatory power to account for how the genetic program can carry out its plans. Geneticist Francois Jacob comments: "[O]utside the cell, without the means to carry out the plans, without the apparatus necessary for copying or transmitting, [the DNA program] remains inert. No more than memory of a computer can the memory of heredity act in isolation. Able to function only within the cell, the genetic message can do nothing by itself. It can only guide what is being done."[57]

Additionally, Barbara McClintock realizes the shortcomings of the reductionist view when she writes:

> [T]he genome is a highly sensitive organ of the cell that monitors genomic activities and corrects common errors, senses unusual and unexpected events, and responds to them often by restructuring the genome. We know about the components of genomes that could be made available for such restructuring. We know nothing, however, about how the cell senses danger and instigates responses to it that often are truly remarkable.[58]

In other words, the mechanistic/reductionist view is unable to provide an account for how DNA is able to accomplish its organizational role. Put simply, DNA needs a driver.

Other dualists, particularly those of a materialistic bent, consider the notion of a substantial form (or soul) an obstacle for the intelligibility

56. Moreland and Rae, *Body & Soul*, 210 and 296.
57. Cited in Shuster, "Determinism and Reductionism," 122.
58. See McClintock, "Significance of the Genome."

of the organism view. John Lizza, for example, criticises Alan Shewmon's position along these lines. Recognizing that Shewmon evokes the notion of "a spiritual soul as what gives life to a body," Lizza suggests that the idea of a soul containing in itself the capacities for intellect and will is conceptually problematic. For Lizza, intellect and will are the defining features of human persons and in the absence of any physical conditions there is "no rational basis for determining when such a radical power or potency for intellect and will is present in a thing."[59] He suggests further why mere membership in the human species is insufficient to signify the presence of a human person. For example, if all members of the human species have the potential for intellect and will, then it follows that one would be committed to count "Jeremy Bentham and the pharaohs (perhaps more completely preserved) as human beings with the potential for intellect and will."[60] These inadequacies, according to Lizza, render the organism/substance view lacking in its intelligibility.

Although a thorough critique of Lizza's view, along with other consciousness-based definitions of death, will be provided in chapter 5, two responses are in order. First, the proponent of the substance view could agree with Lizza that intellect and will represent defining features of human persons. However, where they part company is with regard to what grounds a certain organism as presently having these person-making capacities. Under the substance view, as presented above, the physical conditions in the organism (a properly functioning brain) are a necessary condition only regarding the *present* exhibition of certain higher-order capacities, such as consciousness. Since substantial form is the organizing principle of the material components of body, it is also the locus of the ultimate capacities of personhood. Thus, PVS and brain-dead patients may lack the necessary lower-order capacities for the actualization of higher-order capacities, but by virtue of their continued organic functional unity, higher-order capacities remain intact due to the continued presence of their inner nature, which is what makes them persons. Contrary to Lizza, the rational basis for determining person-hood under the substance view rests on the persistence of organizational unity.

The second response segues from the claim that mere membership in the human species is sufficient reason to ascribe personhood under

59. Lizza, *Persons*, 106.
60. Ibid.

the substance view. The implication given by Lizza is that dead specimens would also have to be considered belonging to the natural kind, hence possessing the real potential for intellect and will. But clearly this is a straw man. For Aristotle, a dead body is no longer a human organism, since it lacks substantial soul to inform its parts into an organized whole. Hence, a dead organism is no organism at all, but merely the remains of parts, which naturally disintegrate into smaller compounds because they lack the organizing principle that once gave them direction and identity.

Two other arguments employed by J. McMahan demonstrate the difficulty of postulating organizational numerical identity as intuitively preferred to psychological continuity.[61] The first involves cases of diacephalus (two-headed) twinning, in which the zygote does not divide completely resulting in twins conjoined below the neck. McMahan employs the case of Abigail and Brittany Hensel, each having "her own private mental life and her own character, each [feeling] sensations only on her own side of the body, and each [having] exclusive control over the limbs on her side."[62] Although there are two distinct persons, McMahan argues, there seems to be only one organism shared between them. This suggests that, since the two persons, Abigail and Brittany, share the same organism, then there can be no numerical identity between them and the organism. Additionally, since there seems to be no reason to think that diacephalus twins are different types of beings from persons in general, then this suggests that no person is essentially an organism.

A second argument employed by McMahan is derived from the example of hemispheric commissurotomy. Hemispheric commissurotomy is a procedure in which the corpus callosum, which is responsible for communication between the two cerebral hemispheres of the brain, is severed usually to alleviate epileptic seizures. Some studies on hemispheric commissurotomy indicate that when each hemisphere is presented with different stimuli, each can be unaware of what the other is experiencing.[63] This suggests that a person's consciousness could be divided.[64]

61. McMahan, *Ethics of Killing.*

62. Ibid., 35.

63. Puccetti, "Case for Mental Duality."

64. This suggestion is controversial and challenged by Robinson, "Personal Identity and Survival."

Based on this idea, McMahan suggests that if hemispheric commissurotomy were performed on an individual at birth with each hemisphere presented with different stimuli over the course of many years, this procedure would produce two different minds with different sets of experiences, memories, dispositions and beliefs.[65] If this happens, McMahan argues, there would be two persons co-existing in the same organism. As in the first example, since there is no fundamental reason to think these two individuals would be any different from any other human person, then there is good reason to think human persons are not essentially organisms.

Although it is beyond the scope of this chapter to offer a thorough critique of these criticisms, specific to those advanced by McMahan, several critiques appear in the literature.[66] Matthew Liao, for example, argues that with respect to the dicephalus case, there are in fact two organisms though not completely independent. In McMahan's example, Abigail and Brittany each have her own stomach, heart, brainstem and spine. Moreover, regarding the modified commissurotomy case, in somewhat parallel cases, such as Dissociative Identity Disorder (DID), just because someone has two sets of experiences does not mean that there are two distinct persons.

Most of these objections are given by those who advocate alternative definitions of death to the standard paradigm as advanced by the President's Commission. In the chapter that follows, attention will be given to some of these alternatives.

CONCLUSION

The focus of this chapter was on the definitional challenge to brain death. Specifically, the overall challenge concerned the relation between the implications of the definition of death advanced by the President's Commission and the brain-death criterion. This chapter began by disclosing that both Bernat and the President's Commission opted for a definition that centers on an organism-oriented view of human persons. For them, loss of integrated functioning of the organism as a whole

65. McMahan, *Ethics of Killing*, 38.

66. See for example George and Tollefsen, *Embryo*; Lee and George, *Body-Self Dualism*; and Liao, "Organism View Defended."

constitutes the death of the person. The line of reasoning employed by brain-death advocates who focus on organizational unity typically represents a traditional, substance metaphysics. The substance view represents a long and respected tradition that can be traced back to the philosophical anthropology of Aristotle and Aquinas. It provides an account of the human person based on the notion that humans are valuable because of the sort of things they are, (i.e., organisms of a substantial kind).

Further analysis suggests a lack of conceptual consistency of brain death with the substance view. If humans are by nature, as substance advocates suggest, "rational moral agents" associated with a particular sort of organism, then as long as this organism exists, it remains identical to itself, despite its failure to fully express functions and activities normally associated with fully developed, healthy adult humans. Rather than discriminate the self from the organism based on the present exhibition of certain favorable functions or activities, the substance view advocate asks, "What sort of thing is it that exists?" Once that question can be answered, it is argued, one has sufficient grounds for establishing whether the thing in question is deserving of the respect due to persons. In other words, even if a person lacks the ability to think rationally, due to lack of development or a disability, a person remains a person because of his or her inner nature. It is the inner nature, or the substantial form, that constitutes the continued presence of its ultimate capacities.

If, as substance advocates suggest, a distinct human organism comes to be at conception, the substantial person comes to be, and through an internally structured unity develops herself to be the thing she is by virtue of her inner essence. In other words, persons are what they are prior to the expression of all their ultimate capacities. The process by which these capacities are actualized is characterized by an internally driven orientation toward self-organization, self-expression, and self-communication with others.

The substance view represents a claim of broad inclusiveness for the human community[67] and achieves symmetry when carefully applied to brain-dead persons by virtue of their continued organizational unity despite medical interventions to supplement functional loss. Mechanical ventilation, the administration of vassopressors, and a host of other life-sustaining interventions, may portray dependency for life, but if the

67. Campbell, "No-Brainer."

life of the organism as a whole is sustained, then dependency becomes irrelevant. As Potts notes, "[A] 'whole brain dead' individual can continue to function as a unified organism, although she is *dependent* on machines . . . The brain dead patient's dependence on machines, even permanent dependence on machines, for continued organic functioning is irrelevant to whether or not he or she is alive."[68]

Advocates argue that the explanatory power of the substance view lies in its ability to account for the continued life and existence of the organism when technological support seemingly blurs access to the status of the life of the organism through the window of traditional life signs. Because the substance view recognizes a distinction between lower-order and higher-order capacities, supplementation of lower-order capacities fails to constitute loss of organizational unity. As long as higher-order capacities for organizational life continue, the organism remains the same thing it was prior to lower functional loss. Since the substantial person is identical to a physical organism belonging to a natural kind, as long as that organism continues to exist, the substance-view advocate has sufficient grounds for maintaining the continued existence of the person under the brain-death criterion. Thus, substance advocates who embrace brain death do so on grounds inconsistent with their own metaphysical categories.

Critics of the substance/organism view approach the issue from an entirely different metaphysical viewpoint. Based on a body-self dualism, Hasker, Lizza, and McMahan maintain that the organism view fails to correspond to basic intuitions about what it means to be a person. Whether these criticisms are successful remains to be seen, as there is considerable ongoing debate on these issues. What is clear, however, is that the definition of death, along with the metaphysical foundation upon which it is based, is inconsistent with the brain-death criterion.

This analysis falls short in assessing various alternatives to the standard paradigm dominating the discussion over the past thirty or so years. The following chapter will consider alternatives to, as well as modifications of brain death. Particular attention will be given to the higher-brain model of death proposed by various prominent thinkers. These models will be evaluated for their conceptual coherence. In addition, attention will be devoted to suggestions regarding donation apart from the dead-donor rule, particularly their potential effects on

68. Potts, "Pro-Life Support," 133.

the medical community and society in general. Other proposals involving the adoption of conscience clauses for those who oppose the legal standard of death will be examined as well.

5

Advancing Alternatives to
Brain Death

THE WELL-PUBLICIZED "ACUTE SHORTAGE of organs for transplantation"[1] has led to numerous suggestions designed to increase the
pool of organ donors. At the heart of these suggestions is the idea that
the current standard of death is in need of refinement either by way of
extension or modification. The fact that advances in technology have
allowed for the creation of patients in suspended states has given rise
to questions about previous conceptions of life and death. At the same
time, some thinkers recognize that certain of these patients are ideal
candidates for organ procurement, given their greatly diminished physiological and cognitive capacities. They suggest that an expansion of
death criteria to include higher-brain death is better capable of meeting
the challenges presented by patients in these slippery states, while at the
same time furthering the prospects for increasing organ supply.

Others have gone further suggesting that death is indefinable on a
social level and that social policy should allow for reasoned diversity on
issues as personal as death and donation. Although varying in detail, the
common thread among these proposals, whether a motivating factor or
logical corollary, is the idea that organ procurement ought to proceed
apart from the dead donor rule, which according to the standard paradigm is necessarily connected to the definition of death.

However, some thinkers argue that society can better tolerate individual freedom at the definitional level. They suggest the

1. Veatch and Pitt, "Myth of Presumed Consent," 1888.

implementation of conscience clauses allowing for personal choice with regard to death criteria.

This chapter assesses various alternatives and modifications to death criteria put forward for the purpose of expanding the pool of potential organ donors. In particular, attention is given to higher-brain models of death. These models will be evaluated for their philosophical coherence and with current neurological evidence. The chapter also explores suggestions regarding donation apart from the dead donor rule, particularly with respect to their potential effects on the medical community and society in general. Moreover, this chapter considers proposals involving the adoption of conscience clauses for those who oppose the legal standard of death. Finally, an overall assessment and summary will be provided.

HIGHER-BRAIN MODELS

Higher-brain models of death began to gain support following a landmark *Lancet* article published in 1971.[2] J. D. Brierly and colleagues affirmed that neocortical death could be accurately diagnosed, and that neocortical death represents a sufficient condition for diagnosing permanent unconsciousness. Since that time, several theorists have attempted to justify a conceptual basis for human death that centers on the permanent loss of certain functions associated with the higher regions of the brain.[3] Though there is considerable debate as to what those functions are, higher brain advocates are, as Michael B. Green and Daniel Wikler note:

> . . . united on the point that our decision about what constitutes the death of the human being must reflect what is essentially significant to human nature, and that the permanent cessation of (embodied) consciousness qualifies, since it is a necessary condition for any of the uniquely human capacities individuals possess in different measure.[4]

2. Brierly et al., "Neocortical Death after Cardiac Arrest."

3. Green and Wikler, "Brain Death and Personal Identity"; Veatch, "Whole-Brain Oriented Concept of Death."

4. Gervais, "Advancing the Definition of Death," 159.

Since humans have much in common with other species, particularly with regard to organismic functions, the focus should be placed on functions pertaining to our ontological distinctiveness, including the capacity for consciousness, thinking, reasoning, feeling, and awareness. And since these capacities are attributable to the higher portions of the brain, it is argued, one need not assess the integrative lower functions of the brain stem.

Though higher-brain advocates insist that the mind must be present for the human person to be considered alive, they vary in focus on the required conditions necessary for personhood. Some thinkers, such as Green and Wikler, focus on personal identity, which is sustained only in virtue of psychological continuity. For them, the central issue is whether the conscious self, which includes a set of mental qualities such as consciousness, memory, character, and intentions, is sufficiently intact that one is justified in saying that the same person exists over time. It is important to note that for Green and Wikler, it is not the brain tissue per se that is sufficient in establishing personal identity, but rather the "brain processes, carried out through microstructural and microfunctional registrations in the brain tissue."[5] Patients suffering from neocortical death have suffered permanent loss of personal identity since they lack the necessary qualities or functions to sustain their psychological identity. Hence, such patients are properly considered dead.

Respondents to this position cite numerous counter-intuitive arguments demonstrating its insufficiency for grounding personal identity. The problem seems to be the difficulty of defining death in terms of the loss of personal identity.[6] Francis Beckwith provides a counter example to illustrate the problem.[7] Beckwith suggests imagining that one's uncle, call him Uncle Jed, is in a terrible car accident that results in him being in a coma from which he may or may not awake. Suppose, however, that after two years he awakens. Beckwith queries, "Could the physicians have killed Uncle Jed—the living organism we refer to as 'Uncle Jed'—during that time because he did not exhibit certain functions or have certain present capacities?"[8] If one holds that personal identity is contingent upon certain mental qualities or functions, then it is difficult

5. Ibid., 126.
6. Lizza, "Conceptual Basis for Brain Death Revisited."
7. Beckwith, "Explanatory Power."
8. Ibid., 37.

to say why it would be wrong to end the life of Uncle Jed while he was in a coma. Since Uncle Jed, while in a coma, lacked the necessary functions for personal identity, ending the life of the organism associated with Uncle Jed constitutes no harm to him. But suppose the personal identity advocate claims that what makes it wrong to kill Uncle Jed while in a coma is the psychological continuity between his past functioning and the probability that he will do so in the future. However, pushing the illustration further reveals a difficulty. Beckwith writes:

> For imagine that *while in the coma* Uncle Jed's physician *tells you* that your uncle will come out of the coma, but when he comes out he will *not* have any of the memories, beliefs, or knowledge that he once possessed, though he will be able to regain his prior abilities and accumulate new memories and experiences over the years following his recovery through the normal process of learning and development.[9]

Now it is obvious that the psychological disconnect between Uncle Jed's pre-coma, coma, and post-coma conditions forces the personal identity advocate to accept the permissibility of ending the life of the organism associated with Uncle Jed despite the fact that he will retain his basic capacities as a human being.

Robert M. Veatch[10] and Karen Grandstrand Gervais[11] also criticize the view of Green and Wikler as insufficient to conceptualize human death. Veatch suggests that some cases of dementia and amnesia pose serious problems for the personal identity view of Green and Wikler. Under their view, psychological continuity would cease to exist in patients who suffered from these conditions, and by implication such patients have died. Gervais agrees, arguing that as long as the biological substrate for conscious experience remains intact, despite the loss of past experiences in the form of memories, death has not occurred. Veatch and Gervais both propose that designating such individuals as dead poses counter-intuitive problems for the personal identity proponent

---

9. Ibid., 38. Beckwith claims that Uncle Jed would be in the same position as a fetus and argues that just as it would be wrong to kill Uncle Jed while in a coma, so it would be wrong to kill a fetus. If this argument works in the first respect, then I think the argument also works in its application to Green and Wikler's position.

10. Veatch, "Impending Collapse."

11. Gervais, *Redefining Death*

thereby suggesting that the conceptual criteria for determining human death lies elsewhere.

Veatch is well known for his advocacy of a consciousness related model of death. As early as 1975[12], he challenged the whole brain concept of death advocating in its place a form of higher brain death consistent, in his view, with the Judeo-Christian tradition. For Veatch, human life, in the morally significant sense, is characteristic of "humans with '*embodied* capacity for consciousness.'"[13] A human being, therefore, is an essential union of body and mind. When the capacity for consciousness is permanently lost, as in cases of patients in a permanent vegetative state, the essential union is lost. Veatch contends, "[A] functional body without any capacity for mental function lacks the essential integration of body and mind."[14] Hence, death in the morally significant sense has occurred.

Veatch's model stands out as one that is less concerned about the loss of some mental function, such as consciousness or personhood, and more concerned about the integration of bodily and mental function, which he considers the critical feature of human life. Given the fact that the term *personhood* is so ambiguous, disputes about personhood are irrelevant to the definition of death debate. For some the term refers to all living humans, even if they have lost all brain function. More controversial are those definitions that limit personhood to humans who possess some key mental capacity, such as the ability to have a self-concept or possess self-awareness. Hence, some biologically integrating and even some conscious humans, such as newborns and some of the senile, would be non-persons by this conceptualization. Moreover, the term is sometimes applied to non-embodied entities, "such as the being that would exist if one could download an individual's memories into a sophisticated computer."[15] Still others apply it to departed human souls, angels, and divine persons. To the extent that the term can be applied in so many ways, analytically the question of whether one is a person or not has nothing to do with whether one is a human being, at least in the moral sense. Thus, "Being a living human,"

---

12. Veatch, "Whole-Brain Oriented Concept of Death."

13. Ibid., 370.

14. Ibid.

15. Ibid., 367.

writes Veatch, "is totally independent of possessing either personhood or continuity of personal identity."[16]

What this means, more concisely, is that for Veatch the definition of death debate should be understood as a moral or policy controversy about when certain death behaviors are appropriate. These could include, stopping life-supporting treatment, reading the will, initiating life insurance payment, procuring organs for transplantation, etc., all of which were in the past triggered by an event called death. Unbundling these death behaviors may be appropriate at certain times prior to the moment of death. Indeed, as medicine advanced in its ability to slow down the dying process, society recognized that certain of these behaviors are more appropriately triggered at different stages in a series of dying events.

What is at issue, then, is not merely whether all biological human life has ceased; rather, whether one has lost the full moral standing society affords equally to all members of the human moral community.[17] Included in the concept of possessing full moral standing is a set of rights designating the duties certain other humans have toward these individuals. Death in this sense occurs when an individual has lost his or her moral standing, and this is best characterized when the essential union of mind and body is permanently severed.

Some have characterized Veatch's model as a functionalist view,[18] a charge that Veatch vehemently denies.[19] Unlike Veatch who eschews any interest in the personhood debate, John Lizza argues that how one conceptualizes persons and personal identity directly affects "the evaluation of issues in bioethics, particularly the problem of defining death."[20] For him, higher-brain advocates like Veatch, Green, and Wikler rely on a problematic way of understanding the relation between person and organism. Instead of focusing on persons as substantive entities or subjects, these thinkers identify "the person with certain abilities and qualities of awareness."[21] This qualitative or functionalist approach treats the person as a set of mental qualities and has its origins in the thinking

16. Ibid.
17. Ibid.
18. Gervais, *Redefining Death*; Lizza, *Persons.*
19. Veatch, "Death of Whole-Brain Death."
20. Lizza, *Persons*, xi.
21. Lizza, "Conceptual Basis for Brain Death Revisited," 53.

of John Locke and David Hume. To illustrate this point, Lizza recalls the hypothetical case presented by Locke of the prince and cobbler who swap bodies. Since personal identity is constitutive of psychological states and memories, if the bodies of the prince and cobbler woke up one day with the psychological states and memories of each having been exchanged, Locke concludes that the prince and cobbler would have swapped bodies.[22] Hence, for Locke personal identity consists of psychological continuity over time irrespective of the biological substrate underlying the psychological states at any given time.

Locke's view finds contemporary expression in functionalist theories of mind.[23] For the functionalist, mind is a set of mental states defined "in terms of causal relationships between a system's external input, causal output, and internal causal relations."[24] In this sense, mind is similar to a computer program. And since computer programs are capable of functioning in a variety of intrinsically different hardware platforms, minds, at least in the functionalist sense, are also capable of being realized in multiple physical systems. It is not hard to imagine, therefore, downloading the mind of an individual from one biological substrate, into a new physical support system without losing the essential features of consciousness that ground personal identity.

Although Veatch acknowledges that a "disembodied mind that has been downloaded from a previous embodiment but remains capable of thinking, feeling, remembering, and so forth, would surely have some important moral standing,"[25] he denies that his view entails that one must say it is the same human being as it was when embodied. According to Veatch, it is the functional relation of mind and body that constitutes a human being. Thus, the suggestion that a disembodied mind is just as much a living human being as an embodied mind would be, is a conclusion that Veatch, "and most scholars within the Judeo-Christian tradition, must reject."[26] Moreover, since the hallmark of his view is embodied consciousness, a body-swap would entail a recombination of the two essential features of the previous people resulting in the creation of two new individuals. Yet the creation of these new individuals would involve

22. Ibid.

23. Lizza cites Derek Parfit as an example. See Parfit, *Reasons and Persons*.

24. Garcia, "Artificial Intelligence and Personhood," 42.

25. Veatch, "Death of Whole-Brain Death," 371.

26. Ibid.

Another way to understand this problem is to consider the essential unity belonging to substances. Recall that Veatch understands the essential unity of human beings to be that of mind and body. In the event that no such unity obtains, as in cases of brain death, permanent vegetative state, and anencephaly, a declaration of death is appropriate. He also asserts that this view comports closely with the Judeo-Christian tradition. The problem with this view is that it fails to appreciate the remaining unity, which is most evidently displayed in the organisms' capacity for internal self-direction. More consistent with the Judeo-Christian tradition is the view that human organisms are substances by virtue of the internal relation of the parts to the whole. Each part receives its identity by virtue of its irreducible function and internal relatedness to the organism taken as a whole. This is why the organism is said to be ontologically prior to its parts. The functions of the parts reflect "the internal structure of capacities in the essence of the soul."[41] If one understands the soul as the organizing life principle of the body, then the soul is "the efficient cause of the characteristics of the human body."[42] Various bodily parts are best understood as instrumental causes that the soul utilizes to actualize its various capacities and traits. It therefore follows that as long as organizational unity obtains, despite physiological or cognitive impairment attributable to a lack in some part, the organizational principle, or soul, remains intact.

Lizza claims conceptual space for his view in the metaphysics of Aristotle and Aquinas. Recall that the argument involves a reversal of the succession of souls in the Aristotelian/Thomistic notion of embryogenesis. A necessary condition for the receiving of a rational soul (or ensoulment) is a sufficiently developed body to enable its proper operations. Similarly, when the body loses necessary structural integrity to support the operations of the rational soul, a substantial change has occurred. Hence, permanently unconscious patients manifest only the operations (and presence) of either a sensitive or a vegetative soul lacking any capacity indicative of the presence of a rational soul. The remaining body is nothing more than a humanoid animal or a mere vegetable. However, this view rests on dubious interpretive grounds. First, the ancient and medieval understanding of human embryology, which is the basis for this view, was seriously lacking in development.

41. Moreland and Rae, *Body & Soul*, 206.
42. Ibid. One might note that for Aristotle, the soul is the formal cause.

As some Thomistic scholars contend, "If Aquinas had known the facts of embryology he would have held that the human soul is present from conception."[43] Divorced from erroneous embryonic assumptions, the metaphysics of Aristotle and Aquinas, coupled with the facts of modern embryology, simply fail to support the idea of de hominization.[44]

A second interpretive problem lies in the failure to recognize logical distinctions from ontological ones. Jason Eberl notes that while Aquinas [and by implication, Aristotle] observe that when one "mentally abstracts the concept of rationality from the definition of a human being, the concept of animality will yet remain," he in no way implies "that this is what happens in the process of human death."[45] A careful assessment of Aquinas's entire treatment of the issue reveals a strong contention for the *unicity* of a human being's vegetative, sensitive, and rational capacities residing in one substantial form; namely, a rational soul. Thus the higher brain interpretation invokes an unnecessarily complex metaphysical explanation. As Eberl explains:

> Accepting the higher-brain interpretation entails the following metaphysical description of how human death occurs: there exists first a rational substance informed by a rational soul, and then

43. Haldane and Lee, "Aquinas on Human Ensoulment." Also see Heaney, "Aquinas and the Presence of the Human Rational Soul"; and Finnis, *Aquinas*. Haldane and Lee observe, "The reasons which led Aquinas to hold late human ensoulment are basically four, three embryological points and one metaphysical. First, on his Aristotelian view, the male is the sole active cause; second, the material (the menstrual blood) upon which the semen (as instrument of the male) works has only a very low degree of perfection or organization, not even possessing vegetative life; third, as a consequence, the distance between the initial point (menstrual blood) and the end point (a body sufficiently organized to receive a human soul) is quite long."

44 Haldane and Lee observe, "Modern embryology shows that the female provides a gamete (the ovum) which is already a highly organized living cell, containing highly complex, specific information, in the genetic structure of the nuclear chromosomes. This information (together with that provided by the genetic structure in the chromosomes of the male sperm) helps guide the development of the new living organism formed by the fusion of the sperm and the ovum. Hence the ovum is actually very close to readiness for rapid embryological development; it only requires fusion with the sperm and the activation that occurs with that fusion. To a certain extent the gradual transition from the simple to the complex that Aquinas sought actually occurs during gametogenesis (of which, of course, he was unaware). Thus, applying Aquinas's metaphysical principles to the embryological facts uncovered since his time leads to the conclusion that the human being is present from fertilisation on." Haldane and Lee, "Aquinas on Human Ensoulment."

45. Eberl, "Thomistic Understanding," 37.

possibly a non-rational animal substance informed by a sensitive soul, and finally a merely living substance informed by a vegetative soul before its final transformation into a lifeless corpse. This description violates Ockham's Razor, which states that *ceteris paribus* the simplest explanation of a given phenomenon—i.e., the explanation that is the least metaphysically complex by requiring the postulation of the least number of entities—is the explanation to which one ought to give assent.[46]

It is worth observing that higher-brain models of death depend on a body-self (or body-person) dualism that supposes the human person ceasing to be at one time and the human organism at another. According to this view, permanent loss of consciousness renders the person dead, and the relevance of the remaining organism is contingent on the prior wishes of the person with which it was formerly associated. A logical corollary of this dualistic view is the problem of accounting for the wrongness of intentionally creating unconscious cloned humans whose healthy organs can be used for transplant purposes or spare parts for the person from which the organism was cloned.[47] Given that these organisms lack the potential for consciousness, and hence the usual rights afforded persons, it is not clear how the creation and use of such organisms for morally good reasons is morally wrong. Dan Brock acknowledges this reality and argues that these body-clones could not be harmed since they "lack the capacity for consciousness."[48] Yet, he acknowledges, most people would likely find the intentional creation of permanently unconscious cloned humans appalling and immoral. It is not clear on Lizza's account how the moral repugnance many people would feel about this could be accounted for, given that his view is open to the moral warrant for these gruesome activities. Alternatively, under the traditional substance view, not only is the moral warrant for the creation and use of these organisms removed, but also an explanation for the moral repugnance felt by most people is more easily identified (see chapter 4.)[49]

46. Ibid., 40.

47. Beckwith, "Explanatory Power."

48. Brock, "Cloning Human Beings," E1–E15, as cited in Beckwith, "Explanatory Power."

49. While some might find counter-intuitive arguments of this sort unconvincing, they are nonetheless a valuable and common form of argumentation. The point of this type of reasoning is not to offer a knock-down argument, such as would be the case with a *reductio ad absurdum*, but rather to appeal to as wide a range of intuitions as possible.

Finally, notwithstanding the metaphysical problems of determining when death occurs, higher brain death also engenders epistemic uncertainties. Typically, higher brain death relies on the accuracy of diagnosis of the condition known as *persistent vegetative state*. The persistent vegetative state (PVS) diagnosis predicts a relatively poor prognosis for most patients. However, there is a small fraction of PVS patients who do make subsequent cognitive gains over time. In an effort to avoid prognostic error, some physicians make a distinction between a *persistent* vegetative state and a *permanent* vegetative state, a condition much more tricky to diagnose.[50] It is described as a probabilistic diagnosis regarding the future and requires a substantially longer period of time to diagnose, depending on patient age and the nature of brain damage.

Recent reports of some PVS patients awakening years after diagnosis raises questions about whether society would be willing to accept a higher-brain death criterion.[51] A report in the journal *Neurorehabilitation*, which documents the arousal of PVS patients through medication, proposes further complexities surrounding the potential cognitive status of these patients.[52] Moreover, neuroscience is changing previous conceptions that the grounding of consciousness is exclusively in the neocortex. As Stephen Miles points out, "Consciousness requires neocortical activation by lower brain structures, although there is no clear understanding of the status of consciousness when the activation of the neocortex is destroyed but neocortical activity remains, as is evidenced by neurophysiological studies."[53] Indeed, some cases of persistent vegetative state may be a higher form of the condition known as "locked-in state" in which the neocortex is completely isolated.

Complicating matters further is the cognitive state of patients with severe brain injury resulting in a minimally conscious state (MCS). Distinguished from PVS and coma, the MCS "is characterized by inconsistent but clearly discernable behavioral evidence of consciousness" clearly differentiated from reflex behavior.[54] Recently published data in the journal *Neurology* indicates that functional magnetic resonance im-

50. Plum, "Clinical Standards."

51. Martin and Nancarrow, "Woman Who Woke Up"; Smith, "Coma Recovery after 19 Years."

52. Clauss and Nel, "Drug Induced Arousal."

53. Miles, "Death in a Technological and Pluralistic Culture," 312.

54. Giacino et al., "Minimally Conscious State."

aging (fMRI) can be a very powerful tool in the evaluation of "awareness" of patients in this state. The findings were so remarkable that Dr. Joy Hirsch, director of the Functional MRI Research Center at Columbia University Medical School and an author of the study, said,

> The most consequential thing about this is that we have opened a door, we have found an objective voice for these patients, which tells us they have some cognitive ability in a way they cannot tell us themselves. The patients are more human than we imagined in the past, and it is unconscionable not to aggressively pursue research efforts to evaluate them and develop therapeutic techniques.[55]

One therapeutic technique, still in its experimental stage, is deep brain stimulation (DBS).[56] Although some patients may emerge from a MCS and regain a greater degree of consciousness without intervention, others may regain cognitive and physical abilities through DBS, which involves the electrical stimulation of the thalamus. Because of the extensive connections between the thalamus and the cortex, activating the thalamus may in turn reactivate the cortical functions resulting in an increased awareness of self, others, and the environment for these patients. Though multiple questions remain as to the therapeutic potential of DBS, recent findings "suggest that patients in MCS retain the physiological substrate necessary for cognitive tasks at much higher levels than might be demonstrated by overt behaviors on clinical examination."[57] DBS provides these patients with an expressive vector to the outside world that otherwise would render them cognitively isolated. These new technologies are challenging the degree to which our ability in the past to detect consciousness in many cognitively impaired patients is definitive.

Recognizing the uncertainty of the capacity for consciousness in many of these patients, some higher brain proponents recommend that organ donation from the permanently unconscious be limited to those patients declared brain dead under the current standard.[58] Since the likelihood of these patients regaining consciousness is nil, brain death

---

55. Schiff et al., "Fmri Reveals Large-Scale Network."

56. Schiff et al., "Deep Brain Stimulation."

57. Ibid.

58. Truog and Robinson, "Role of Brain Death"; Whetstine, "Examination of the Bio-Philosophical Literature."

is the minimal threshold under which donation should be permitted for the permanently unconscious.

Despite attempts to maintain a consciousness-based definition of death mediated through brain death, the epistemic quandary remains a serious challenge for all neurologically based criteria. Sometimes overlooked in the West, the public debate about brain death in the country of Japan evidences the relevance of the phenomenological perspective of family members. Several reflective reports by writers who witnessed the brain death of their relatives document the personal experiences between family members and their brain-dead loved ones.[59] These reports evidence a kind of intercorporeal communication, in the form of stabilization of heart rate and blood pressure, suggesting the felt presence of relatives by brain-dead patients. Another overlooked area relevant to the issue concerns the growing body of literature documenting the extraordinary reports of near-death experiences among patients in critical medical situations. Reports of heightened, lucid conscious experiences of patients with flat EEG readings, lack of cerebral blood flow, and no clinical life signs are suggestive of an epistemological gap in the understanding of the nature of consciousness.[60] Indeed, to conclude that a certain capacity, X, is present through the observation of its corresponding activity, Y, does not entail that in the absence of activity Y, capacity X is no longer present. It is therefore fallacious to infer that a PVS or brain-dead patient lacks any rational capacity on the sole basis of not having observed any rational or neural activity.[61] To illustrate the problem further, a recent article in the magazine *Wired* reports that, despite advancements in neuroscience, "Almost nothing is known about how the brain produces awareness, and current models of brain function don't accord with the little that is known."[62] The article goes on to highlight five major problems that are yet to be overcome before any model can begin to be constructed for explaining consciousness.[63] These problems

59. Sugimoto et al., *Kita Kamoshirenai Seifuko*; Yanagida, "Sakurifaisu: Waga Musuko Noshi No 11 Nichi," as cited in Steineck, "'Brain Death,' Death, and Personal Identity."

60. The literature in this area is vast and diverse. However, for an excellent work detailing the implications of NDEs to brain death, see van Lommel, "About the Continuity of Our Consciousness."

61. Eberl, "Thomistic Understanding."

62. Anderson, "Never Mind the Singularity."

63. These include: 1) No one knows how the mind is synchronized; 2) Current

are so acute that the prospects of constructing a coherent model of consciousness based on the classic physics governing neuroscience today seem unlikely.

In light of these shortcomings, some commentators maintain that the focus on defining death is ill conceived. They contend that a social consensus at the definitional level is an unlikely goal, given the various perplexities surrounding death and donation. Rather, it is suggested that social policy should be sensitive to reasoned diversity on issues as personal as death and donation. In the next section consideration is given to the proposal that organ procurement ought to proceed apart from the dead donor rule, which is necessarily connected to the definition of death.

CHANGING THE DEAD DONOR RULE

An important goal of the transplant community is to discover ways to increase the pool of organ donors in a manner that respects donor choice. Given that the number of patients waiting for transplants continues to rise while the number of donors remains unchanged, it is becoming difficult to realize such a goal without offering alternatives that challenge current standards governing organ donation. Currently, decisions about organ donation are made in accordance with the *dead donor rule*. Simply stated, the dead donor rule says that a patient must be dead before vital organs can be removed for transplantation. The purpose of the rule is to temper the utilitarian goal of increasing organ supply with the deontological concern of respecting persons. n this way, two key protections for patients are supported: 1) patient choice, and 2) protection from "futile and callous medical intervention."[64] Moreover, the dead donor rule provides protection for the medical community in general and the moral ethos of the physician in particular by limiting the scope of intrusion into the lives of patients. The practice of medicine is built upon public trust. If the public perceives that medical practitioners are

---

brain maps are of little use in explaining awareness; 3) The brain's computations may be a trillion times faster than previously thought; 4) Our current understanding of how anesthesia works flatly contradicts the notion that consciousness arises from firing neurons;)5 Understanding consciousness may have to wait for a new physics. See Anderson, "Never Mind the Singularity"

64. Pernick, "Brain Death in Cultural Context."

overstepping their boundaries to the point of hastening or prematurely ending the lives of patients, this trust is seriously compromised.

Recently, there has been some discussion about whether the dead donor rule remains capable of mediating these utilitarian and deontological goals. Elysa R. Koppelman argues that given the lack of consensus on a definition of death, the dead donor rule can no longer arbitrate between these moral goals, and in some cases we are right to "sever the connection between determinations of death and organ procurement."[65] For those who advocate the dead donor rule, a consensus definition of death is necessary in order to determine the moral status of taking organs from patients. However, since the concept of death is elusive, the establishment of a consensus turns out to be nothing more than a legal fiction created to resolve pragmatic concerns. Koppelman writes: "The attempt to develop a consensus definition of death was unsuccessful largely because this effort was entangled with other social and moral agendas."[66] As a result, the moral status of removing organs in many cases remains unresolved.

Accepting the premise that death is an ambiguous concept, Koppelman suggests two possible approaches to resolving the policy problem. First, continue to adhere to the dead donor rule, with its focus on the distinction between life and death, and address how social policy should handle the lack of consensus. Second, eliminate the dead donor rule thus severing the connection between definitions of death and organ procurement. Koppelman opts for the second approach suggesting that a focus on patient history provides for truer patient respect without undermining efforts to at least sustain the current pool of organ donors.[67]

Contrasting her view with Veatch's, who attempts to embrace ambiguity and establish social policy respecting pluralism, Koppelman begins by maintaining that the rationale of the dead donor rule is to protect potential organ donors from a kind of harm, (i.e., the harm of being disrespected). However, respect for persons is not necessarily achieved by

65. Koppelman, "Dead Donor Rule," 2. Koppelman cites Youngner, Arnold, and DeVita who likewise suggest: "Perhaps our society can accept a frank discussion about relaxing the dd rule in borderline cases better than it can tolerate efforts by the transplant community to minimize or ignore uncertainty and disagreement [bout the concept of death] within the scholarly community." Youngner et al., "When Is Dead?"

66. Koppelman, "Dead Donor Rule."

67. Ibid.

distinguishing between life and death. She remarks, "The point of death does not mark the point at which a person can no longer be harmed."[68] It is something other than life itself which entitles one to respect. Thus, to focus merely on the line of demarcation between life and death fails to adequately ground respect for persons—it must be found elsewhere.

Relying on the Kantian maxim, "Act in such a way that you always treat humanity, whether in your own person or in the person of another, never simply as a means but always at the same time as an end,"[69] Koppelman argues that to treat people as a means is to fail to regard them as subjects, i.e., as persons with reason who have established ends or interests. Disrespecting persons, therefore, constitutes violating their abilities to set ends.

Some theorists contend that many patients who are not dead would suffer no violation of interests by allowing removal of vital organs prior to death.[70] In particular, patients in a permanent vegetative state, with no prospect of cognitive recovery, and patients whose planned death through withdrawal of life-sustaining treatment has been chosen as the morally preferred choice are ideal examples.

Robert Truog and Walter Robinson[71] "propose that the ethics of organ donation be based on the ethical principles of non-maleficence and respect for persons rather than on brain death and the dead donor rule." They suggest "that sometimes the harm of dying is sufficiently small that patients should be allowed to voluntarily accept that harm if it makes organ donation possible." To advance the case for organ retrieval from still living patients, Truog and Robinson further suggest the necessity of "shifting the key ethical question from 'Is the patient dead' to 'Are the harms of removing life sustaining organs sufficiently small that patients or surrogates should be allowed to consent to donation?'"[72] By doing so, the prospects of overcoming the problems surrounding the orchestration of death in NHBD protocols would be achieved, in addition to "optimizing both the number and viability of the organs obtained."[73] In the event that society recognizes that the dead donor rule is no longer

68. Ibid., 5.

69. Kant, "Groundwork of the Metaphysics of Morals," 96.

70. Frost, "Unimportance of Death," 173.

71. Truog and Robinson, "Role of Brain Death."

72. Ibid.

73. Ibid.

morally necessary for the procurement of organs, Truog and Robinson contend that the "concept of brain death will then disappear from textbooks, illustrating the degree to which the concept was never more than a social construction, developed to meet the needs of the transplantation enterprise during a crucial phase of its development."[74]

Some theorists have taken this line of reasoning further. They argue that certain patients lack the ability to have any interests, and in such cases the dead donor rule need not apply to them.[75] Lacking these interests removes not only the ethical harm of treating them as a means to an end, but also the ethical or legal obligations to continue aggressive care.

Koppelman finds this line of reasoning misguided. Relying on Thomas Nagel's analysis, she argues that persons do not lose interests merely by virtue of their categorical position. She writes, "The fact that a patient is brain-dead or in PVS does not mean that she has no interests or ends. Clearly there is a sense in which there are still ends in such situations; what is absent is the person's awareness of her own ends."[76] An example by Nagel is helpful here. He argues that a man betrayed and ridiculed by his friends suffers harm even if he never finds out about the betrayal. What makes betrayal bad is not that upon discovery it makes one unhappy, but rather it makes one unhappy because it is bad. The fact that one may be unaware of the harm being done to him or her has no bearing on our obligation to treat an individual as an end. Indeed, argues Nagel, one often considers a person whose reputation has been ruined or whose will is ignored after he or she has died a victim of harm.[77] He concludes, "And if people who have already died can be harmed, then people who are unaware of having any ends can be harmed too."[78]

Transferring this to the issue at hand, society's obligation to treat someone as a subject of respect, as an end and not merely as a means to an end, is achieved neither by a focus on life and death distinctions nor by focusing on a particular moment in time. Rather, the focus should be on a patient's history in which personal ends in the form of interests and values are discoverable. A person who has expressed the desire to donate organs and has an advance directive indicating the desire to forego

74. Ibid.

75. Robertson, "Dead Donor Rule."

76. Koppelman, "Dead Donor Rule," 6.

77. T. Nagel, "Death," as cited in Koppelman, "Dead Donor Rule."

78. Ibid.

life-sustaining treatment while in a PVS or if brain dead is harmed when he or she is denied "the opportunity to donate in a way that has the best chance for success."[79] In such cases, the application of the dead donor rule fails to help the patient achieve the fate he or she has chosen.

For Truog and Robinson, the issue is framed a bit differently. Recognizing that brain-dead individuals are alive, in the interest of patient respect, they find it morally acceptable to remove their organs for transplantation, provided prior consent has been obtained. To avoid the charge of promoting homicide in order to obtain organs, they attempt to collapse the distinction between *killing* and *allowing to die*, a distinction well established in legal precedence and traditional morality. They argue:

> In both ventilator withdrawal and organ procurement, the physician acts, and this act is the most proximate cause of the patient's death. In both cases, the physician is not morally responsible for the patient's death—the morally relevant cause of death is the patient's disease. In both cases, the physician is acting with the patient's consent in ways that respect the wishes of the patient and that are in the pursuit of morally worthwhile ends.[80]

One might claim that the position advocated above would lead us down a slippery slope. Once we accept that patients in these states can donate organs apart from a declaration of death, what's to stop individuals who are perfectly healthy from donating vital organs? Koppelman believes the answer to this question lies with Kant. She writes, "Kant holds that treating people as ends is an obligation only if their goals or projects are rational or moral."[81] Hence, donating one's organs when not in a suspended state is an end that is almost always irrational and immoral, while donating one's organs in a suspended state is not. Although Kant thought suicide to relieve one's sufferings was wrong, he left open the question whether suicide to save one's country or to escape impending madness was immoral. Koppelman suggests that "ending one's life in a suspended state by donating organs seems to be more analogous to committing suicide to save one's country." While there seems to be nothing immoral about donating organs in a suspended state, donating them when one is not in such a state seems immoral. "Doing so," she writes,

---

79. Ibid., 7.
80. Truog and Robinson, "Role of Brain Death."
81. Koppelman, "Dead Donor Rule," 8.

"violates the categorical imperative as it fails to celebrate or recognize one's humanity."[82]

Respondents to the above proposal vary in their criticism. Mark D. Fox, for example, suggests there is less ambiguity surrounding brain death than Koppelman suggests. For him, the ambiguity concerning the criteria for brain death is less certain than the manner in which "we talk about states of neurologic devastation."[83] People often speak of brain-dead individuals as being kept alive by machines. Although life-support machines may maintain their physiology, since they lack vital respiratory function, which is a necessary criterion for a declaration of brain death, these individuals are easily distinguishable from patients in a persistent vegetative state. "Thus," writes Fox, "our verbiage is more ambiguous than our criteria."[84]

As important as respect for autonomy is, the social context of transplantation often goes unrecognized. The unique nature of the gift exchange aspect of transplantation cannot be viewed as simply a private act between two people. It involves the entire transplant community, at a minimum, whose values matter. Moreover, because transplantation "requires active societal involvement to be complete," mediation between donor preference and communal values is necessary for its continued success.[85] Thus, given that the entire transplantation enterprise is dependent upon public trust, Laura A. Siminoff suggests the necessity of establishing a stronger societal consensus with regard to both the definition of death and the circumstances for organ donation—something that the above proposal fails to accomplish.[86]

Robert Veatch, who is sympathetic to Koppelman's (and by default, Truog and Robinson's) proposal that "it is acceptable to take critical organs...from those who have irreversibly lost higher-brain function," wonders why it is necessary to abandon the dead donor rule rather than simply defining "the persistently vegetative as dead."[87] If the dead donor rule is abandoned, he argues, not only would almost every state in the US and most jurisdictions in the world have to amend current statutes

82. Ibid.
83. Fox, "Stewards of a Public Trust," v.
84. Ibid.
85. Ibid.
86. Siminoff, "Dead Donor Rule," 30.
87. Veatch, "Dead Donor Rule," 10–11.

in order to declassify brain death as death, but "homicide laws would also have to be amended to make clear that procuring organs and causing death in these humans was not murder."[88] Speaking for the bioethics community in general, Veatch asks whether it makes sense after having persuaded, with great effort, "many legislators, judges, transplant professionals, clergy, and philosophers that these beings are dead...to do an immediate about face and retrain these professionals to once again refer to these people as living."[89] And even if one were to retain the brain-death standard, legislatures would still have to address the legal status of the physicians who procure organs from still living, though permanently unconscious humans beings.

Michael Potts and David W. Evans, in their response to Truog and Robinson's proposal, offer two criticisms worth noting. For one thing, the argument that organ removal from a mechanically ventilated apnoeic comatose patient is no different than the removal of ventilator support to allow a patient to die is seriously flawed. They write, "When a ventilator is removed from an apnoeic comatose patient, it is the disease or injury that causes the loss of the patient's ability to breathe spontaneously . . . . The situation is different when vital organs are removed from a patient." When unpaired vital organs are removed from these patients, it directly causes the death of these individuals. Hence, it is the surgery itself that kills the patient, not the illness or disease. Second, Potts and Evans register their concern with the idea of doctors being involved in killing patients. Since abandoning the dead donor rule involves a form of justified killing, they charge that such a proposal "fundamentally distorts the nature of medicine itself."[90] Given the fact that the practice of medicine primarily involves an imbalanced relationship between the health-care provider, empowered with knowledge and skill, and the patient, whose characteristic vulnerability is exacerbated when ill, the idea of physicians directly ending the lives of patients "involves a dangerous use of medical power."[91] The danger lies in the potential for misuse of power, particularly regarding the weakest members of society, who depend upon the virtues of medicine for protection. Additionally, despite Koppelman's reliance upon Kantian rationality as a safeguard, as

88. Ibid.
89. Ibid.
90. Potts and Evans, "Does it Matter?"
91. Ibid.

Fox notes, "Taking Koppleman's proposal to its logical extreme offers no solid basis for denying an individual with decision-making capacity the opportunity to commit suicide by donation of vital organs."[92]

If abandoning the dead donor rule fails to conceptually satisfy the goals of organ procurement and patient respect, further exploration is necessary. One particular avenue of thought suggests that balance is better obtained when patient choice is placed at the level of defining death rather than at overturning the dead donor rule. Given the social values of autonomy and pluralism, some thinkers, such as Robert Veatch, have suggested social policy "that would permit individuals, while competent, to execute documents choosing alternative definitions of death that are, within reason, not threatening to significant interests of others."[93] Veatch's policy invites a larger menu of death criteria that includes higher-brain death (or neo-cortical death) and cardiopulmonary death with the current brain-death criterion serving as the "default definition of death." This policy purports to protect autonomy in a pluralistic society and expand the pool of possible organ donors under the current dead donor rule. This approach is the subject of discussion in the section that follows.

CONSCIENCE CLAUSES

Recognizing the ongoing controversy over the definition of death is primarily a religious and philosophical matter, some commentators have attempted to restructure the debate by proposing new ideas concerning human death and organ donation—ideas that potentially may affect how future social policy will be shaped. At the heart of these ideas is the concern for respect with regard to diverse conscientious positions about death, dying, and organ donation that conflict with present social policy. This concern has already found expression in New Jersey's religious exemption claim enacted in 1991[94] allowing for religious persons to choose cardiopulmonary death, as opposed to brain death, as their personal bottom line standard. The Act seeks to protect the religious convictions of its Orthodox Jewish community which opposes a

92. Fox, "Stewards of a Public Trust."
93. Veatch, *Transplantation Ethics,* 137.
94. Olick, "Brain Death."

neurological criterion for determination of death. The state of New York also provides for some discretion, based on family objections to brain death.[95] However, the discretion is primarily given to the physician contemplating a brain death declaration, and dissenting family members are dependent on whether their physician will accommodate their wishes. Until recently, the country of Japan rejected brain death as a legal standard. After much open public debate, Japanese law now permits the use of the brain death criterion, provided that the individual, while alive, has clearly expressed consent for both brain death and organ procurement, and this only after the family also consents.[96]

Given the social values of autonomy and pluralism, some higher brain advocates, such as Robert Veatch and John Lizza, have suggested social policy conscientious exemptions similar to New Jersey's religious exemption Act. Robert Veatch suggests an inclusion "that would permit individuals, while competent, to execute documents choosing alternative definitions of death that are, within reason, not threatening to significant interests of others."[97] By way of a statutory model, Veatch proposes a policy that allows individuals to select a definition of death, provided they choose, based on reasons of personal conscience, from a menu of acceptable definitions set forth in the policy. As the default definition, Veatch elects brain death. The policy begins by stating:

> An individual who has sustained irreversible loss of all functions of the entire brain (excluding cellular level and hormonal regulatory functions) is dead. This shall be referred to as the "default" definition of death. A determination of death must be made in accordance with accepted medical standards.[98]

In order to respect individuals who may conscientiously object to brain death, Veatch's policy allows competent individuals to choose from two other acceptable definitions. The first is higher brain death, which the policy describes as "sustained irreversible cessation of all consciousness."[99] The second is the traditional cardiopulmonary, which occurs when an individual "has irreversibly lost all circulatory and re-

---

95. Veatch, *Transplantation Ethics*, 114–35.
96. Ibid. Also see Lock, *Twice Dead*.
97. Veatch, *Transplantation Ethics*, 137.
98. Ibid., 138.
99. Ibid.

spiratory functions."[100] If an individual, while competent, chooses one of the alternative definitions, that definition "shall serve as the definition of death for all legal purposes."[101] The policy continues that, "unless an individual has, while competent, selected a definition of death to be used for his or her own death pronouncement, the legal guardian or next of kin (in that order) may so do relying on substituted judgment in so far as that information is available about the patient's wishes."[102] However, when no such information is available, decision makers must rely on a best-interest standard; otherwise, the default definition will be used.

Veatch's proposal differs from the New Jersey conscience clause in two ways. First, Veatch expands the choices to include higher brain death, a conscious-based definition. Under this definition, individuals in a persistent vegetative state, as well as anencephalic children, could be declared dead, since the capacity for consciousness for these individuals is virtually non-existent. Second, Veatch expands the conscience clause beyond religious preference. The New Jersey conscience clause was originally crafted for Orthodox Jews who preferred the traditional cardiopulmonary standard for religious reasons. Veatch's policy favors "variation based on any conscientiously formulated position."[103] In other words, individuals may choose alternative definitions of death for reasons other than religious. Hence, the policy recognizes that individuals capable of formulating a conscience-based conception of death, for either religious or non-religious reasons, should be given the opportunity to choose the definition that best fits their ideas about death.

Veatch's policy recommendation is commendable in its attempt to respect personal autonomy through the respect of diverse values as they affect personal choices concerning death and organ donation. Public policy should be crafted in the broadest terms possible to respect freedom of choice in a pluralistic society. A favorable aspect of his policy is, to be sure, that it allows individuals who conscientiously object to brain death to opt out of the standard. Nevertheless, there are several problems with Veatch's proposal that, on balance, outweigh its favorable aspects. First, Veatch's proposal includes higher brain death as a viable option. This is unacceptable for medical reasons, which were previously

100. Ibid.
101. Ibid., 139.
102. Ibid., 138.
103. Ibid.

addressed in this chapter. For instance, there are reported cases of PVS patients who recover under exceptional conditions and develop the capacity to write and speak.[104] Moreover, neuroscience is also finding that consciousness may not be entirely dependent on the neo-cortex, which suggests the possibility that PVS is "the highest form of locked-in state in which the cranial nerve communication that remains possible (e.g. as eye blinking) when the brain stem is intact is lost because the neo-cortex is completely isolated."[105] Finally, the clinical tests to determine irreversible loss of consciousness are not as definitive as those for other death criteria.[106] These medical facts pose difficult problems for the acceptability of higher brain death that by far exceed those of brain death. In light of these concerns, it would seem that even personal autonomy fails to justify its acceptability.

Second, Veatch's policy fails to correct the misgivings concerning the acceptability of brain death by reducing it to the default presumption. Veatch attempts to dismiss the inconsistencies of brain death by relegating them to a simple exclusionary clause (e.g., excluding cellular level and hormonal regulatory functions). However, the degree to which these remaining functions contribute to the body as a whole suggests that they ought not be so easily dismissed. As previously noted, there is growing unease from both the medical community as well as the general public with respect to brain death as an accurate diagnosis concerning the body's lack of organic integration. Evident from the analysis of brain death in previous chapters is that the loss of brain function is not necessarily indicative of the loss of integrative organic functioning of the organism as a whole. Indeed, few seem willing to dispute this.[107] Yet, Veatch's policy not only catalogues it as an acceptable option, but also places it as the default definition of death. With a growing number of commentators and medical practitioners calling into question the legitimacy of brain death, it is difficult to imagine how any proposed policy that regards brain death as the default definition ought to be considered good social policy.

---

104. See Arts et al., "Unexpected Improvement"; Higashi et al., "Five-Year Follow-up Study"; Morioka, "Reconsidering Brain Death."

105. Miles, "Death in a Technological and Pluralistic Culture."

106. Youngner and Arnold, "Philosophical Debates," 529.

107. Notably, even Veatch recognizes this problem, as well as the deficiency of brain death as a whole. See chapter 5, Veatch, *Transplantation Ethics*.

Third, Veatch's policy implicitly promotes a utilitarian drive to increase the pool of potential organ donors. As previously noted, the primary impetus behind the Harvard Committee's recommendation of brain death was to make it possible for physicians to procure organs under the dead donor rule. Youngner and Arnold note that utilitarian appeals "were the only justification given by the Harvard Committee for their new definition of death" and "were being accepted into law and clinical practice years before Bernat and the President's Commission came up with the first widely circulated, coherent philosophical justification that these patients were indeed dead."[108] Now that the conception seems seriously flawed, the means for procuring organs for transplantation is equally questionable. What is needed is policy that works to correct this problem. Veatch's policy recommendation fails to offer a corrective alternative, but instead continues to advance the problems that many commentators suggest demonstrate the need for abandoning brain death.

CONCLUSION

A common recognition among those who propose alternatives to the standard paradigm is the failure of brain death's conceptual basis. Nevertheless, as a means of retaining brain death as a feasible criterion, two general suggestions are proposed. First, some higher-brain advocates, working from a consciousness-based definition of death, suggest amending the dual standard to include a higher-brain criterion. The resulting triad (cardiopulmonary, whole-brain, and higher-brain criteria) is meant to assure the permanent loss of consciousness and thereby increase the pool of organ donors. Second, recognizing the uncertainties about the capacity for consciousness under the higher-brain criterion, others suggest a more certain way to guarantee that a patient has suffered permanent loss of consciousness exists in the current dual standard. This, it is argued, removes the moral hazard of prematurely ending the lives of patients whose cognitive capacities are in question.

Endemic to these proposals are questions regarding the ontological and moral status of the permanently unconscious. Philosophically, consciousness-based definitions of human life and death lack adequate

108. Youngner and Arnold, "Philosophical Debates," 533.

explanatory power to account for society's moral offence concerning the logical consequences entailed by higher-brain conceptions. There seems to be no reason in principle to object to the creation and use of "humanoid bodies" for the purposes of medical experimentation or organ harvesting. The logical entailments of focusing on cognitive capacity as a means for determining personhood status are at best, disturbing, striking at the heart of our moral intuitions about the value of human life. Indeed, one embarks on an uncertain path when society accepts certain groups of humans as non-persons, partially informed by the need for transplantable organs and the cost of continued treatment and care.

But there remains sufficient warrant for questioning the acceptability of any neurologically based criterion for death. Epistemological gaps regarding the status of awareness remains uncertain given the personal experiences reported by family members regarding brain-dead loved ones. Working from a highly formalized, impersonal method of ascertaining the presence of a person, modern science tends to dismiss as invalid the content of phenomenal cognition family members experience with brain dead loved ones as well as the personal experiences of those near-death. The dominant assumption driving most higher-brain proponents is that consciousness is identical to brain processes, the activity of which can be correlated with neural events. A closer look at recent findings in cognitive science, however, suggests that consciousness is not wholly identifiable with brain processes and that reductionism lacks the necessary empirical moorings many assume it has.[109]

Due to the inconsistencies and epistemic problems of neurologically based definitions of death, it seems more plausible that death does not occur until the human body ceases to function as a unified integrated organism. More consistent is the traditional substance view which maintains that the rational soul is not only the seat of a human being's cognitive and rational capacities, but is also the substantial form of the body and hence the source of its vegetative and sensitive capacities.

Other strategies that emphasize defining death as a purely private matter out of respect for autonomy and pluralism must be measured by their potential effects upon society as a whole. While public policy should be crafted in the broadest terms possible to respect freedom of choice, the question of whether exceptional cases translate into good social policy must not be shortsighted in deliberation. For example,

---

109. See LaRock, "Is Consciousness Really a Brain Process?"

important consideration must be given to the long-term pedagogical affects of law. It might be worth asking how sanctioning a medical procedure (organ procurement) that directly ends the lives of patients, no matter how altruistically conceived, will affect the moral sensibilities of both the public and medical community with regard to the value of human life. More specifically, if power is given to medical practitioners to directly end the lives of the permanently comatose, how might such a policy affect public trust with regard to the practice of medicine? Or more importantly, would public policy of this sort unwittingly desensitize the populace resulting in greater intrusions into the prohibitions against killing? These important considerations reflect the issues addressed in the remaining chapters.

6

An Ethical Analysis of Brain Death

To THIS POINT IN this investigation the analysis has been more descriptive than normative. The task has been to identify the major areas in which discussions about brain death have taken place. These include the historical, medical, social, and philosophical domains of inquiry all of which contribute to the overall framework and content necessary for an ethical assessment. It is tempting to conclude that the development of medical and social consensus over the last thirty years is sufficient to establish the ethical acceptability of brain death. However, this fact alone does not make brain death right from an ethical perspective. What is needed is a careful ethical analysis that takes all the domains of ethical assessment into consideration prior to an evaluative deliberation.

In many ways, this chapter is the most important, in that it attempts to bring all the relevant data from the previous chapters together in order to assess the ethical viability of brain death as it relates to organ donation.

The procedure for this chapter is as follows. First, the chapter deals with the application of traditional medical ethics to problems revealed in previous chapters concerning brain death. Second, the principles of biomedical ethics and relevant case law are applied to the issue of informed consent for organ donors under the brain-death standard. Finally, this chapter considers the ethical feasibility of grounding brain death on pragmatism as a sufficient reason for its continued use.

TRADITIONAL MEDICAL ETHICS AND BRAIN DEATH

It is important to begin by laying out the basic principles and concepts that have largely influenced moral reasoning relating to end of life issues. While a thorough discussion of these principles is beyond the scope of this investigation, a synopsis will suffice for the purposes of this ethical analysis. In American bioethics the ethical treatment of patients at the end of life has been informed and shaped by two traditions. The oldest of these is the Hippocratic tradition. This tradition maintains that the primary duty of the physician is to do no harm.[1] This precludes the administration of poisons in order to prematurely end the lives of patients. The Hippocratic ethos conceives the primary practice of medicine as the relief of suffering wrought by disease. When medicine can no longer accomplish this end, the physician and patient ought to recognize the futility of medicine and withdraw or withhold its use as evidenced in the following two passages from Hippocrates:

> First, I will define what I conceive medicine to be. In general terms it is to do away with the sufferings of the sick, to lessen the violence of their diseases, and to refuse to treat those who are overmastered by their diseases realizing that in such cases medicine is powerless.
>
> Whenever therefore when a man suffers from an ill that is too strong for the means at the disposal of medicine he surely must not expect that it can be overcome by medicine.[2]

Thus, this tradition asserts that the purpose of medicine is to relieve suffering associated with sickness and disease and that when medicine can no longer achieve this goal, the physician should no longer employ medicine. The implication is that the extension of medicine beyond its purpose could potentially cause greater harm to patients in hopeless medical conditions.

Another important influence on American medical ethics is the Roman Catholic moral tradition.[3] In conjunction with the Hippocratic tradition, Roman Catholic medical ethics draws out two important

---

1. Beauchamp and Childress, *Principles of Biomedical Ethics*, 149. The obligation is expressed in the Oath as follows: "I will use treatment to help the sick according to my ability and judgment, but I will never use it to injure or wrong them."

2. Hippocrates, *On the Art*, as cited in Pellegrino, "Physician-Assisted Suicide and Euthanasia," 94.

3. Kelly, *Critical Care Ethics*.

distinctions that remain well embedded in American law and ethics. While recognizing an obligation to heal, there exists no moral obligation to extend life at all costs. As the *Catechism of the Catholic Church* says: "Discontinuing medical procedures that are burdensome, dangerous, extraordinary, or disproportionate to the expected outcome can be legitimate."[4] The traditional means for determining whether care is beneficial or not is found in the distinction between *ordinary* and *extraordinary* care.[5] Ordinary care refers to any treatment modality that has reasonable benefit for the patient, as determined by the patient. According to the Roman Catholic moral tradition, foregoing these sorts of treatments is morally prohibited. Extraordinary care refers to any treatment modality that does not provide reasonable benefit to the patient, as determined by the patient. These sorts of treatments may be foregone.

There is also the distinction between *killing* and *allowing to die*.[6] While the Catholic tradition prohibits the direct killing of an innocent human person, allowing someone to die is sometimes morally right.[7] For instance, a patient may decide not to employ certain medical treatments to prolong his or her life. Withholding such treatment, if the treatment is deemed extraordinary by the patient, is morally acceptable even though it will result in the death of the patient. In another case a patient may decide to stop a medical treatment or procedure that has already begun. In cases of this sort, withdrawing treatment is considered morally permissible if such treatment is considered extraordinary by the patient. Finally, when the administration of pain medication contributes to a patient's death, the general consensus is that in such cases the intention to relieve pain qualifies the act as an indirect cause or hastening of death. In these cases, the consensus views the underlying condition as the direct cause of death. This distinction has a thorough basis in medical ethics and American jurisprudence.

---

4. *Catechism of the Catholic Church,* 29.

5. Kelly, *Critical Care Ethics.*

6. Ibid.

7. Kelly clarifies the issue when he says, "The norm is not that it is always wrong to kill and always right to allow people to die; dismissing the norm on the basis that it is not always right to allow people to die misses the basic point. Clearly, it is sometimes wrong to allow people to die of their illnesses." Kelly, *Contemporary Catholic Health Care Ethics,* 134.

Consider, for example, the line of reasoning of the U.S. Supreme Court in *Vacco v. Quill*.[8] The question before the Court concerned whether New York's prohibition on assisted suicide violated the Equal Protection Clause of the Fourteenth Amendment. Quill, et al argued that the refusal of life-sustaining treatment is the same thing as physician-assisted suicide, since the effects are identical. Thus, cases in which patients desire to end their lives due to the prospects of progressive loss of bodily integrity and increased pain and suffering, constitute an equivalency with those cases in which patients refuse treatment in order to end their lives. The Court argued, contrary to the respondents, that the distinction between letting a patient die and making a patient die concerns the legal principle of causation and intent. Writing for a unanimous court, Justice William H. Rehnquist cited a plethora of legal cases and medical sources recognizing that "when a patient refuses life-sustaining treatment, he dies from an underlying fatal disease or pathology; but if a patient ingests lethal medication prescribed by a physician, he is killed by that medication." Furthermore, he argued, "A physician who withdraws, or honors a patient's refusal to begin life-sustaining medical treatment purposefully intents, or may so intend, only to respect his patient's wishes"[9] to cease from futile and degrading treatment that no longer benefits the patient. Thus, the Court maintained a patient's right to refuse medical treatment and rejected its equivalency with a right to hasten death.[10]

The application of these principles to brain death is further elucidated by the conclusions reached in previous chapters in which a careful consideration of the justifications and weaknesses of the brain-death criterion were considered. In the analysis that follows, the basic thrust of these conclusions will be highlighted, although the chapters that address

8. "Dennis C. Vacco, Attorney General of New York, Et Al."

9. Ibid., 2298–99.

10. Some bioethicists, such as Beauchamp and Childress, contest the distinction. For instance, they write: "Intentional actions and intentional effects include any action and any effect willed in accordance with the plan, including tolerated as well as wanted effects." Beauchamp and Childress, *Principles of Biomedical Ethics*, 209. But this is misleading in that it fails to be properly nuanced with respect to the moral complexity of actions. Foreseeing and tolerating an effect is not the same thing as directly willing it. While it is true that physicians are often causal agents in bringing about circumstances affecting the timing of a patient's death, unless a physician uses known lethal means to directly affect a patient's death, it is more proper to view the lethal disease as the direct cause of death that the physician has no power to prevent.

the various issues should be consulted for the full range of analysis leading to the conclusions.

Any ethical analysis offered at this point must be based upon the consensus governing current practice. Representative of the consensus, though by no means universal, is the current paradigm that includes the brain-death criterion, the tests for diagnosing the criterion, and the definition of death as the death of the organism as a whole. The relation between the parts of the paradigm must be consistent. If not, then certain ethical consequences will follow. For instance, if the criterion fails to furnish evidence of correspondence with the definition, then it follows that brain-dead patients are not dead and organ procurement under this criterion is the direct cause of death for these patients. The argument may be summarized as follows:

1. If brain-dead patients are not dead (i.e., the criterion fails to correspond to the definition), then the procurement of their vital organs for transplantation is the direct cause of their deaths.

2. Brain-dead patients are not dead.

3. Therefore, the procurement of their vital organs is the direct cause of their deaths.

The second premise is supported by the medical data gathered in Chapter 2 as follows. First, it may be noted that the tests do not match the criterion. This is due to the fact that although patients may pass the clinical tests for brain death, a litany of non-brain integrative functions continues in many of these patients. Hence, the tests have no correspondence to the permanent cessation of all functions of the entire brain, including the brain stem. Second, the criterion lacks correspondence with the definition. There is substantial evidence that somatic integrative life continues in brain-dead patients. Although the length of time varies, some brain-dead patients have been shown to survive for extended periods of time, seriously challenging the somatic integration hypothesis which seats the brain as the organ of integration. As D. Alan Shewmon notes, "Under ordinary circumstances the brain participates intimately and importantly in this mutual interaction, but it is not a *sine qua non*; the body without brain function is surely very sick and disabled, but not dead."[11] Thus, it would seem that brain-dead individuals are alive

11. As Shewmon writes: "Under ordinary circumstances the brain participates intimately and importantly in this mutual interaction, but it is not a *sine qua non*; the body

since they continue to exhibit at least one integrative bodily system (the circulatory system being the key).[12]

Ultimately then, the procurement of vital organs from brain-dead patients is the direct cause of their deaths. With regard to the ethical and legal consensus detailed at the beginning of this section, it is clear that the procurement process constitutes a direct killing. Since brain-dead patients are mechanically sustained for the purpose of organ donation, the surgical procedure is what ends their lives. If discontinuing life-support preceded the surgical removal of vital organs, then perhaps a different outcome would emerge.[13]

Nonetheless, as demonstrated in chapter 1, in medical conditions commonly referred to as brain death, many life-sustaining interventions would represent extraordinary means. Patients who have been diagnosed as brain dead, although still very much alive, will not long survive in most cases. This is due primarily to damage to other bodily organs and systems prior to the onset of brain death. As Shewmon once again notes, "The process of *brain* damage leading up to '*brain death*' frequently induces secondary damage to heart and lungs. Therefore, the tendency to early cardiac arrest in the majority of patients is attributable more to somatic factors than to mere absence of *brain* activity per se."[14] In chapter 1, Josef Seifert argued that there is no moral obligation to continue life-sustaining treatment in such cases, although some may choose to do so. Medicine, in most of these cases, simply prolongs life that may be less than meaningful to many patients. The proposal of the Harvard Committee to expand death criteria based partly on the extraordinary and costly care needed to sustain brain-dead patients is thus both unnecessary and ethically questionable. As early as 1957 recognition was made regarding the moral permissibility of withdrawing extraordinary care measures.[15] Since then, legal guidance has been much clearer, specifically as exemplified in two landmark cases.

---

without brain function is surely very sick and disabled, but not dead." Shewmon, "Brain and Somatic Integration," 473.

12. Potts, "A Requiem."

13. I will address this possibility in chapter 7 as an alternative to current practice.

14. Shewmon, "Brainstem Death." Emphasis in original.

15. Pope Pius XII, "Prolongation of Life."

The first of these involved a 1975 New Jersey Supreme Court case.[16] In 1975, twenty-one-year-old, Karen Ann Quinlan slipped into a coma and was later diagnosed as PVS. Karen was admitted to an ICU and placed on a vent because of her inability to breathe properly. Her parents were Roman Catholic and remained hopeful until a meeting in which Karen's physicians informed them that Karen would not recover. They understood the Catholic teaching as not requiring extraordinary means to prolong life and felt they knew their daughter's wishes. With this in mind Karen's parents asked the physicians to remove the ventilator and after signing a release form the physicians at the hospital agreed. However, the next day one of the physicians informed the Quinlans he could not remove the vent unless they obtained a court order allowing the action. Mr. Quinlan then launched the battle for guardianship of Karen and the right to remove his daughter from the ventilator. The Quinlans lost their first round in the New Jersey Superior Court but they prevailed in the New Jersey Supreme Court and Mr. Quinlan was granted guardianship. The Quinlan's attorney filed for removal of the ventilator under: 1) the First amendment: Freedom of Religious Beliefs, 2) The Eighth amendment: Cruel and Unusual Punishment, 3) The Fourteenth amendment: liberty principle. The New Jersey Supreme Court agreed that the case involved the liberty principle concerning intimate personal decision-making and the ventilator was removed. To the surprise of many, Karen was able to breathe on her own and lived for another nine years. During the interval, Karen's father did not want to remove her feeding tube, without which Karen would have died in a few weeks.

The second case involved a U.S. Supreme Court case.[17] In 1983 a motor vehicle crash left twenty-five-year-old Nancy Cruzan in a persistent vegetative state, permanently unconscious and without any higher-brain functioning. She was kept alive with a feeding tube. After seven years in this state, Nancy's parents went to the circuit court on her behalf to ask that the feeding tube be removed. Nancy's parents argued that if it was not for the feeding tube she would die of her head injury and the circuit court judge agreed. However, the Missouri attorney general appealed to the Missouri Supreme Court and the decision was reversed. The court ruled that 'the state's interest in life is unqualified' and that clear and convincing evidence was needed when life was hanging in the balance. The

16. *In Re Quinlan.*
17. "Cruzan v. Director, Missouri Department of Health."

Cruzans appealed to the U.S. Supreme Court and with a 5 to 4 vote the U.S. Supreme Court ruled that the Cruzans needed to meet that state's clear and convincing evidence standard. Later, due to the publicity of the case, new evidence emerged from some of Nancy's friends who testified that she had mentioned how she would not want useless treatment. The family then went back to the Missouri courts and the courts ruled to remove the feeding tube based on the new evidence, since it now rose to the level of "clear and convincing." Nancy died within a few days of having the tube removed. The case was influential in three ways: 1) State courts can decide to require clear and convincing evidence when life is hanging in the balance. 2) There is no right to die but instead a right to liberty, which recognizes the right to refuse any treatment, including life-sustaining treatment. 3) The case was instrumental in Congress passing the *Patient Self Determination Act.*

In both cases, the recognition of the right to refuse any treatment was upheld as a liberty right based on the Fourteenth Amendment. While recognizing states interests in the preservation of life, the prevention of suicide, third party interests, and the furtherance of ethics in the medical profession, these cases demonstrate how these interests must be tailored to the unqualified right to refuse treatment. Moreover, these cases ensure that this right does not diminish when patients become incompetent. When applied to patients in a condition such as brain death, the right to refuse treatment allows patients or their surrogates to withdraw or refuse life-sustaining treatment they deem extraordinary. This constitutional right also protects physicians from legal reprisals when acting on behalf of their patients who want to discontinue life-support. Thus, it is unnecessary to employ the medical and legal fiction of brain death to justify the removal of life measures when patients or their surrogates choose to discontinue.

The preceding discussion suggests several implications. Specifically, the ethical and legal concepts governing end of life matters distinguish between a direct killing and the refusal of medical treatment, even when it is life sustaining. Regarding the status of brain-dead patients, since the criterion fails to comport with the definition, then brain death is not the death of the organism as a whole. Thus, the surgical removal of organs from brain-dead patients is the direct cause of their deaths and is unethical and illegal under the current paradigm. Moreover, brain death is also unnecessary as a means for discontinuing life-support. The ethical and legal parameters discussed above allow for the removal of life-sustaining treatment when patients or their surrogates make the decision. Since in practically all cases, brain death is a condition out of which no one recovers, the withdrawal of life-support is consistent with the Hippocratic and Catholic moral traditions as well as with the ethical and legal principles set forth in court cases concerning end of life decision-making. Nevertheless, the ethical and legal problems surrounding brain death do not end here. They include the difficulty of honoring the informed consent process, which is a hallmark of patient autonomy in medical ethics as set forth in American law. The extent of this difficulty will be discussed in the following section.

PRINCIPLES OF BIOETHICS AND BRAIN DEATH

The current approach in American medical ethics, which in some respects is beholding to the Hippocratic and Catholic traditions, is the "principle-to-problems" approach as represented by Tom L. Beauchamp and James F. Childress. In *Principles of Biomedical Ethics*[18], Beauchamp and Childress propose a four-tiered principled bioethics aimed at providing a practical methodology for shared decision-making among a diverse people with varying views on place of values in medicine, religion, and philosophy. The proposed four-tiered approach sets forth a hierarchy of principle-based rules founded upon ethical theories for the purpose of justifying medical decisions. The theory as a whole promises to extend to all people and is not limited to any particular community.

The approach of Beauchamp and Childress yields the following principles: autonomy, non-maleficence, beneficence, and justice. The principle of respect for autonomy includes respecting the values and actions of patients. It involves disclosing information to competent individuals to enable them to act autonomously. Disrespecting autonomy involves "attitudes and actions that ignore, insult or demean others' autonomy" thus denying "a minimal equality to persons."[19] Therefore, in the context of organ donation, respect for autonomy requires that individuals receive accurate information about the procedure prior to signing organ donor cards. Since the dead donor rule requires that

18. Beauchamp and Childress, *Principles of Biomedical Ethics*.
19. Ibid., 103.

patients must neither be alive during organ procurement nor killed by the procedure, relevant information pertaining to the current practice of organ procurement is required. In the absence of prior consent, it is ethically imperative that next of kin be fully informed about the procedure as well.

According to the second principle of biomedical ethics, the principle of non-maleficence, there is an obligation not to inflict harm intentionally. The concept of *harm* refers to "thwarting, defeating, or setting back some party's interests."[20] More specifically, the concept of harm includes "physical harms, including pain, disability, and death" as well as "mental harms and setbacks to one's interests."[21] While some harmful actions may be justifiable in certain social circumstances, the particular emphasis is on "intending, causing, and permitting death or risk of death."[22] Thus, if the diagnostic procedure to determine brain death, or the process of organ procurement under the brain-death criterion causes harm in the above-prescribed manner, an ethical violation occurs.

While non-maleficence requires the non-infliction of harm, the principle of beneficence requires taking positive steps to protect and defend the rights of others.[23] There is little doubt that protecting physicians, who act for the good of their patients, from undue prosecution and advancing life-saving organ transplantation enhances the good of society in general. Nonetheless, it is still necessary to require positive acts that respect the informed consent of the dying or newly dead. By taking steps to ensure disclosure of the relevant details of diagnosis, process, and controversy regarding a medical modality is to act in accordance with the principle of beneficence. When beneficence is pursued in this way, not only do patients benefit, but the practice of medicine benefits as well.

Finally, the last principle to be considered is justice. Justice is generally understood as "fair, equitable, and appropriate treatment in light of what is due or owed to persons."[24] In the interest of justice thus construed, failure to disclose information necessary for informed decision-making is an omission of respect, which is owed to persons. Equitable

20. Ibid., 152.
21. Ibid., 152–53.
22. Ibid.
23. Ibid., 197.
24. Ibid., 241.

treatment requires that respect for patients and their families include the obligations of veracity, fidelity, and confidentiality.[25] To dismiss the responsibility to disclose information for fear of an undesirable outcome is to fail to act with respect. Furthermore, to deny vulnerable individuals respectful treatment just because they hold the potential means to alleviate other burdens is to act unjustly.

The way in which these principles apply to the issue at hand will be the subject matter for the discussion that follows. Since law, medicine, and ethics play significant roles in shaping social perspectives, it will be necessary to disclose how each has contributed to society's understanding of values, rights, and justice as it pertains to healthcare in general and death and donation in particular.

The place where these four principles coalesce, at least for the purposes of this ethical analysis, is in the area of informed consent. The doctrine of informed consent has assumed a prominent place in healthcare due to several factors. Among these are the growing emphases on personal autonomy, the importance of biomedicine in people's lives, and skepticism over "expertise" in many spheres.[26] Medical ethics today has been largely shaped by the influence of these concerns.

Over the last thirty years, a patient's right to give informed consent to medical treatment has been well established in law and medical ethics. In particular, the courts have come to recognize the following: the unequal relationship between doctor and patient, that patients have autonomous rights, and that it is incumbent upon physicians not to deal with patients at arms length. An important case that was instrumental in bringing out the legal concepts for the doctrine is *Canterbury v. Spence.*[27] In this case a physician failed to disclose a one percent risk of paralysis to his patient, Jerry Canterbury, following back surgery. A day after the surgery, Canterbury fell from his bed and the lower half of his body was paralyzed. This court set precedence regarding a physician's duty of care to inform his or her patient "of any risks to his well being" of material consequence (would make a difference) to the decision of the patient. The duty itself is based upon the concept that "every human being of adult years and sound mind has a

25. Ibid., 289.
26. President's Commission, *Making Health Care Decisions*
27. "Canterbury, Appellant, v. William Thornton Spence."

right to determine what shall be done with his own body . . . "[28] and this includes the disclosure of information material to the decision-making process. The court further reasoned that "True informed consent to what happens to one's self is the informed exercise of a choice. . . ."[29] Failure on the part of Canterbury's physician to disclose a risk, no matter how small, or for fear that the patient might forego a beneficial therapy, nonetheless constitutes a breach of duty to inform.

Further development of the doctrine is exemplified in *Moore v. Regents of the University of California*.[30] John Moore, who had been undergoing treatment for leukemia, was unaware that his physician was using his cells for research and profit. The plaintiff attempted to state thirteen causes of action against the defendants.[31] The superior court only considered conversion as the cause of action. However, the Supreme Court of California, while not applying conversion liability, struck a balance between a competent patient's right to make informed autonomous decisions, based on the longstanding principles of fiduciary duty and informed consent, and the need to avoid threatening potentially useful research with civil liability. The court ruled in favor of Moore in regard to his complaint stating a cause of action for breach of fiduciary duty and lack of informed consent.

From these two cases a framework consisting of a duty of care to inform and a duty to obtain consent emerges. The duty to inform includes disclosing risks (including side effects), benefits, and options. The duty to obtain consent includes ensuring that patient choice is made competently, voluntarily and with understanding. These duties necessitate a meaningful conversation between a physician and his or her patient. Obtaining a quick signature or checking a box on a form is no substitute for the dignity of a conversation necessary for true informed consent.

There are several factors relevant to the ethical and legal principles discussed above that allow for an ethical analysis of brain-dead organ donors. In particular, organ donors in most cases simply check a box on a form or answer a simple "yes" or "no" question given by an individual at a driver's license office who, more than likely, knows little about the

28. Ibid.

29. Ibid.

30. "Moore v. Regents of the University of California."

31. These include: 1) conversion; 2) lack of informed consent; 3) breach of fiduciary duty; 4) fraud and deceit; 5) unjust enrichment; 6) quasi contract; etc.

extent of one's anatomical gift or the retrieval procedures involved. As discussed in Chapter Three, ambiguities in consent instruments concerning uncommon or controversial research on brain-dead "corpses" constitute insufficient disclosure, particularly when public trust in the medical profession is at stake.[32] To make matters worse, if the brain-dead are not dead, then how are potential donors consenting to post-mortem research? Given that the medical profession potentially receives multiple benefits from donors, disclosure is required under the legal concepts of fiduciary duty and informed consent, consistent with the court's reasoning in the *Moore* case.[33]

In addition, material to the consent process is the fact that, should donation occur under the brain-death criterion, donors' vital organs will be procured while their heart-beating bodies are still warm, pink, and pulsating with life to the extent that muscle-paralyzing agents will have to be used in the surgical procedure.[34] Additionally, donors should be made aware of the controversy surrounding the criterion, (i.e., that the criterion is based on an unproven theory).[35] Undoubtedly this raises the related question of the extent to which donors are capable of understanding the theory behind brain death. As noted in Chapter Three, it is questionable whether patients or their families can understand the complexity of terms meant to convey various levels of cognitive impairment, the details of which their own physicians may be uncertain. Statistically, there is great confusion. In survey after survey misunderstanding and doubt exist in both the general population, and medical profession, an indication of which implies informed consent is seriously deficient.

A lack of universal testing criteria for brain death (see Chapter Two) and statutory irregularities (see Chapter Three) highlight the problem further. The degree to which there is no agreed upon testing criteria gives the impression that the application of any set of testing criteria is arbitrary.[36] Advancing the problem further are the statutory

32. Wicclair, "Informed Consent."

33. Allowing donors to limit the scope of their anatomical gifts is one way to increase awareness, in that further disclosure would be necessary to satisfy the requirements of informed consent.

34. Typical anaesthetic protocol for the procurement surgery for brain-dead donors is anticipatory in regard to haemodynamic and hypotension responses, indicating the frequency of their occurrences. See Gelb and Robertson, "Anaesthetic Management."

35. Karakatsanis, "Brain Death."

36. Wijdicks, "Diagnosis of Brain Death."

inconsistencies between jurisdictions, implying that the difference between being alive and being dead is geographically determined. If medical professionals and law makers vary in the way they understand the criterion and its clinical application, how is it possible for potential donors and their families to know that to which they are consenting?

Given these stark realities, it is unlikely that the principles of autonomy, beneficence, non-maleficence, and justice, can be followed with any consistency. Although Chapter Seven will propose policy suggestions to attempt to rectify these problems, some of the groundwork is already being laid. Respect for patient autonomy requires that patients receive accurate information about the procedure prior to signing organ donor cards. While there may be no intention to cause harm (nonmaleficence) in withholding such information, certain non-intentional harms, such as the bodily interests of patients and the veracity of the medical profession, both of which concern states' interests, are compromised. Both beneficence and justice require taking steps to ensure disclosure of the relevant details of diagnosis, process, and controversy regarding a medical modality. To fail to do so is to fail to act equitably for patients and their families in a way that is reflective of the obligations of veracity, fidelity, and confidentiality. As is evident from this discussion, it is questionable whether these principles can be followed under the current system.

Some might argue that donation would be seriously compromised should disclosure to the extent as suggested above is implemented—a legitimate concern echoed in the *Moore* case regarding the need to avoid undermining potentially useful research and life-saving therapy. Closer examination from previously discussed case law is helpful here. As the court reasoned in *Canterbury v. Spence*, a physician's duty of care to inform his or her patient "of any risks to his well being" is predicated on the well-established concept that all competent adult persons have bodily rights determined solely by the individual, not the medical profession. Withholding any information material to the decision-making progress constitutes a breach of duty to inform, even if such disclosure may diminish the willingness of a patient to consent. Thus, failure to inform, even when a physician judges the information irrelevant or potentially threatening to a patient's consenting to a medical procedure is both unethical and illegal.

As the preceding discussion demonstrates, it is unlikely that informed consent for organ donors under the brain-death criterion is obtainable. Consideration of the medical and social reality of brain death as applied to the principles of biomedical ethics and case law renders the process of informed consent practically impossible to achieve. This calls into question the ethical and legal veracity of organ donation under the brain-death standard. Nonetheless, some brain death advocates continue to support its application based primarily upon its pragmatic benefits. Whether these justifications are ethically feasible will be discussed in the section that follows.

PRAGMATISM AND BRAIN DEATH

As the historical analysis in chapter 1 discloses, it is evident that supporters of brain death have assumed, either implicitly or explicitly, the sufficiency of a pragmatic basis for justifying its use in medical practice. Pragmatism is the idea that truth or value is determined by practical results that further specific aims. It is an "empirically based philosophy that defines knowledge and truth in terms of practical consequences."[37] Although there are differing forms of pragmatism,[38] the best known of the so-called neo-pragmatists is Richard Rorty. According to Rorty, the longstanding traditional view (from Plato to present day) that truth is correspondence to reality is positively mistaken and should be abandoned. Consequently, writes Rorty, "For the pragmatist, true sentences are not true because they correspond to reality, and so there is no need to worry what sort of reality, if any, a given sentence corresponds to—no need to worry about what 'makes' it true."[39] Pragmatism, therefore, is anti-essentialist and anti-foundationalist. Notions of progress toward an objective reality or internal coherence are illusory. Simply put, truth is not something to be discovered, but rather is constructed by the vocabulary or concepts one brings to the world in efforts to effect desired

37. Soccio, *Archetypes of Wisdom*, 550.

38. Early pragmatists include William James (1842–1910), Charles Sanders Price (1839–1914), and Johen Dewey (1859–1952). More recently, the following thinkers are considered pragmatic philosophers: Hilary Putnam, Nochols Rescher, Jurgen Habermas, Susan Haack, Robert Brandom, and Cornel West.

39. Rorty, *Consequences of Pragmatism*, 16.

results.[40] Commenting along these lines, Youngner and Arnold observe how the Harvard Committee justified its new criterion on what it could accomplish for the medical field. They write: "First, it allowed physicians to turn off respirators without fear of legal consequences, and, second, it allowed organ procurement without violating the dead donor rule (patients must neither be alive when organs are removed nor killed by the process.)"[41] They further observe that these pragmatic and utilitarian appeals "were the only justification given by the Harvard Committee for their new definition of death" and "were being accepted into law and clinical practice years before Bernat and the President's Commission came up with the first widely circulated, coherent philosophical justification that these patients were indeed dead."[42]

Those who maintain that the current legal standard on death has worked and does not require that society should rethink brain death, do so largely on the basis of its pragmatic success. The means for measuring success is determined exclusively on its social acceptance, its avoidance of legal challenges and its success in procuring organs for transplantation, not on whether it is theoretically coherent and understandable for satisfying informed consent.[43]

In arguing against the conceptual and medical coherence of brain death, some critics nonetheless promote organ donation on pragmatic grounds. Capitalizing on surveys of an (arguably) uninformed public, Truog suggests that society no longer needs the legal fiction of brain death to retrieve organs for donation.[44] Since both brain death and the dead donor rule no longer represent the views of the public, then the door to organ retrieval from consenting patients prior to a diagnosis of death becomes a viable alternative.

Along similar lines, other thinkers propose that "death is ultimately a social construct" that can be altered in accordance with desired

40. Noteworthy is the fact that some pragmatists, including Rorty, do not see coherence as a necessary condition for the truth either.

41. Youngner and Arnold, "Philosophical Debates," 533.

42. Ibid.

43. Capron, "Bifurcated Legal Standard for Determining Death"; Wikler, "Brain Death."

44. Truog, "Is It Time to Abandon Brain Death?" Truog, "Organ Donation without Brain Death?"

outcomes or goals.[45] Those who view death in this way often do so on the basis that notions of personhood are socially constructed as well. Lizza, for example, suggests, "Personhood is a dynamic concept that is subject to change in light of new knowledge and possibilities."[46] Thus, personhood and definitions of death are subject to changing paradigms as "new knowledge and possibilities" construct new social norms.

Several points can be made, however, that call into question the sufficiency of such reasoning. One concerns the argument from consensus. Although brain death is accepted by many religions and is legal in many countries, there is something deceiving about the way in which such a consensus has been achieved. As Ari R. Joffe remarks:

> This general acceptance of BD [brain death] by non-medical society suggests the concept is sound. However, this is a circular argument. A primary reason law and religion have accepted BD is that the medical profession informed the public that BD is the irreversible loss of integration of the organism as a whole, and of all brain (including brain stem) functions…these are now known to be mistaken facts.[47]

Added to this problem is the fact that the legal and social acceptance of brain death is not a philosophical argument as much as a locus for philosophical investigation. As Joseph Koterski remarks, "Neither legal nor social reception of a definition can make something to be the case if the reality is otherwise."[48] To suggest, as the pragmatist does, that our notions of death and personhood are temporally relative to the changing paradigms of societal norms apart from any objective standard invites the possibilities of gross injustices. Koterski notes how the same culture that "tolerated slavery and allowed some human beings to be treated as if they were property rather than persons with unalienable rights has sometimes later come to recognize the gross injustice of such a practice."[49] The shift in understanding, however, if it is not one that is guided by a clearer picture of the ontological status of the beings in question, can just as likely be reversed, or worse, lead to a slippery slope in which other beings are devalued resulting in further injustices. Koterski con-

45. Youngner and Arnold, "Philosophical Debates," 532.

46. Lizza, *Persons,* 49.

47. Joffe, "Neurological Determination of Death," 17–18.

48. Koterski, "Book Review," 387.

49. Ibid., 386.

tends the central problem is that the pragmatist "Confuses the cultural question of our social esteem for persons with the ontological question of the presence or absence of personhood." Continuing, he writes, "... The shift that one witnesses in any such change in social awareness and moral understanding 'in light of new knowledge and possibilities' in no way changes the ontological status of the beings in question—either they were already persons or they were not."[50]

Aside from the metaphysical problems this objection raises, the slippery slope argument is worth exploring in some detail. There are those who fear that if concessions are made with regard to the moral or ontological status of certain cognitively impaired human beings, the path to devaluing other less impaired individuals becomes dangerously more probable.[51] In other words, even those who are severely mentally ill and unable to interact with others or their environment might be considered dead. However, others retort that the likelihood of "a public that is quite accepting of whole-brain death would ever come to believe that the profoundly retarded or senile are dead" is highly improbable.[52] But given the social realities of the past, the slippery slope argument cannot be ignored. Edmund Pellegrino warns against ignoring the past with respect to the potential of failing to appreciate the consequences of moral compromise indicative of pragmatic concessions when he remarks:

> In any case, the slippery slope is not a myth. Historically it has been a reality in world affairs. Once a moral precept is breached a psychological and logical process is set in motion which follows what I would call the law of infinite regress of moral exceptions. One exception leads logically and psychologically to another. In small increments a moral norm eventually obliterates itself. The process always begins with some putative reason, like compassion, freedom of choice, or liberty. By small increments it overwhelms its own justifications. The histories of the French Revolution, the Holocaust, and partial birth abortion are representative examples.[53]

In addition, the slippery slope may be aided by the use of euphemisms, which have the potential to shape the way society thinks about

50. Ibid.

51. Bernat, "How Much of the Brain Must Die?"

52. Ott, "Defining and Redefining Death," 20.

53. Pellegrino, "Physician-Assisted Suicide and Euthanasia," 98.

issues in healthcare.[54] The steady use of reductive terminology of the brain dead such as, "humanoids," "merely breathing bodies," "remains," "biological artifacts", and "biomorts"[55] has over time weakened previous resistance to accept that the brain-dead patient is dead.[56] Furthering the slippery slope of social acceptance is the influence of physicians on their patients and the influence of law on both. Law does have pedagogical and psychological effects on behavior and opinion.[57] Once a standard of behavior is either embraced or rejected by law, the potential for societal desensitization (or sensitization) of certain behaviors and thought patterns is present. Great care must be taken in contemplating the influence the change in longstanding proscriptions might entail. While the pragmatist might intend to satisfy an important goal, shortsightedness may entail non-intended consequences. As the old adage reminds, "Before you tear down a fence, pause long enough to find out why it was put up in the first place."

Perhaps the most fatal challenge to the sufficiency of a pragmatic moral justification lies in its own self-stultification. In recent years several leading philosophers are now endorsing their contentions that the prospects of a moral system built upon pragmatic principles is bleak, if not impossible.[58] The problem resides in the wholesale rejection of metaphysical realism without which no standards of objectivity exist. In the course of denying any objective standard, the pragmatist, in sense, has cut off the branch upon which he or she stands. In his noteworthy volume entitled, *The Collapse of the Fact/Value Dichotomy,* Hilary Putnam takes Rorty to task for failing to inquire into the unintelligibility of the sort of metaphysical realism he rejects. Such a failure is endemic to Rorty's consideration of other sorts of realism, and more importantly, undermines the intelligibility of his own position. As Putnam remarks, "…if it is unintelligible to say that we *sometimes* succeed in representing things as they are in themselves, then it is equally unintelligible to say

54. Mitchell, "Nazi Germany's Euphemisms."

55. Lizza, *Persons.*

56. See the progression of this as illustrated in various surveys documented in chapters 1 and 3.

57. Glendon, *Rights Talk.* Glendon's study of how law guides one's conduct and opinions is instructive on this point.

58. Boghossian, *Fear of Knowledge*; Delsol, *Icarus Fallen*; Nagel, *Last Word*; Putnam, *Collapse of the Fact/Value Dichotomy*; Rescher, *Objectivity.*

that we *never* succeed in representing things as they are in themselves."[59]
More to the point, if the pragmatist contends that all ideologies are nothing more than social constructions with no objective correspondent, or
if all values have only local and limited application, then pragmatism
itself is nothing more a social construct and is too limited in its application. Thus, pragmatism can offer no compelling reason as to why it
should be accepted as a viable theory.

All this is brought out more fully, however, in the deleterious logical consequences of a society that embraces unstintingly the principles
of pragmatism. Commenting along these lines, Leszek Kolakowski notes
that when a real distinction between good and evil, independent of our
decisions is renounced, "then no moral boundary prevents us from
engaging in any action for no better reason than that it promotes the
success of a tendency which, by definition, will be legitimate if it suc-
ceeds, even if it carries the name of Hitler or Stalin."[60] Documenting the
real-world consequences of a worldview divested of any *a priori* moral
principles, Edward A. Purcell in his noteworthy volume, *The Crisis of
Democratic Theory*[61], traces the surrogation of traditional legal theory
with legal realism. Like pragmatism, legal realism divests the world of
all absolute structures thereby reducing all economic, political, ethical,
and theological systems to symbols of government conjured by men to
"explain the world in terms that pleased them."[62] While useful, these
symbols are false and contradictory. Thus the only real laws were the
completed actions of government officials. Such notions remained un-
challenged until the totalitarian regimes of the Second World War posed
a serious threat to neighboring nations. Yet the position of the legal re-
alists not only deprived them of any standard by which to criticize or
condemn Nazi terror, but actually sanctioned as law the horrific acts
of the Nazis. In short, the denial of any referential standards outside,
as it were, of all cultures and systems of government undermines any
inducements of avoidance or condemnation. Once a system is criticized
or condemned, it may be taken as an explicit admission of an external
order. Chantal Delsol poignantly expresses this point on an individual
level when she writes:

59. Putnam, *Collapse of the Fact/Value Dichotomy*, 101.
60. Kolakowki, *Modernity on Endless Trial*, 47.
61. Purcell Jr., *Crisis of Democratic Theory*.
62. Ibid., 112.

The identification of an absolute evil forces us to believe that an order exists beyond our will, beyond our capacity as creators of order. This identification puts into doubt not only the subjective morality of our times, but the very possibility if its being. We cannot decree that each individual has the sovereignty to invent his own values and at the same time point our finger at an intolerable and permanent universal. We cannot proclaim, "To each his own morality," and at the same time decry racism and apartheid.[63]

The central point this discussion discloses is that of the inability of pragmatism to provide a sufficient basis for moral justification.[64] Not only is pragmatism self-refuting, it also is inept to foment any standard to safeguard individuals from social injustices. While pragmatic appeals may be instructive and perhaps necessary starting points in the deliberation process, by themselves they reveal little beyond what is desirable. By relying solely on pragmatic justifications, the Harvard Committee, although seeking admirable goals opened the door to many unaccountable circumstances, not the least of which are those surrounding the issue of informed consent.

CONCLUSION

The conclusions in this chapter build upon conclusions developed throughout this investigation. The ethical assessment provided in this chapter discloses several important implications. Specifically, the ethical and legal concepts governing end of life matters are unsustainable under the current paradigm. If medical practice and statutory law continue to sanction the use of the brain death criterion (which does not comport with the death of the organism as a whole), then the removal of vital organs for transplantation violates the dead donor rule. This net result constitutes a direct killing violating the traditional distinction between killing and allowing to die. Consequently, the continued use of brain death as a means to remove organs from brain-dead

63. Delsol, *Icarus Fallen*, 53.

64. The attractiveness of pragmatism may lie in its relation to the order of truth. The distinction between a necessary and sufficient condition bears out this possibility. "Sufficient conditions are what is *enough* for something to be the case. Necessary conditions are what is *required* for something to be the case." Baggini and Fosl, *Philosophers Toolkit*, 158. Pragmatism may be a necessary condition but not a sufficient condition in ethics.

patients is the direct cause of their deaths and is unethical and illegal under the current paradigm.

A related though distinct point is that despite the rationale of the Harvard Committee, brain death is an unnecessary medical and legal construct for discontinuing life-support in hopeless cases. Traditional ethics and case law allow for the removal of life-support for patients who consent. Brain death is representative of a condition many would consider requiring extraordinary care, and hence not morally required. Additionally, the law recognizes the unqualified right of patients to refuse medical treatment of any kind. No legal barriers exist for discontinuing treatment when requested by patients or their surrogates. Thus, physicians who follow the directives of patients under these circumstances are immune from legal reprisals.

It is also highly questionable that informed consent for organ donors under the brain-death criterion is obtainable. When consideration of the medical and social reality of brain death is applied to the principles of bioethics and case law, the process of informed consent is seriously compromised. Confusion and uncertainty of the meaning of diagnosis and testing for the condition exists universally, and it is doubtful that under the current *modus operandi* any resolution is possible.

Those who wish to justify the use of brain death on purely pragmatic grounds also face difficult ethical obstacles. Pragmatism, in principle lacks the facility to provide a sufficient basis for establishing ethical direction and thus is open to abuse. In addition, pragmatism also lacks intellectual and practical coherence. In the attempt to utilize brain death in medical practice on a pragmatic basis, the Harvard Committee seemingly paved the way to the furtherance of problems elucidated throughout this chapter.

In the chapter that follows, attention will be given to alternatives to the way in which organ donation is conducted under the brain-death criterion. Specifically, the chapter will highlight current research that promises to advance organ transplantation apart from cadaver donation under the current system. Moreover, attention will be given to how donation might proceed apart from the brain-death criterion within the confines of law and ethics as currently conceived. Finally, some policy guidelines will be proposed as an attempt to encapsulate how such a practice might be worked into social policy.

7

Proposing a New Model for Death and Donation

THE SCOPE OF THIS investigation has come full circle. This work explored the major areas of discussion concerning the distinct though interrelated issues of brain death and organ donation. Each chapter provided a detailed disclosure and analysis of a segment of the ethical issues surrounding death and donation as construed today, which taken together furnishes a sufficient basis for assessing the central thesis of this investigation.

This investigation began with the proposal that brain death, under the current paradigm is problematic to the point that it cannot be sustained on ethical grounds as a means for procuring transplantable organs. In an effort to sustain this notion, it was necessary to investigate the historical, medical, legal, philosophical, and ethical spheres of influence that have contributed to the vast complexity of the issues surrounding death and donation. First, this chapter summarizes the findings of previous chapters in order to demonstrate how this investigation proffers support for the central thesis of this work. Consequently, sustaining this thesis leaves a significant gap in a longstanding life-saving practice that could have enormous ramifications in both the medical community and society at large. For this reason, the chapter investigates some of the emerging technologies that may eliminate the need for heart-beating cadaveric organ and tissue donors. Taking into consideration the fact that many of these technologies are nascent in their development, the chapter furnishes a possible means of organ procurement consistent with the general consensus currently embraced in health care law and ethics. Specifically, the chapter provides a tentative suggestion for organ procurement apart from brain death that is consistent with the ethical consensus governing the practice of health care today. Finally, in conjunction with the provisionary evocation offered in this chapter, the groundwork for a new standard of death and donation for policy consideration is offered.

BRAIN DEATH IS NOT DEATH

As the analyses in the previous chapters illustrate, difficulties exist that call into question the ethical sustainability of brain death as a means for organ procurement. The summary that follows indicates the force of these problems as discussed in detail in each chapter. The following summary statements are offered in support of the thesis of this work.

From its inception, some thinkers have criticized brain death as an *arbitrary* and *ad hoc* criterion. It is ad hoc because it was created as a solution to the problem of obtaining viable transplantable organs. Historically brain death emerged in close proximity to organ transplantation (see chapter 1). Less than a year after the first publicized heart transplant in 1967, an Ad Hoc Committee from the Harvard Medical School recommended brain death as a criterion for death for the purpose of turning off ventilators and retrieving organs for transplantation. A closer look into the rationale of the committee indicates that transplantation was the primary motive. The problem with the Harvard Committee's recommendation is that it provided no biological or philosophical conceptual basis that supported the idea that brain death is death. Instead, the Committee justified brain death on pragmatic grounds. As chapter 6 indicated, pragmatic reasons alone are insufficient to justify its use.

It is arbitrary because there are no good reasons to think that the diagnostic tests conform to the criterion. In the decade that followed the Harvard Committee's recommendation, numerous sets of diagnostic criteria and state statutes were constructed in an attempt to advance brain death into policy and practice. Lack of a conceptual foundation, however, resulted in confusion and inconsistency in its application in law and medical practice. Attempting to solve these problems, the President's Commission issued a report in 1981 that provided a conceptual basis and model statute in an effort to make death uniform. Despite this attempt, the next two and a half decades proved to be challenging for the new criterion as new physiologically enlightened research revealed that the conceptual basis is flawed (see chapters 2 and 3). In short, since the diagnostic criteria disregard certain neurological activity, the tests fail to conform to the criterion. Presently, the data indicates that brain death cannot be confirmed prior to autopsy following cardiopulmonary death. Furthermore, the diagnostic sets vary so widely that the same individual who is declared brain dead in the emergency room could still be alive in the intensive care unit, depending on which diagnostic set is chosen.

Compounding these problems is the fact that the brain-death criterion fails to conform to the definition (see chapter 4). If one maintains that human persons are essentially physical organisms of a substantial kind, then as long as the organism as a whole is functioning, despite mechanical ventilation, the administration of vassopressors, and a host of other life-sustaining interventions to supplement a diffused brain, then death has not occurred. Those who attempt to either maintain brain death or further advance death criteria to increase the pool of organ donors do so on dubious grounds (see chapter 5). The inconsistencies and epistemological gaps endemic to all neurologically based criteria render them suspect in light of advancing cognitive science. Moreover, given that death is not a purely private matter, the expansion of death criteria on the basis of autonomy and pluralism needs to be carefully measured in light of the unintended pedagogical effects on society a move of this sort might have.

The aim of this work was to investigate brain death as a criterion of death for the procurement of transplantable organs. Ultimately, an ethical assessment informed by the historical, medical, legal, and philosophical data renders brain death as a means for organ procurement so problematic that it ought to be abandoned as a viable criterion for determining death (see chapter 6). Not only is informed consent unobtainable under the current paradigm, but the rationale for its utilization is unsustainable as well. Thus, this investigation confirms the thesis of this work.

The consequence of this conclusion suggests that the already short supply of transplantable organs will further deteriorate. While it is not the primary focus of this investigation, in the sections that follow, consideration of various alternatives to brain death will be briefly discussed as a means to suggest possible ways to move forward in order to preserve the life-saving practice of organ transplantation. It is not the purpose of these sections to provide a detailed analysis of the alternatives presented, but rather to set the direction for further exploration and development in the inseparable matters of death and donation.

POSSIBLE ALTERNATIVES TO BRAIN DEATH

In recent years, discussion concerning alternatives to organ procurement under the current paradigm has been on the increase. While some of these discussions emanate from the reports of popular news agencies, not all do. For this reason a degree of caution regarding the conclusions that can be drawn from some of these reports should be maintained. Nevertheless, the most interesting component of these potential alternatives pertains to the irrelevance of brain death as a factor in their implementation. Specifically, not only do many of these alternatives eliminate the need for brain death as a means for securing donatable organs, they also purport to remove many of the ethical and medical hazards concurrent in the bifurcated standard.

For example, advances in pharmacology and technology may eventually supplement the current need for organ donors. Some reports suggest that improved diagnostic and surgical procedures are beginning to show promise in reducing the need for many organ transplants. *AV Magazine*, published under the auspices of the American Anti-Vivisection Society, reports that, "a simple surgical technique, ventricular remodeling, has removed a significant number of patients from heart transplant waiting lists."[1] The article goes on to report that physicians at Columbia Presbyterian Medical Center have used positron emission tomography (PET) machines to discover that approximately forty percent of patients waiting for heart transplants needed only bypass surgery. Supporting similar alternatives is Japanese cardiologist Yoshio Watanabe who suggests concentrating on the development of "a more effective pharmacological regimen and new therapeutic modalities."[2] With newly devised drugs, he contends, heart-patients on waiting lists "are now surviving as long as

1. McArdle, "Xenotransplantation," 1998.
2. Watanabe, "Brain Death and Cardiac Transplantation," 185.

those who received heart transplants."[3] This is significant, given that under the current system many recipients of donor hearts do not survive any longer than those left on waiting lists.[4] This is due primarily to the fact that the pre-existing weakened condition of heart patients is further compromised by the surgical procedure and the ensuing immune-suppressant diseases characteristic of organ recipients. Watanabe suggests efforts be made to develop a totally transplantable heart as the final solution to donor heart shortages.

As far back as 1982, cardiologist David Evans suggested, "The development of the mechanical heart offers a much better prospect for the future."[5] Today, many patients who suffer from severe heart failure do benefit from the use of artificial hearts. However, the limitations of these devices provide impetus for further development. *Nature Medicine* reports on the prospects of a new biologic heart in which blood is pumped by actual heart muscle rather than by metal and plastic.[6] Though there are still many hurdles to overcome, one such hurdle was breached when researchers demonstrated that a bioartificial heart could be created using a matrix platform composed of immuno-compatible cardiac cells.

Other high-tech solutions to donor organ "shortage" include the creation of tissues and organs without donors. In August of 2005, a study funded by the UK Government, and led by researchers from Kingston University's School of Life Sciences, disclosed that the research team had grown an artificial liver from umbilical cord stem cells.[7] Hailed as the first step in creating a fully artificial liver for transplantation, researcher Dr. Colin McGuckin said, "The transplant of a section of liver grown from cord blood could be possible within the next ten to fifteen years."[8]

Other sources in the popular media report that a breakthrough in the growth of transplantable human bladders from tissue taken from recipients' own defective bladders.[9] The bladder cells were cultured in a nutrient bath in a laboratory, and after two months, new bladders were fully grown. Not only were the transplants successful, but the recipients

3. Ibid.
4. Deng, "Effect of Receiving a Heart Transplant."
5. Evans, "Heart Transplants."
6. Ott et al., "Perfusion-Decellularized Matrix."
7. BBC News, *Liver Cells Grown from Cord Blood.*
8. Ibid.
9. BBC News, *US Scientists Have Successfully Grown Fully Functioning Bladders.*

were free of side effects, including tissue rejection. The Wake Forest University team of scientists is currently working on ways to grow twenty different tissues and organs.

Additionally, another news source reports that, "US scientists have coaxed recycled hearts taken from animal cadavers into beating in the laboratory after reseeding them with live cells."[10] If this procedure is extended to humans, the potential "for almost limitless supply of hearts, and possibly other organs" could diminish the need for heart-beating cadaver organ donors. The theory behind the procedure involves developing "transplantable blood vessels or whole organs that are made from your own cells" thus eliminating the need for immunosuppressive drugs. Dr. Richard Horton, editor of *The Lancet*, the journal that reported the new research, comments, "A lot more work needs to go into this, but over the next ten years or so, we are going to see a revolution in transplantation."[11] The prospects of transplantable organs derived from recipients' own cells are clearly preferable to the current organ and tissue procurement system. Not only would it eliminate much of the controversy that surrounds the means of procurement for transplantation under the bifurcated standard, but it also would advance survival rates for recipients.[12]

Another approach that could significantly reduce the demand for organ transplants would be the sustained, committed, long-term emphasis on disease and injury prevention.[13] John McArdle suggests that if health-care industries, government agencies, and individuals seriously enacted such measures, it would not only "eliminate the need for all but a small fraction of current transplantation procedures," but also "provide additional benefits in all areas of medicine and public health."[14] Wolfgang Bünnagel, a heart transplant survivor, notes how many sufferers owe their conditions to unhealthy lifestyles due in large measure to

10. Ibid.

11. Ibid.

12. Reports like the ones above are becoming regular. Recently the AP reported another breakthrough in the transplant of a windpipe grown from stem cells from the recipient's own stem cells. See Associated Press, *Doctors Transplant Windpipe with Stem Cells*.

13. McArdle, "Xenotransplantation."

14. Ibid.

excessive consumption of fat, alcohol, and tobacco.[15] He suggests that improved care of organs while still healthy is a better solution to organ disease than transplants. Noting that the "majority of patients for liver transplants are . . . suffering from liver disease due to alcohol consumption," he advocates that, "we change our ways of working, living and eating . . . and find daily routines that better fit our bodies."[16] Perhaps if incentives were offered to physicians and patients, many people would be more prone to adopt healthier lifestyles.[17] However, while some human suffering is self-inflicted, one cannot wholly ascribe all organ disease to lifestyle choices. Nonetheless, preventative medicine could help reduce the need for organ donors.

As the preceding discussion demonstrates, some experimental alternatives to brain death may lie just over the horizon. Although most are in the beginning stages of development, given the rapid advancement of recent biotechnologies in medicine in the last decade, it is possible that some of these alternatives could be realized in the near future. On the whole, a multi-pronged approach to the organ donor shortage, in which several possible alternatives to organ donation are pursued, is advantageous for at least two significant reasons. First, these alternatives promise to relieve many of the ethical concerns endemic to current social policy and medical practice for procuring organs for transplantation. Second, these alternatives promise greater health benefits and survival rates for patients. Nonetheless, many of these alternatives are experimental and may never be realized. During the interval, some mediating alternative is required to fill the gap left by the abandonment of brain death as a means for organ procurement. In the next section, some tentative considerations for organ procurement during the latter stages of the dying process will be presented. It is necessary that such considerations remain consistent with the ethical consensus governing the practice of health care as discussed in the previous chapter.

---

15. Bünnagel, "Living with My New Heart." It is worth noting that the first recipient of a donor heart was suffering from heart disease wrought by excessive alcohol and tobacco use. See chapter 1.

16. Ibid.

17. Schlett, *Insurers Turning to Incentives to Promote Healthy Lifestyles.*

TENTATIVE CONSIDERATIONS FOR A NEW STANDARD

The implication of the discussion to this point suggests that there is no immediate alternative to brain death as means for procuring unpaired viable organs for transplantation. Indeed, some may worry that returning to a single criterion of death would be to turn back time and thus undermine the progress that has been made during the last thirty-five years in transplantation efforts.[18] However, as previous chapters have demonstrated, this "progress" has been at a cost. Nothing less than the public trust and the integrity of the medical profession are at stake. Modesty in the claims of medical experts is required, particularly in the light of the history of medical practice in which ethical violations were justified for the purported benefits that would be reaped by society as a whole (see chapter 1). Any proposal, therefore, must be in accord with the ethical and legal principles outlined in chapter 6. Otherwise, the proposal will be no better than what it purports to replace.

At first blush, the suggestion may sound overly ambitious. To begin with, the idea of returning to a qualified form of the cardiopulmonary single standard of death suggests that society might well find itself back in a 1960s era of medical practice, once again plagued by the attendant problems that were overcome through the introduction of brain death. Moreover, to suggest that organ donation, in particular heart donation, can proceed apart from brain death seems to push the ethical boundaries beyond acceptable limits. This rationale does not promise to solve all difficulties surrounding death and donation. No policy proposal is without its problems. Rather, this rationale paves the way for the implementation of social policy with the aim of accomplishing that for which the brain-death criterion was created, apart from the vast majority of ethical problems with which it is associated.

There are several reasons why the cardiopulmonary single standard criterion is preferred. First, the cardiopulmonary criterion provides an ethically safer environment for determining death. As previous chapters indicate, neurological criteria for determining death rest on uncertain and unproven grounds. Commenting on the Italian legislation on brain death and capturing the essence of the problem in general, Massimo Bondi writes,

---

18. Veatch, "Dead Donor Rule." This was Veatch's concern in this important article.

It is well-known that our knowledge of the brain functions only cover a bare 10% of their spectrum; therefore art.1 of law 578/93 (of the Italian legislation) stating that "death is the irreversible cessation of all functions of the entire brain" is scientifically an absurdity, because it is not possible to declare an unknown function to be "ceased."[19]

The uncertainty surrounding the moment of death lingers in the minds of many, despite technological advances. Because of this, Hans Jonas' suggestion that, "Since we do not know the exact borderline between life and death, nothing less than the maximal definition of death will do,"[20] remains relevant. The criteria for death primarily should be based on patient care, and secondarily on the economic and pragmatic interests of others. As Barry Bostrom observes,

> . . . law, medicine and health care should be designed to err, if at all, on the side of the preservation of life and the establishment of rational principles for the protection of the most vulnerable persons in society—those who are medically dependent and disabled.[21]

Second, it is easier to satisfy informed consent under the cardiopulmonary criterion. As previous chapters indicate, satisfying the demands of the doctrine of informed consent under the brain-death criterion is, for all practical purposes, impossible. David Price, commenting on the Danish Council on Ethics' *Report on Death* notes the importance of the establishment of a concept of death that relates to the common person's every day experience:

> In 1988, the Danish Council on Ethics, in a Report on Death, drew attention to a perceived divide on "scientific" (unseen) and "ordinary" (seen) views of death. It stated that "The concept of death must relate to the everyday experience," according to which "the identity of the person relates no less to the body than to the mind," and recommended that the standard of death should be cessation of respiration and cardiac activity.[22]

19. Bondi, *J'accuse*.

20. Jonas, *Philosophical Essays*, 130.

21. Bostrom, "Euthanasia in the Netherlands."

22. Price, *Legal and Ethical Aspects*.

Commenting on her personal experiences with family members of brain dead patients, researcher Michi Nakajima observes:

> During my five-month visit to the ICU, I felt one thing as most peculiar in the beginning. None of the family members would take the hand of the patient, nor shed a single tear at the news that their husband, wife, or a beloved child was brain death. At first, I thought I accidentally came across people who were cold-hearted or logical-minded. However, I soon understood that no one really felt that the brain dead person was truly dead.

Later, the same researcher notes:

> But the same people, without exception, burst into tears or wiped their eyes when the brain dead person's heart ceased beating and the respirator was removed. At this point, they truly realized their relative's death.[23]

As noted in chapter 3, it is unlikely that informed consent for organ donation under the brain-death criterion is obtainable. The central problem emanates from the complexity of the condition and the uncertainty of the diagnosis. However, most people would have little difficulty accepting death as occurring at the permanent cessation of heart and respiratory functions.[24] What remains at this point is some qualification on the particulars.

Finally, cardiopulmonary death, which is the most consistent criterion under the current definition, enjoys an already established consensus. As Josef Seifert contends, "Everyone will agree that after the end of the biological life of the human organism as a whole there is no human life present in the body." He continues noting that, "A complete consensus is possible with regard to the thesis that no human life is present before the beginning or after the end of the biological life of the human organism." Since no consensus can be established regarding any other limit, he concludes that the "most natural, unambiguous definition and

---

23. Nakajima, *Invisible Death,* 12–13.

24. Veatch objects to the idea that cardiopulmonary death can be a criterion for heart donors. He writes, "One cannot say a heart is irreversibly stopped, if, in fact, it will be restarted." O'Reilly, *Redefining Death.* This is precisely why we are concerned not with mere heart stoppage but with the permanent cessation of the cardiopulmonary functions. In this sense we are concerned with the entire system that is responsible for fluid flow of oxygenated blood necessary for the life of the organism as a whole.

criterion of human death . . . is preferable to any other criterion or definition of death."[25]

Taken as a whole, the cardiopulmonary criterion can provide an ethically safer environment for determining death, can more readily satisfy the demands of informed consent, and has an already established consensus. Exactly how organ donation may proceed that respects the principles and distinctions embedded in American law and ethics will be discussed next.

Based on discussions in previous chapters, at least three alternatives emerge, each of which has major problems. In chapter 5, a proposal, with varying rationales, was offered by Koppelman, Truog, and Robinson. Recognizing that brain death is not death, they suggest that while cardiopulmonary death should be the default criterion of death, excepting the dead donor rule for organ donation in cases where the patient is dying is acceptable provided prior consent is obtained. However, as the critique in chapter 5 demonstrates, this proposal would necessarily involve the collapse of the traditional distinction between killing and allowing to die, thereby inviting a new direction in how the practice of medicine is conceived. Not only would it involve a dangerous use of medical power, it also would provide no basis against the use of the practice of organ donation as a means of suicide by individuals with decision-making capacity. In short, this proposal, while recognizing the problems of organ donation under brain death, fails to maintain consistency with the ethical consensus governing the practice of medicine today.

Another possibility is the suggestion made by D. Alan Shewmon which was briefly alluded to in chapter 1.[26] Shewmon proposes a form of controlled Non-Heart Beating Organ Donation (NHBD), with a short asystole time, as a means for procuring organs for transplantation. Further elucidation of this proposal shows promise in satisfying the ethical demands as discussed in chapter 6. As Shewmon reminds, successful heart transplants in the 1960s were carried out without the need for the brain-death criterion. Similar to the procedure used by Christiaan Barnard, the process of removing hearts and lungs can be carried out after discontinuation of ventilator support and circulatory standstill. After a latency of sufficient time to ensure moral certainty that spontaneous

25. Seifert, "Brain Death and Euthanasia," 224.
26. Shewmon, "Brainstem Death."

resuscitation will not occur, the removal process may begin. During the interval, preserving medications can be delivered to select organs to ensure their viability. As Margaret Lock notes, "If a patient is perfused with specially prepared cold fluids immediately prior to or after cardiac arrest, then the organs remain in reasonably good condition even after cardiopulmonary death and can be removed for transplant."[27] This elaborate procedure is needed, writes Shewmon, due to the fact that "transplant surgeons never developed a technique for heart-lung retrieval, primarily because the 'brain-death' fiction convinced them that there was no need to do so." For the sake of everyone's consciences, he writes, "I believe that a historically honest and physiologically enlightened appraisal of 'brain death' makes it an ethical requisite."[28]

There are a number of favorable characteristics in this proposed procedure. First, it satisfies the ethical distinctions addressed in chapter 6. The distinction between killing and allowing-to-die, upheld in both law and ethics, permits patients or their surrogates to choose to withhold or withdraw life-sustaining measures that they deem extraordinary. This policy closely adheres to this moral distinction by recognizing a patient's right to refuse medical treatment. Since organ procurement does not proceed until cardiopulmonary death is determined, then there is no reason to extend donation beyond the dead donor rule. Moreover, even if successful cardiopulmonary resuscitation is technically possible, the decision to forego the ventilator "all the more so would be the foregoing of resuscitation immediately thereafter."[29] Second, informed consent can be respected in a more meaningful way. Under the current paradigm, informed consent is not achievable. The complexity of the issues surrounding brain death and its diagnosis renders it practically impossible for patients to understand. However, these problems are greatly lessened in light of the fact that a consensus regarding cardiopulmonary death

27 Lock, *Twice Dead*, 357. It is also important to note that the use of preserving fluids removes the problem of organ deterioration with which transplant surgeons in the 1960s had to contend.

28. Shewmon, "Dead Donor Rule," 293–96.

29. Shewmon, "Brainstem Death." It is noteworthy that the first justification in the Harvard Committee's report can be satisfied without the need of the brain-death criterion. Some question remains as to the possibility of auto-resuscitation. Whetstine suggests, for example, that insufficient research has been done to ascertain the likelihood of its occurrence. See Whetstine, "Examination of the Bio-Philosophical Literature," 206–7.

already exists. Most people accept that when cardiopulmonary functions permanently cease, death has occurred. Third, it could potentially increase the number of organ donors. Many more patients who request to withdraw life-support are potential donors. This includes neurologically devastated patients on life-support. By relieving the decades-old suspicion surrounding brain death that some suggest has been counterproductive to organ procurement, many individuals may be more inclined to become organ donors.[30]

Despite these favorable characteristics, some important problems remain. First, critics of NHBD note that while an asystolic heart can be used as a means for determining death, it is unclear whether heart stoppage is actually reversible if it could be restarted but is not due to a decision to forego resuscitation measures. Robert Veatch explains:

> Death requires irreversible stoppage, yet it is unclear whether that means the heart could not be started again or merely will not be. Even more perplexing is whether an individual should be considered dead during the period when a heart could be restarted by people with expert skills and sophisticated equipment if those people and equipment are not available. The concept of irreversibility has become much more complex.[31]

In the analysis of some, ensuring that spontaneous resuscitation will not occur is unsatisfactory.[32] Given the possibility that if a patient is removed from life-support, and resuscitation efforts are successful in restoring circulation, the patient cannot be said to have been dead when life support was removed. Simply deciding not to resuscitate does not constitute "irreversibility" but rather conflates a prognosis of death with a diagnosis of death.[33]

30. Shewmon, "Brainstem Death." As Shewmon reminds, "There is good reason to believe that a significant factor contributing to the low rate of signing of organ donor cards has been a widespread instinctive suspicion that '*brain dead*' donors are really still alive (though fatally injured), and that historically the '*brain death*' concept was manufactured through 'conceptual gerrymandering' for purely utilitarian purposes."

31. Veatch, *Transplantation Ethics*, 209.

32. Whetstine, "Examination of the Bio-Philosophical Literature"; Youngner et al., "When Is Dead?"

33. Whetstine, "Examination of the Bio-Philosophical Literature," 243. Whestine notes that, based on limited studies, it is impossible to know whether a two minute or a five minute "no touch" protocol is sufficient to exclude auto-resuscitation. Nonetheless, the ability to auto-resuscitate is not the issue, if manual resuscitation efforts could restore circulation function. See pages 199–200.

    A second problem concerning the meaning of irreversibility involves whether brain tissue is dead at the point when heart stoppage is determined to be irreversible. NHBD protocols that employ a short asystole time[34] run the risk of designating a patient dead when a patient's brain continues to be living.[35] Under the current paradigm, a patient in this state is not yet dead. Protocols that do not allow for sufficient time for determining irreversibility may allow for greater viable organ procurement, but run the risk of violating the Dead Donor Rule.

    A third possibility remains. One could employ the cardiopulmonary death criterion, minus the short asystole time to ensure that irreversibility is met to the satisfaction of the concerns expressed above. This would allow the employment of Shewmon's controlled method, though modified with a longer wait period to ensure that the patient is really dead. A consequence of this would be a reduction of viable organs due to the greater length of time necessary prior to procurement to ensure irreversibility is satisfied.[36]

    While no alternative is without its problems, the third suggestion seems to be the least troubling. Although a thorough investigation of these alternatives is beyond the scope of this investigation, this preliminary suggestion is offered as a means to expand discussion in terms of how society might proceed to further organ donation in light of the major problems that call into question the ethical sustainability of brain death as a means for organ procurement. In attempt to further such discussion, the following policy recommendations are presented.

POLICY RECOMMENDATIONS

The following policy recommendations are an attempt to balance autonomy, death, and organ donation in a more meaningful way. First, as suggested in the previous section, social policy should recognize a standard of death that is consistent with current medical science and is generally understandable to the average person. A form of the

34. The Pittsburgh protocol originally called for a death pronouncement after two minutes of asystole. See Arnold and Youngner, "Ethical, Psychological, and Public Policy Implications."

35. Veatch, *Transplantation Ethics*, 209.

36. Organ deterioration could be minimized if organ preserving medications are used during the wait. See Shewmon's suggestion as articulated earlier.

cardiopulmonary criterion, which focuses on the permanent cessation of the circulatory and respiratory functions, is best suited to accomplish these goals. Second, in an effort to satisfy the ethical and legal requirements of informed consent, social policy should respect personal autonomy by requiring transparency through disclosure of the diagnosis of death and the procedure used to procure organs and tissues. This requires that the individual be informed as to the definition and diagnosis of death, the procedures employed in procuring organs and tissues for donation, and be given the opportunity to specify the extent of his or her anatomical gift. Finally, consideration should be given to the means for satisfying the informed consent process. This could be accomplished through the use of a form (advanced directive), containing signatures from the potential organ donor and a physician, indicating the potential donor's informed consent and directive of extent for donation. These policy considerations are offered as a means of furthering discussion specific to safeguarding patient choice and the integrity of the medical profession in general.

Bibliography

Abe, Tomoko. "Philosophical and Cultural Attitudes Against Brain Death and Organ Transplantation in Japan." In *Beyond Brain Death: The Case Against Brain Based Criteria for Human Death*, edited by Michael Potts, Paul A. Byrne, and Richard G. Nilges, 66, 191–200. Dordrecht: Kluwer Academic, 2000.

Alexander, Marc. "The Rigid Embrace of the Narrow House: Premature Burial and the Signs of Death." *Hasting Center Report* 25 (1980).

American Academy of Neurology (Quality Standards Subcommittee). "Practice Parameters for Determining Brain Death in Adults." *Neurology* 45 (1995) 1012–14.

American Academy of Pediatrics. "Report of Special Task Force: Guidelines for the Determination of Brain Death in Children." *Pediatrics* 80 (1987) 298–300.

American Bar Association. *American Bar Association Annual Report* (1978) 100.

Anderson, J. Kerby. "A Biblical Appraisal of Euthanasia." In *Living Ethically in the 90's*, edited by J. Kerby Anderson. Wheaton, IL: Scripture, 1990.

Anderson, Mark. "Never Mind the Singularity, Here's the Science." *Wired Magazine* (2008). Online: http://www.wired.com/medtech/drugs/magazine/16-04/ff_kurzweil_sb.

Aquinas, Thomas. *Treatise on Man*. Translated by James F. Anderson. Westport: Greenwood, 1962.

Arnold, J. D., T. F. Zimmerman, and D. C. Martin. "Public Attitudes and the Diagnosis of Death." *JAMA* 206 (1968) 1949–54.

Arnold, Robert M., and Stuart J. Youngner. "The Dead Donor Rule: Should We Stretch It, Bend It, or Abandon It?" *Kennedy Institute of Ethics Journal* 3:2 (1993) 263–78.

———. "Ethical, Psychological, and Public Policy Implicatons of Procuring Organs from Non-Heart-Beating Cadavers." *Kennedy Institute of Ethics Journal* (1993) 103–278.

Arras, John D., and Bonnie Steinbock. "Defining Death, Foregoing Life Sustaining Treatment and Euthanasia." In *Ethical Issues in Modern Medicine*, edited by John D. Arras and Bonnie Steinbock. Mountain View, CA: Mayfield, 1998.

Arts, W. F. M., et al. "Unexpected Improvement after Prolonged Posttraumatic Vegetative State." *Journal of Neurology, Neurosurgery and Psychiatry* 48 (1985) 1300–1303.

Associated Press. *Doctors Transplant Windpipe with Stem Cells*. 2008. Online: www.lancet.com.

Baggini, Julian, and Peter S. Fosl. *The Philosophers Toolkit: A Compendium of Philosophical Concepts and Methods*. Oxford: Blackwell, 2003.

Barber, Norm. *The Nasty Side of Organ Transplantation: The Cannibalistic Nature of Transplant Medicine.* 3rd ed. Adelaide: Norm Barber, 2007.

Barnard, Christiaan, and Curtis Bill Pepper. *One Life.* Oxford: Macmillan, 1969.

Beauchamp, Tom L., and James F. Childress. *Principles of Biomedical Ethics.* 4th ed. New York: Oxford University Press, 1994.

Beckwith, Francis J. "The Explanatory Power of the Substance View of Persons." *Christian Bioethics* 10 (2004) 33–54.

Beecher, Henry K. "Definition of Irreversible Coma." Manuscript Draft of April 11, 1968. Henry K. Beecher Manuscripts, Holmes Hall, Harvard Medical School.

———. "Ethical Problems Created by the Hopelessly Unconscious Patient." *New England Journal of Medicine* 278 (1968) 1427.

———. "Ethics and Clinical Research." *New England Journal of Medicine* 274 (1966) 1354–60.

Beecher, Henry K., and H. I. Dorr. "The New Definition of Death: Some Opposing Views." *International Journal of Clinical Pharmacology* 5 (1971) 120–24.

Belkin, Gary S. "Brain Death and the Historical Understanding of Bioethics." *Journal of the History of Medicine* 58 (2003) 325–61.

Berger, Jeffrey T, Fred Rosner, and Eric J. Cassell. "Ethics of Practicing Medical Procedures on Newly Dead and Nearly Dead Patients." *Journal of General Internal Medicine* 17:10 (2002) 774–78.

Bernat, James L. "A Defense of the Whole-Brain Concept of Death." *Hasting Center Report* 28 (1998) 17.

———. "How Much of the Brain Must Die on Brain Death?" *The Journal of Clinical Ethics* 3:1 (1992) 25.

———. "On Irreversibility as a Prerequisite for Brain Death Determination." In *Brain Death and Disorders of Consciousness.* Edited by Calixto Machado and D. Alan. Shewmon, 161–68. New York: Kluwer Academic, 2004.

———. "Refinements in the Definition and Criterion of Death." In *The Definition of Death,* edited by Stuart J. Youngner, Robert M. Arnold and Renie Schapiro, 83–92. Baltimore: The Johns Hopkins University Press, 1999.

Bernat, James L., Charles M. Culver, & Bernard Gert. "On the Definition and Criteria of Death." *Annals of Internal Medicine* 94 (1981) 389–91.

Bernstein, I. M., M. Watson, G. M. Simmons, P. M. Catalano, G. Davis, R. Collins. "Maternal Brain Death and Prolonged Fetal Survival." *Obst Gynecol* 74 (1989) 434–37.

Black, P. "Brain Death." *New England Journal of Medicine* 229 (1978) 338–44.

Bleich, J. David. "Establishing Criteria of Death." In *Jewish Bioethics,* edited by Fred Rosner and J. David Bleich, 297–315. Hoboken, NJ: KTAV, 2000.

Boghossian, Paul. *Fear of Knowledge: Against Relativism and Constructionism.* New York: Oxford University Press, 2007.

Bondi, Massimo. *J'accuse: Against the Heart-Beating Brain Death.* Press Release 8. Canonici Lateranensi: Universita' di Roma, 2006.

Bostrom, Barry A. "Euthanasia in the Netherlands: A Model for the United States?" *Issues in Law and Medicine* 4 (1989) 486.

Brierly, J. D., et al. "Neocortical Death after Cardiac Arrest." *Lancet* 2:7724 (1971) 560–65.

Brock, Dan W. "Cloning Human Beings: An Assessment of the Ethical Issues Pro and Con." In *Ethical Issues in Human Stem Cell Research*, II, E1–E15. Rockville, MD, 1999.

———. "The Role of the Public in Public Policy on the Definition of Death." In *The Definition of Death*, edited by Stuart J. Youngner, Robert M. Arnold, and Renie Schapiro, 293–307. Baltimore: The Johns Hopkins University Press, 1999.

Brody, Baruch A. "How Much of the Brain Must be Dead?" In *The Definition of Death: Contemporary Controversies*, edited by Stuart J. Youngner, Robert M. Arnold, and Renie Schapiro, 71–82. Baltimore: The Johns Hopkins University Press, 1999.

Bünnagel, Wolfgang. "Living with My New Heart." *Curative Education & Social Therapy* (Christmas/New Year 1996) 17–19.

Byrne, Paul A., Sean O'Reilly, Paul M. Quay, and Peter W. Salsich Jr. "Brain Death-the Patient, the Physician, and Society." *Gonzaga Law Review* 18 (1982/83) 429–516.

Byrne, Paul A., and Walt F. Weaver. ""Brain Death" Is Not Death." In *Brain Death and Disorders of Consciousness*, edited by Calixto Machado and D. Alan Shewmon, 43–50. New York: Kluwer Academic, 2004.

Campbell, Courtney S. "Fundamentals of Life and Death: Christian Fundamentalism and Medical Science." In *The Definition of Death: Contemporary Controversies*, edited by Stuart J. Youngner, Robert M. Arnold, and Renie Schapiro. Baltimore: The Johns Hopkins University Press, 1999.

———. "Harvesting the Living? Separating "Brain Death" and Organ Transplantation." *Kennedy Institute of Ethics Journal* 14:3 (2004) 301–18.

———. "A No-Brainer: Criticisms of Brain-Based Standards of Death." *Journal of Medicine and Philosophy* 26:5 (2001) 539–51.

Caplan, Arthur L., and Daniel H. Coelho. *The Ethics of Organ Transplants: The Current Debate*. Buffalo, NY: Prometheus, 1999.

Capron, Alexander Morgan. "The Bifurcated Legal Standard for Determining Death: Does it Work?" In *The Definition of Death*, edited by Stuart J. Youngner, Robert M. Arnold, and Renie Schapiro, 117–36. Baltimore: The Johns Hopkins University Press, 1999.

———. "Brain-Death: Well Settled yet Still Unresolved." *The New England Journal of Medicine* 344:16 (2001).

———. "Legal Definition of Death." *Annals of the New York Academy of Science* 315 (1978) 349–56.

Capron, Alexander Morgan, and L. R. Kass. "A Statutory Definition of the Standards for Determining Human Death." *University of Pennsylania Law Review* 121 (1972) 87–118.

Carson, Ronald A., Jaime L. Frias, and Richard J. Melker. "Research with Brain-Dead Children." *IRB* (1981) 5–6.

Catechism of the Catholic Church. Mahwah, NJ: Paulist, 1994.

Center, National Catholic Bioethics. *Faq's on Brain Death*. Online: http://www.ncbcenter. org/FAQ_BrainDeath.asp.

Chiong, Winston. "Brain Death without Definitions." *Hasting Center Report* 35:6 (2005) 20–30.

Clarke, W. Norris. *Explorations in Metaphysics*. South Bend, IN: University of Notre Dame Press, 1994.

Clauss, Ralf, and Wally Nel. "Drug Induced Arousal from the Permanent Vegetative State." *Neurorehabilitation* 21:1 (2006) 23–28.

Coimbra, C. G. "Implications of Ischemic Penumbra for the Diagnosis of Brain Death." *Braz J Med Biol Res* 32 (1999) 1479–87.

Coller, Barry S. "The Newly Dead as Research Subjects." *Clinical Research* 37 (1989) 487–94.

Cranford, Ronald E. "The Persistent Vegetative State: The Medical Reality." *Hasting Center Report* 18 (1988) 27–32.

"Cruzan v. Director, Missouri Department of Health." U.S. Supreme Court, 1990.

Damian, Maxwell S. "Neuroprotection Becomes Reality: Changing Times for Cerebral Resuscitation." In *Brain Death and Disorders of Consciousness*, edited by Calixto Machado and D. Alan Shewmon, 143–50. New York: Kluwer Academic, 2004.

Daneffel, M. B., J. E. Kappes, D. Waltmire, et al. "Knowledge and Attitudes of Health Care Professionals About Organ Donation." *Journal of Transplant Coordination* 2 (1992) 127–30.

de Frias, Casado, F. Balboa de Pas, A. Perez Martinez, and C. Palacio Mestres. "Inappropriate Secretion of Antidiuretic Hormone and the Effect of Lithium on Its Treatment." *Journal of Pediatrics* 96 (1980) 153–55.

"Death." In *Iowa Code*, Section 702.8, 1999.

"Death and Disposition of the Body." In *Texas Statute*, Title 8.

"A Definition of Irreversible Coma: Report of the Ad Hoc Committee of the Harvard Medical School to Examine the Definition of Brain Death." *Journal of the American Medical Association* 205 (1968) 337–40.

Delmonico, F. L., and J. G. Randolph. "Death: A Concept in Transition." *Pediatrics* 51 (1973) 234–39.

Delsol, Chantal. *Icarus Fallen: The Search for Meaning in an Uncertain World.* Translated by Robin Dick. Wilmington: ISI, 2003.

DeMere, M. "Statement." In *Hearing Before the Missouri Select Committee on the Definition of Death*, 1976.

Deng, Mario C. "Effect of Receiving a Heart Transplant: Analysis of a National Cohort Entered on to a Waiting List, Stratified by Heart Failure Severity." *British Medical Journal* 231 (2000) 540–45.

"Dennis C. Vacco, Attorney General of New York, Et Al., Petitioners v. Timothy E. Quill Et Al." U.S. Supreme Court, 1997.

The Determination of Brain Death and its Relationship to Human Death. Edited by R. J. White, H. Angstwurm, and I. Carrasco de Paula. Vatican City: Pontificia Academia Scientarum, 1989.

"Determination of Death." In *Code of Virginia*, 54.1–2972.

"Determination of Death." In *Delaware Laws*, Title 24.

"Determination of Death." In *Oregon Statute*, ORS 432.300, 1997.

DeWeese, Garett J., and J. P. Moreland. *Philosophy Made Slightly Less Difficult.* Downers Grove, IL: InterVarsity, 2005.

Dorff, Elliot N. *Matters of Life and Death: A Jewish Approach to Modern Medical Ethics.* Philadelphia: The Jewish Publication Society, 1998.

Dorff, Elliot N., and Louis E. Newman, editors. *Contemporary Jewish Ethics and Morality: A Reader.* New York: Oxford University Press, 1995.

Döşemeci, L., M. Cengiz, M. Yilmaz, and A. Ramazanoğlu. "Frequency of Spinal Reflex Movements in Brain-Dead Patients." *Transplant Proc* 36 (2004) 17–19.

DuBois, James M. "Organ Transplantation: An Ethical Road Map." *The National Catholic Bioethics Quarterly* 2:3 (2002) 413–53.

Dyck, Arthur J. *Life's Worth: The Case Against Assisted Suicide*. Grand Rapids: Eerdmans, 2002.

Eberl, Jason T. "A Thomistic Understanding of Human Death." *Bioethics* 19 (2005) 29–48.

Edwards, Steven D., and Kevin Forbes. "Nursing Practice and the Definition of Death." *Nursing Inquiry* 10:4 (2003) 229–35.

Elliot, J. M. "Brain Death." *Trauma* 5 (2003) 23–42.

Engelhardt, H. Tristram, Jr. "Redefining Death: The Mirage of Consensus." In *The Definition of Death: Contemporary Controversies*, edited by Stuart J. Youngner, Robert M. Arnold and Renie Schapiro, 319–31. Baltimore: The Johns Hopkins University Press, 1999.

Evans, C. Stephen. "Human Persons as Substantial Achievers." *Philosophia Reformata* 58:1 (1993) 100–112.

Evans, David W. "The Demise of 'Brain Death' in Britain." In *Beyond Brain Death: The Case Against Brain Based Criteria for Human Death*, edited by Michael Potts, Paul A. Byrne and Richard G. Nilges, 66, 139–58. Dordrecht, The Netherlands: Kluwer Academic, 2000.

———. "Heart Transplants: Some Observations and Objections." *Cambridge Review* 103 (1982) 338–39.

Evans, David W., and L. C. Lum. "Brain Death." *Lancet* 2 (1980a) 1022.

Feinberg, John S., and Paul D. Feinberg. *Ethics for a Brave New World*. Wheaton, IL: Crossway, 1993.

Field, D. R., E. A. Gates, R. K. Creasy, A. R. Jonsen, and R. K. Laros. "Maternal Brain Death During Pregnancy." *JAMA* 260 (1988) 816–22.

Finnis, John. *Aquinas: Moral, Political, and Legal Theory*. Oxford: Oxford University Press, 1998.

Focke, Renate. "Renate Focke's Story." *The Life Guardian*. Online: http://thelifeguardian.com/?action=mother_greinert.

Fost, Norman. "Research on the Brain Dead." *Journal of Pediatrics* 96 (1980) 54–56.

Fox, Mark D. "Stewards of a Public Trust: Responsible Transplantation." *The American Journal of Bioethics* 3:1 (2003) v–vii.

Frame, John M. *Medical Ethics: Principles, Persons, and Problems*. Phillipsburgh, NJ: P. & R., 1988.

Franz, H. *Study of Donor and Nondonor Families*. Washington, DC: Presented at the Annual Meetings of the Division of Transplantation, 1996.

Frost, Norman. "The Unimportance of Death." In *The Definition of Death: Contemporary Controversies*, edited by Stuart J. Youngner, Robert M. Arnold, and Renie Schapiro, 161–78. Baltimore: The Johns Hopkins University Press, 1999.

Futterman, Laurie G. "Presumed Consent: The Solution to the Critical Donor Shortage?" *American Journal of Critical Care* 4:2 (1995) 383–88.

Garcia, Robert K. "Artificial Intelligence and Personhood." In *Cutting-Edge Bioethics*, edited by John F. Kilner, C. Christopher Hook, and Diann B. Uustal, 39–51. Grand Rapids: Eerdmans, 2002.

Geisler, Norman L. *Christian Ethics: Options and Issues*. Grand Rapids: Baker, 1989.

Gelb, Adrian W., and Kerri M. Robertson. "Anaesthetic Management of the Brain Dead for Organ Donation." *Canadian Journal for Anaesthesia* 37:1 (1990) 806–12.

George, Robert P., and Christopher Tollefsen. *Embryo: A Defense of Human Life*. New York: Doubleday, 2008.

Gervais, K. G. "Advancing the Definition of Death: A Philsophical Essay." *Medical Humanities Review* 3:4 (1989) 7–9.

———. *Redefining Death*. New Haven: Yale University Press, 1986.

Giacino, J. T., S. Ashwal, N. Childs, R. Cranford, B. Jennett, D. I. Katz, J. P. Kelly, J. H. Rosenberg, J. White, R. D. Zafonte, N. D. Zasler, "The Minimally Conscious State: Definition and Diagnostic Criteria." *Neurology* 58 (2002) 349–53.

Giacomini, Mita. "A Change of Heart and a Change of Mind? Technology and the Redefinition of Death in 1968." *Social Science Medicine* 44:10 (1997) 1465–82.

Glannon, W. "Neurostimulation and the Minimally Conscious State." *Bioethics* 22 (2008) 337–45.

Glaves-Innis, Georgetta. "Organ Donation and Incompetents: Can They Consent? Comparative Analysis of American and Canadian Laws of Consent and Brain Death Determination." *Touro International Law Review* 10 (1994) 155–63.

Glendon, Mary Ann. *Rights Talk: The Impoverishment of Political Discourse*. New York: Free, 1991.

Graham-Rowe, Duncan. "World's First Brain Prosthesis Revealed." March 12, 2003. Online: www.newscientist.com.

Green, M. "Aristotle and Modern Biology." *Journal of the History of Ideas* 33 (1972) 411.

Green, Michael B., and Daniel Wikler. "Brain Death and Personal Identity." *Philosophy and Public Affairs* 9 (1980) 105–33.

Greenberg, Gary. "As Good as Dead." *The New Yorker*, August 13, 2001, 36–41.

Greinert, Renate. "Renate Greinert's Story." *The Life Guardian*. Online: http://thelifeguardian.com/?action=mother_greinert.

Grene, Marjorie. "Aristotle and Modern Biology." *Journal of the History of Ideas* 33:3 (1972) 395–424.

Grossman, Kathy Lynn. "When Life's Flame Goes Out: Death is Difficult to Define, Legally and Morally." *USA Today*, October 5 2005, D1.

Guerit, Jean-Michel. "The Concept of Brain Death." In *Brain Death and Disorders of Consciousness*, edited by Calixto Machado and D. Alan Shewmon, 15–22. New York: Kluwer Academic, 2004.

"Halakhah." In *Encyclopedia Judaica*, edited by Cecil Roth, 7:1156–57. Philadelphia: Coronet, 1994.

Haldane, John, and Patrick Lee. "Aquinas on Human Ensoulment, Abortion and the Value of Life." *Philosophy* 78 (2003) 255–78.

Hasker, William. *The Emergent Self*. Ithaca: Cornell University Press, 1999.

———. "Persons as Emergent Substances." In *Soul, Body, and Survival: Essays on the Metaphysics of Human Persons*, edited by Keven Corcoran, 107–19. Ithaca, NY: Cornell University Press, 2001.

Heaney, Stephen. "Aquinas and the Presence of the Human Rational Soul." *The Thomist* 56 (1992).

Higashi, K., et al. "Five-Year Follow-up Study of Patients with Persistent Vegetative State." *Journal of Neurology, Neurosurgery and Psychiatry* 44 (1981) 552–54.

Hill, David J. "Brain Stem Death: A United Kingdom Anaesthetist's View." In *Beyond Brain Death: The Case Against Brain Death Criteria for Human Death*, edited by Michael Potts, Paul A. Byrne, and Richard G. Nilges, 159–69. Dordrecht: Kluwer Academic, 2001.

Hippocrates. *Hippocrates, Vol. I: Ancient Medicine, Airs, Waters, Places, Epidemics 1 &*
2. Oath, Precepts, Nutriment. Translated by W. H. S. Jones. Cambridge: Harvard
University Press, 1984.

Iserson, Kenneth V. "Live Verses Death: Exposing a Misapplication of Ethical Reasoning."
Journal of Clinical Ethics 5 (1994) 261–66.

Ivanhoe Newswire. "Artificial Brain Parts on the Horizon." May 30, 2006. Online: http://
news14.com.

Iwai, A., T. Sakano, M. Uenishi, H. Sugimoto, T. Yoshioka, T. Sugimoto. "Effects of
Vasopressin and Catecholamines on the Maintenance of Circulatory Stability in
Brain-Dead Patients." *Transplantation* 48 (1989) 613–17.

"Jerry W. Canterbury, Appellant, v. William Thornton Spence and the Washington
Hospital Center, a Body Corporate, Appellees." In *150 U.S. App. D.C. 263*, 464 F, 2d
772: United States Court Of Appeals For The District of Columbia Circuit, 1972.

Joffe, Ari R. "The Neurological Determination of Death: What Does it Really Mean?"
Issues in Law and Medicine 32:2 (2007) 119–40.

Joffe, Ari R., and Natalie Anton. "Brain Death: Understanding of the Conceptual Basis
by Pediatric Intensivists in Canada." *Archives of Pediatrics & Adolescent Medicine*
160:7 (2006) 747–52.

"John Moore v. Regents of the University of California." In *51 Cal.3d 120*, 271 Cal.Rptr.
146, 480: Supreme Court of California, 1990.

John Paul II, Pope. *Address of John Paul II to the 18th International Congress of the*
Transplantation Society. Vatican City, 2000. Online: http://cnservero.nkf.med.
ualberta.ca/misc/Rome/Encyclical.htm.

———. "Discourse of John Paul II to the Participants of the Working Group." In *Working*
Group on the Determination of Brain Death and its Relation to Human Death, edited
by R. White, H. Angstwurm & I Carrasco de Paula, xxv. Vatican City: Pontificia
Adacemis Scientiarum, 1992.

———. *Evangelium Vitae.* Vatican City, 1995. Online: http://www.vatican.va/holy_
father/john_paul_ii/encyclicals/documents/hf_jp-ii_enc_25031995_evangelium-
vitae_en.html.

Jonas, Hans. *Philosophical Essays: From Ancient Creed to Technological Man.* Chicago:
University of Chicago Press, 1974.

Jones, D. A. "Metaphysical Misgivings About 'Brain Death.'" In *Beyond Brain Death: The*
Case Against Brain Based Criteria for Human Death, edited by Michael Potts, Paul
A. Byrne, and Richard G. Nilges, 91–119. Dordrecht: Kluwer Academic, 2000.

Jouvet, M. "Diagnostic Electrosouscorticographique Da La Mort Du Systeme Nerveux
Central Au Cours De Certains Comas." *Electroencephalography and Clinical*
Neurophysiology 3 (1959).

Kafetsios, Konstantinos, and Eric LaRock. "Cognition and Emotion: Aristotelian
Affinities with Contemporary Emotion Research." *Theory & Psychology* 15:5 (2005)
639–57.

Kagan, Shelly. *Normative Ethics.* Boulder, CO: Westview, 1998.

Kant, Immanuel. "Groundwork of the Metaphysics of Morals." In *Kants' Groundwork of*
the Metaphysics of Morals. New York: Harper & Row, 1964.

Karakatsanis, K. G. "'Brain Death': Should it be Reconsidered?" *Spinal Cord* 46 (2008)
396–401.

Karakatsanis, K. G., and J. N. Tsanakas. "A Critique of the Concept of 'Brain Death.'"
Issues in Law and Medicine 18:2 (2002) 127–41.

Kelly, David F. *Contemporary Catholic Health Care Ethics.* Washington, DC: Georgetown University Press, 2004.

———. *Critical Care Ethics: Treatment Decisions in American Hospitals.* Kansas City: Sheed & Ward, 1991.

Kilner, John F., Nigel M. de S. Cameron, and David L. Schiedermayer, editors. *Bioethics and the Future of Medicine.* Grand Rapids: Eerdmans, 1995.

Kolakowki, Leszek. *Modernity on Endless Trial.* Chicago: University of Chicago Press, 1990.

Koppelman, Elysa R. "The Dead Donor Rule and the Concept of Death: Severing the Ties that Bind Them." *The American Journal of Bioethics* 3:1 (2003) 1–9.

Korein, Julius, and Calixto Machado. "Brain Death: Updating a Valid Concept for 2004." In *Brain Death and Disorders of Consciousness,* edited by Calixto Machado and D. Alan Shewmon, 1–14. New York: Kluwer Academic, 2004.

Koterski, Joseph. "Book Review of John Lizza's *Persons, Humanity, and the Definition of Death.*" *International Philosophical Quarterly* 47:3 (2007) 385–87.

Lamb, David. *Death, Brain Death, and Ethics.* London: Croom Helm, 1985.

Lang, Christoph J. G., and Josef G. Heckmann. "How Should Testing for Apnea be Performed in Diagnosing Brain Death?" In *Brain Death and Disorders of Consciousness,* edited by Calixto Machado and D. Alan. Shewmon, 169–74. New York: Kluwer Academic, 2004.

LaRock, Eric F. "Dualistic Internaction, Neural Dependence, and Aquinas's Composite View." *Philosophia Christi* 3:2 (2001) 459–72.

———. "Is Consciousness Really a Brain Process." *International Philosophical Quarterly* 48 (2007) 201–29.

Lee, Patrick. *Abortion and Unborn Human Life.* Washington, DC: Catholic University of America Press, 1996.

———. "Human Beings are Animals." In *Natural Law and Moral Inquiry: Ethics, Metaphysics, and Politics in the Work of Germain Grisez,* edited by Robert George, 135–51. Washington, DC: Georgetown University Press, 1998.

———. "The Pro-Life Argument from Substantial Identity: A Defense." *Bioethics* 18:3 (2004) 249–63.

Lee, Patrick, and Robert P. George. *Body-Self Dualism in Contemporary Ethics and Politics.* New York: Cambridge University Press, 2007.

Lee, Patrick, and Robert P. George. "The Wrong of Abortion." In *Contemporary Debates in Applied Ethics,* edited by Andrew I. Cohen and Christopher Wellman, 13–26. New York: Blackwell, 2005.

Liao, Matthew. "The Organism View Defended." *The Monist* 89:3 (2006) 334–50.

Lizza, John P. "The Conceptual Basis for Brain Death Revisited: Loss of Organic Integration or Loss of Consciousness?" In *Brain Death and Disorders of Consciousness,* edited by Calixto Machado and D. Alan Shewmon, 51–60. New York: Kluwer Academic, 2004.

———. *Persons, Humanity, and the Definition of Death.* Baltimore: The Johns Hopkins University Press, 2006.

Lock, Margaret. "Inventing a New Death and Making it Believable." *Anthropology & Medicine* 9:2 (2002) 97–115.

———. *Twice Dead: Organ Transplants and the Reinvention of Death.* Berkeley: University of California Press, 2002.

Machuga, Ric. *In Defense of the Soul: What it Means to be Human*. Grand Rapids: Brazos, 2002.

Marti-Fabregas, J., et al. "Decerebrate-Like Posturing with Mechanical Ventilation in Brain Death." *Neurology* 54 (2000).

Martin, Lauri, and David Nancarrow. "Woman Who Woke Up After 6 Years Relapses." Online: http://www.kktv.com/home/headlines/6347997,html2007.

Martyn, Susan R. "Using the Brain Dead for Medical Research." *Utah Law Review* 1 (1986) 1–28.

McArdle, John. "Xenotransplantation: An Opportunity to Promote Alternatives." *AV Magazine* (1998) 6–9.

McCarthy, Michael. "Study Surveys Brain-Death Guidelines in 80 Nations." *The Lancet* 359 (2002) 139.

McClintock, Barbara. "The Significance of the Genome to Challenge." *Science* 226 (1984) 792–801.

McMahan, J. *The Ethics of Killing: Problems at the Margins of Life*. Oxford: Oxford University Press, 2002.

Menikoff, Jerry. *Law and Bioethics: An Introduction*. Washington, DC: Georgetown University Press, 2001.

Miles, Stephen. "Death in a Technological and Pluralistic Culture." In *The Definition of Death*, edited by Stuart J. Youngner, R. M. Arnold, & Renie Schapiro, 311–18. Baltimore: The Johns Hopkins University Press, 1999.

Mitchell, C. Ben. "The Church and the Cultural Imperative." In *Bioengagement*, edited by Nigel M. de S. Cameron, Scott E. Daniels, & Barbara J. White, 211–19. Grand Rapids: Eerdmans, 2000.

———. "Nazi Germany's Euphemisms." In *Dignity and Dying*, edited by John F. Kilner, Arlene B. Miller, and Edmund D. Pellegrino. Grand Rapids: Eerdmans, 1996.

Mohandas, A., and S. N. Chou. "Brain Death: A Clinical and Pathological Study." *Journal of Neurosurgery* 35:2 (1971) 211–18.

Molinari, Gaetano F. *The Nincds Collaborative Study of Brain Death: A Historical Perspective*. Monograph No. 24. Washington, DC: U.S. Department of Health and Human Services, 1980.

Mollaret, P., and M. Goulon. "A State Beyond Coma. Preliminary Report." *Revue Neurologique* 101 (1959) 3–15.

Moreland, J. P. "Humanness, Personhood, and the Right to Die." *Faith and Philosophy* 12:1 (1995) 95–112.

Moreland, J. P., and Scott B. Rae. *Body & Soul: Human Nature & the Crisis in Ethics*. Downers Grove: InterVarsity, 2000.

Morioka, Masahiro. "Reconsidering Brain Death: A Lesson from Japan's Fifteen Years of Experience." *Hasting Center Report* 31:4 (2001) 41–46.

Nagel, T. "Death." In *The Metaphysics of Death*, edited by J. M. Fischer, 63–72. Stanford: Stanford University Press, 1993.

Nagel, Thomas. *The Last Word*. New York: Oxford University Press, 2001.

Nakajima, Michi. *Invisible Death*. Mienai Shi: Bungei Shunju, 1985.

National Institute of Health. "An Appraisal of the Criteria of Cerebral Death: A Summary Statement. A Collaborative Study." *JAMA* 237:10 (1977) 982–86.

Neslon, Stephen N. "'The Least of These': A Christian Moral Appraisal of Vital Organ Procurement from 'Brain-Dead' Patients." *Ethics & Medicine* 20:1 (2004) 7–19.

Nevins, Daniel S. "Dead or Alive? Halakhah and Brain Death." *Conservative Judaism* 57:2 (2005) 3–29.

"New Jersey Declaration of Death Act." In *New Jersey Statutes Annotate*, 23, 1991.

New York Task Force on Life and The Law. *The Determination of Death.* New York, 1986.

News, BBC. *Liver Cells Grown from Cord Blood.* October 31, 2006. Online: http://news. bbc.co.uk/2/hi/health/6101420.stm.

———. *US Scientists Have Successfully Grown Fully Functioning Bladders in the Lab, and Implanted them into Patients with Bladder Disease.* 2006. Online: http://news.bbc. co.uk/1/hi/health/4875244.stm.

Nilges, Richard G. "Organ Transplantation, Brain Death, and the Slippery Slope: A Neurosurgeon's Perspective." In *Beyond Brain Death: The Case Against Brain Based Criteria for Human Death*, edited by Michael Potts, Paul A. Byrne, and Richard G. Nilges, 66, 249–58. Dordrecht, The Netherlands: Kluwer Academic, 2000.

Novak, David. "Judaism." In *Encyclopedia of Bioethics*, edited by Warren T. Reich, 3:1302. New York: Macmillan, 1995.

Olick, R. S. "Brain Death, Religious Freedom, and Public Policy: New Jersey's Landmark Legislative Initiative." *Kennedy Institute of Ethics Journal* 1:4 (1991) 275–92.

O'Reilly, Kevin. *Redefining Death: A New Ethical Dilemma.* American Medical News, 2009. Online: http://www.amednews.com.

Orr, Robert D., and Gilbert Meilander. "Ethics and Life's Ending." *First Things* 145 (2004) 31–37.

Ott, Barbara B. "Defining and Redefining Death." *American Journal of Critical Care* 4:6 (1995) 476–80.

Ott, Harald C., Thomas S. Mathiesen, Saik-Kai Goh, Laren D. Black, Stefan M. Kren, Theoden I. Netoff, and Doris A. Taylor. "Perfusion-Decellularized Matrix: Using Nature's Platform to Engineer a Bioartificial Heart." *Nature Medicine* 14:2 (2008) 213–21.

Parfit, Derek. *Reasons and Persons.* Oxford: Oxford University Press, 1986.

Pellegrino, Edmund D. "Physician-Assisted Suicide and Euthanasia: Rebuttals of Rebuttals—The Moral Prohibition Remains." *Journal of Medicine and Philosophy* 26:1 (2001) 93–100.

Pernick, Marin S. "Brain Death in Cultural Context: The Reconstruction of Death, 1968–1981." In *The Definition of Death: Contemporary Controversies*, edited by Stuart J. Youngner, Robert M. Arnold, and Renie Schapiro, 3–33. Baltimore: The Johns Hopkins University Press, 1999.

Pius XII, Pope. "The Prolongation of Life: An Address of Pope Pius XII to an International Congress of Anesthesiologists." *The Pope Speaks* 4 (1958) 393–408.

Plum, Fred. "Clinical Standards and Technological Confirmatory Tests in Diagnosing Brain Death." In *The Definition of Death*, edited by Stuart J. Youngner, R. M. Arnold, & Renie Schapiro, 34–65. Baltimore: The Johns Hopkins University Press, 1999.

Potts, Michael. "Letters: Editor's Choice: Deep Seated Fear." *British Medical Journal* 325 (2002) 598.

———. "Pro-Life Support of the Whole Brain Death Criteria: A Problem of Consistency." In *Beyond Brain Death: The Case Against Brain Based Criteria for Human Death*, edited by Michael Potts, Paul A. Byrne, and Richard G. Nilges, 66, 121–38. Dordrecht: Kluwer Academic, 2000.

————. "A Requiem for Whole Brain Death: A Response to D. Alan Shewmon's 'The Brain and Somatic Integration.'" *Journal of Medicine and Philosophy* 26:5 (2001) 479–91.

Potts, Michael, and D. W. Evans. "Does It Matter That Organ Donors Are Not Dead? Ethical and Policy Implications." *Journal of Medical Ethics* 31 (2005) 406–9.

Potts, Michael, Paul A. Bryne, and Richard G. Nilges. "Introduction." In *Beyond Brain Death: The Case Against Brain Based Criteria for Human Death*, edited by Michael Potts, Paul A. Byrne, and Richard G. Nilges. Dordrecht: Kluwer Academic, 2000.

Powner, David J., Michael Hernandez, and Terry E. Rives. "Variability among Hospital Policies for Determining Brain Death in Adults." *Critical Care Medicine* 32:6 (2004) 1284–88.

President's Commission for the Study of Ethical Problems in Medicine and Biomedical and Behavioral Research. *Defining Death: A Report on the Medical, Legal, and Ethical Issues in the Determination of Death*. Washington, DC: Government Printing Office, 1981.

————. *Making Health Care Decisions: The Ethical and Legal Implications of Informed Consent in the Patient-Practitioner Relationship*. 3 vols. Washington, DC: U.S. Government Printing Office, 1982.

Price, David. *Legal and Ethical Aspects of Organ Transplantation*. Cambridge: Cambridge University Press, 2000.

Puccetti, R. "The Case for Mental Duality: Evidence from Split-Brain Data and Other Considerations." *Behavioral and Brain Sciences* 4 (1981) 93–123.

Purcell, Jr., Edward A. *The Crisis of Demoncratic Theory: Scientific Naturalism and the Problem of Value*. Lexington: University of Kentucky Press, 1973.

Putnam, Hilary. *The Collapse of the Fact/Value Dichotomy and Other Essays*. Cambridge: Harvard University Press, 2002.

Rado, Leslie. "Cultural Elites and the Institutionalization of Ideas." *Sociological Forum* 2:1 (1987) 42–66.

Randell, T. T. "Medical and Legal Considerations of Brain Death." *ACTA Anaesthesiologica Scandinavica* 28 (2004) 139–44.

Repertinger, S., W. P. Fitzgibbons, M. F. Omojola, and R. A. Brumback. "Long Survival Following Bacterial Meningitis-Associated Brain Destruction." *Journal of Child Neurology* 21 (2006) 591–95.

Rescher, Nicholas. *Objectivity: The Obligations of Impersonal Realism*. Notre Dame: University of Notre Dame Press, 1997.

Rix, Bo Andreassen. "Brain Death, Ethics and Politics in Denmark." In *The Definition of Death*, edited by Stuart J. Youngner, Robert M. Arnold, and Renie Schapiro, 227–38. Baltimore: The Johns Hopkins University Press, 1999.

Robertson, John A. "The Dead Donor Rule." *Hasting Center Report* November-December (1999) 6–14.

————. "Research on the Brain-Dead." *IRB* (1980) 4–6.

Robinson, J. "Personal Identity and Survival." *Journal of Philosophy* 85 (1988) 319–28.

Roper, A. H. "Unusual Spontaneous Movements in Brain-Dead Patients." *Neurology* 34 (1984) 1089–92.

Rorty, Richard. *Consequences of Pragmatism*. Minneapolis: University of Minnesota Press, 1982.

Rosner, Fred. "The Definition of Death in Jewish Law." In *The Definition of Death: Contemporary Controversies*, edited by Stuart J. Youngner et al., 210–21. Baltimore: The Johns Hopkins University Press, 1999.

Saposnik, G., J. Maurino, and J. A. Bueri. "Movements in Brain Death." *European Journal of Neurology* 8 (2001) 209–13.

Schiff, N. D., MD, D. Rodriguez-Moreno, MS., A. Kamal, MD, K. H. S. Kim, MD, PhD, J. T. Giacino, PhD, F. Plum, MD, and J. Hirsch, PhD. "Fmri Reveals Large-Scale Network of Activation in Minimally Conscious Patients." *Neurology* 64 (2005) 514–23.

Schlett, James. *Insurers Turning to Incentives to Promote Healthy Lifestyles*. October 3, 2008. Online: http://www.dailygazette.com.

Schoen, Wendy L. "Conflict in the Parameters: Defining Life and Death in Missouri Statues." *American Journal of Law and Medicine* (1990).

Seifert, Josef. "Brain Death and Euthanasia." In *Beyond Brain Death: The Case against Brain Based Criteria for Human Death*, edited by Michael Potts, Paul A. Byrne, and Richard G. Nilges, 201–27. Dordrecht: Kluwer Academic, 2000.

———. "Consciousness, Mind, Brain, and Death." In *Brain Death and Disorders of Consciousness*, edited by Calixto Machado and D. Alan Shewmon, 61–78. New York: Kluwer Academic, 2004.

Seifert, Josef. "Is 'Brain Death' Actually Death?" *Monist* 76:2 (1993) 175–203.

Sgreccia, Elio. "Vegetative State and Brain Death: Philosophical and Ethical Issues from a Personalistic View." *Neuro Rehabilitation* 19 (2004) 361–66.

Shewmon, D. Alan. "The ABC of PVS: Problems of Definition." In *Brain Death and Disorders of Consciousness*. Edited by Calixto Machado and D. Alan Shewmon, 215–28. New York: Kluwer Academic, 2004.

———. "The Brain and Somatic Integration." *Journal of Medicine and Philosophy* 26:5 (2001) 457–78.

———. "'Brainstem Death,' 'Brain Death' and Death: A Critical Re-Evaluation of the Purported Evidence." *Issues in Law and Medicine* 14:2 (1998) 125–46.

———. "Chronic Brain Death." *Neurology* 51 (1998) 1538–45.

———. "The 'Critical Organ' for the Organism as a Whole: Lessons from the Lowly Spinal Cord." In *Brain Death and Disorders of Consciousness*, edited by Calixto Machado and D. Alan Shewmon, 23–42. New York: Kluwer Academic, 2004.

———. "The Dead Donor Rule: Lessons from Linguistics." *Kennedy Institute of Ethics Journal* 292 (2004) 277–300.

———. "The Metaphysics of Brain Death, Persistent Vegetative State, and Dementia." *Thomist* 49:1 (1985) 24–80.

———. "Recovery from 'Brain Death': A Neurologist's Apologia." *Linacre Quarterly* (1997) 30–95.

Shewmon, D. Alan, and Elisabeth Sietz Shewmon. "The Semiotics of Death and its Medical Implications." In *Brain Death and Disorders of Consciousness*, edited by Calixto Machado and D. Alan Shewmon, 89–114. New York: Kluwer Academic, 2004.

Schiff, N. D., J. T. Giacino, and J. J. Fins. "Deep Brain Stimulation, Neuroethics, and the Minimally Conscious State: Moving Beyond Proof of Principle." *Archives of Neurology* 66 (2009) 697–702.

Shuster, Evelyne. "Determinism and Reductionism." In *Gene Mapping: Using Law and Ethics as Guides*, edited by George J. Annas & Sherman Elias. New York: Oxford University Press, 1992.

Siegler, M., and D. Wikler. "Brain Death and Live Birth." *JAMA* 248 (1989).

Siminoff, Laura A. "The Dead Donor Rule: Not Dead Yet." *The American Journal of Bioethics* 3:1 (2003) 30.

Siminoff, Laura A., and Alexia Bloch. "American Attitudes and Beliefs about Brain Death: The Empirical Literature." In *The Definition of Death*, edited by Stuart J. Youngner, Robert M. Arnold, and Renie Schapiro, 183–93. Baltimore: The Johns Hopkins University Press, 1999.

Siminoff, Laura A., Christopher Burant, and Stuart J. Youngner. "Death and Organ Procurement: Public Beliefs and Attitudes." *Kennedy Institute of Ethics Journal* 14:3 (2004) 217–34.

Singer, Peter. "Is the Sanctity of Life Ethic Terminally Ill?" In *Bioethics: An Anthology*, edited by Helga Kuhse and Peter Singer, 292–300. Oxford: Blackwell, 2001.

———. *Rethinking Life and Death*. New York: St. Marin's, 1994.

Smith, David H. "On Being Queasy." *IRB* (1980) 6–7.

Smith, Peter J. "Coma Recovery after 19 Years Poses Questions about Terri Schiao." 2006. Online: http://www.lifesite.net/ldn/2006/jul/06070409.html.

Smith, Tony. "Clincal Freedom." *British Medical Journal* 295:19–26 (December 1987) 1583.

Soccio, Douglas J. *Archetypes of Wisdom: An Introduction to Philosophy*. 6th ed. Belmont: Wadsworth, 2007.

Sperling, Daniel. "Breaking the Silence: The Illegality of Performing Resuscitation Procedures on the Newly Dead." *Annals of Health Law* 13:2 (2003–4).

"State of Connecticut v. Barry Guess." 852: Appellate Court of Connecticut, 1997.

Steineck, Christian. ""Brain Death," Death, and Personal Identity." *KronoScope* 3:2 (2003) 227–49.

Sugimoto, Tateo, Yuko and Chihior. *Kita Kamoshirenai Seifuko*. Tokyo: Nami Shobo, 1986.

"Surgery: The Ultimate Operation." *Time*, December 15, 1967, 64–72.

Taylor, R. "Reexamining the Definition and Criteria of Death." *Seminars in Neurology* 17:3 (1997) 265–70.

Titmuss, R. M. *The Gift of Relationship: From Human Blood to Social Policy*. New York: Vintage, 1971.

Tomlinson, Tom. "The Conservative Use of the Brain-Death Criterion: A Critique." *Journal of Medicine and Philosophy* 9 (1984) 377–93.

Tonti-Filippini, Nicholas. "Revising Brain Death: Cultural Imperialism." *Linacre Quarterly* 65:2 (1998) 51–72.

Tooley, Michael. *Abortion and Infanticide*. New York: Oxford University Press, 1983.

Torrey, R. A., editor. *The Fundamentals*. Grand Rapids: Baker, 2003.

Truog, Robert D. "Organ Donation without Brain Death?" *Hasting Center Report* 35:6 (2005) 3.

———. "Is it Time to Abandon Brain Death?" *Hasting Center Report* 27:1 (1997) 29–37.

Truog, Robert D., and J. T. Fletcher. "Brain Death and the Anencephalic Newborn." *Bioethics* 4 (1990) 199–215.

Truog, Robert D., and W. M. Robinson. "Role of Brain Death and the Dead-Donor Rule in the Ethics of Organ Transplantation." *Critical Care Medicine* 31 (2003) 2391–96.

"Uniform Determination of Death Act." In *South Carolina Code of Laws*, Article 6.

Unos Research Data. Denice Tripp, 2006. Online: http://www.optn.org/data/.

van Lommel, Pim. "About the Continuity of Our Consciousness." In *Brain Death and Disorders of Consciousness*, edited by Calixto Machado and D. Alan Shewmon, 115–32. New York: Kluwer Academic, 2004.

Vautier, B. Holly. "Defining Death." In *Dignity and Dying*, edited by John F. Kilner, Arlene B. Miller, and Edmund D. Pellegrino. Grand Rapids: Eerdmans, 1996.

Veatch, Robert M. "The Dead Donor Rule: True by Definition." *The American Journal of Bioethics* 3:1 (2003) 10–11.

———. *Death, Dying, and the Biological Revolution*. New Haven, CT: Yale University Press, 1976.

———. "The Death of Whole-Brain Death: The Plague of the Disaggregators, Somaticists, and Mentalists." *Journal of Medicine and Philosophy* 30:4 (2005) 353–78.

———. "Generalization of Expertise." *Hasting Center Report* 1:2 (1973) 29–40.

———. "The Impending Collapse of the Whole-Brain Definition of Death." *Hasting Center Report* 23:4 (1993) 18–24.

———. "Research on "Nonconsentables." *IRB* (1981) 6–7.

———. *Transplantation Ethics*. Washington, DC: Georgetown University Press, 2000.

———. "The Whole-Brain Oriented Concept of Death: An Outmoded Philosophical Formulation." *Journal of Thanatology* 3 (1975) 13–30.

Veatch, Robert M., and J. B. Pitt. "The Myth of Presumed Consent: Ethical Problems in New Organ Procurement Strategies." *Transplantation Proceedings* 27:2 (1995) 1888–92.

Wallace, W. A. "St. Thomas on the Beginning and Ending of Human Life." *Studi Tomistici: Sanctus Thomas de Aquino Doctor Hodiernae Humanitatis* 58 (1995).

Warren, Mary Ann. "On the Moral and Legal Status of Abortion." *The Monist* 57:1 (1973) 43–61.

Watanabe, Yoshio. "Brain Death and Cardiac Transplantation: Historical Background and Unsettled Controversies in Japan." In *Beyond Brain Death: The Case Against Brain Based Criteria for Human Death*, edited by Michael Potts, Paul A. Byrne, and Richard G. Nilges, 66, 171–90. Dordrecht: Kluwer Academic, 2000.

Whetstine, Leslie Mary. "An Examination of the Bio-Philosophical Literature on the Definition and Criteria of Death: When is Dead Dead and Why Some Donation after Cardiac Death Donors are Not." PhD diss., Duquesne University, 2006.

White, Hillary. *New Jersey Looking to Harvest More Organs by Easing "Brain Death" Criteria*. LifeSite, 2006. Online: http://www.lifesite.net/ldn/2006/jun/06061605.html.

Wicclair, Mark R. "Informed Consent and Research Involving the Newly Dead." *Kennedy Institute of Ethics Journal* 12:4 (2002) 351–72.

Wiggins, David. *Sameness and Substance*. Cambridge, MA: Harvard University Press, 1980.

Wijdicks, E. F. "Brain Death Worldwide: Accepted Fact but No Global Consensus in Diagnostic Criteria." *Neurology* 58 (2002) 20–25.

———. "The Diagnosis of Brain Death." *New England Journal of Medicine* 344 (2001) 1215–21.

Wijdicks, E. F., and J. L. Bernat. "Chronic 'Brain Death' (Letter)." *Neurology* 53 (1999) 1369–70.

Wikler, D. "Brain Death: A Durable Consensus." *Bioethics* 7 (1993) 239–41.

Wolstenholme, G. E. W., and M. O'Connor. *Ethics in Medical Progress: With Special Reference to Transplantation.* Boston: Little, Brown, 1966.

Yanagida, Kunio. "Sakurifaisu: Waga Musuko Noshi No 11 Nichi." *Bungei shuniju* 72 (1994) 126–51.

Youngner, Stuart J. "Defining Death: A Superficial and Fragile Consensus." *Archives of Neurology* 49 (1992) 570–72.

Youngner, Stuart J., M. Allen, E.T. Barlett, et al. "Psychological and Ethical Implications of Organ Retrieval." *New England Journal of Medicine* 313 (1985) 321–24.

Youngner, Stuart J., R. M. Arnold, and M. A. DeVita. "When Is Dead?" *Hasting Center Report* 29:6 (1999) 14–21.

Youngner, Stuart J., and Robert M. Arnold. "Philosophical Debates About the Definition of Death: Who Cares?" *Journal of Medicine and Philosophy* 26:5 (2001) 527–37.

Youngner, Stuart J., and E. T. Bartlett. "Human Death and High Technology: The Failure of the Whole Brain Formulations." *Annals of Internal Medicine* 99 (1983) 252–58.

Zamperetti, Nereo, Rinaldo Bellomo, Carlo Alberto Defanti, & Nicola Latronico. "Irreversible Apnoeic Coma 35 Years Later: Towards a More Rigorous Definition of Brain Death?" *Intensive Care Medicine* 30 (2004) 1715–22.

Index

APR 2012

DATE DUE

HOLDS

HOLDS

WITHDRAWN

Demco, Inc. 38-293

RA 1063.3 .H46 2011

Henderson, D. Scott.
Death and donation :

Middlesex County College
Library
Edison, NJ 08818